T0283776

Ten Men *of* The Bible

HOW GOD USED IMPERFECT PEOPLE TO CHANGE THE WORLD

·············

UPDATED EDITION

·············

FROM THE WRITINGS OF

MAX LUCADO

Harper*Christian* Resources

Ten Men of the Bible: Updated Edition
© 2015, 2024 by Max Lucado

Published in Grand Rapids, Michigan, by HarperChristian Resources. HarperChristian Resources is a registered trademark of HarperCollins Christian Publishing, Inc.

Requests for information should be sent to customercare@harpercollins.com.

ISBN 978-0-310-17203-1 (softcover)
ISBN 978-0-310-17204-8 (ebook)

Scripture quotations marked CEV taken from the Contemporary English Version®. Copyright © 1995 American Bible Society. All rights reserved.

Scripture quotations marked ESV taken from the Holy Bible, English Standard Version®. Copyright © 2001 by Crossway, a publishing ministry of Good News Publishers. The ESV® text has been reproduced in cooperation with and by permission of Good News Publishers. Unauthorized reproduction of this publication is prohibited. All rights reserved.

Scripture quotations marked KJV taken from the Authorized King James Version.

Scripture quotations marked MSG are from THE MESSAGE, copyright © 1993, 2002, 2018 by Eugene H. Peterson. Used by permission of NavPress. All rights reserved. Represented by Tyndale House Publishers, Inc.

Scripture quotations marked NASB taken from the New American Standard Bible®, Copyright © 1960, 1971, 1977, 1995, 2020 by The Lockman Foundation. Used by permission.

Scripture quotations marked NCV taken from The Holy Bible, New Century Version. Copyright © 1987, 1988, 1991 by Word Publishing Group, a division of Thomas Nelson, Inc. Used by permission. All rights reserved.

Scripture quotations marked NEB taken from The New English Bible. Copyright © Oxford University Press, 1961, 1970, 1989. All rights reserved.

Scripture quotations marked NIV taken from The Holy Bible, New International Version®, NIV®. Copyright © 1973, 1978, 1984, 2011 by Biblica, Inc.® Used by permission. All rights reserved worldwide. www.zondervan.com. The "NIV" and "New International Version" are trademarks registered in the United States Patent and Trademark Office by Biblica, Inc.®

Scripture quotations marked NKJV taken from the New King James Version®. Copyright © 1982 by Thomas Nelson, Inc. Used by permission. All rights reserved.

Scripture quotations marked NLT taken from the Holy Bible, New Living Translation, copyright © 1996, 2004, 2015 by Tyndale House Foundation. Used by permission of Tyndale House Publishers, Inc., Carol Stream, Illinois 60188. All rights reserved.

Scripture quotations marked NLV taken from the New Life Version, copyright © 1969 and 2003. Used by permission of Barbour Publishing, Inc., Uhrichsville, Ohio 44683. All rights reserved.

Scripture quotations marked NRSV taken from the New Revised Standard Version, Updated Edition. Copyright 2021 by the National Council of Churches of Christ in the United States of America. Used by permission. All rights reserved worldwide.

Scripture quotations marked TEV taken from Today's English Version. Copyright © 1966, 1971, 1976, 1992 by American Bible Society.

Scripture quotations marked TJB taken from The Jerusalem Bible © 1966 by Darton Longman & Todd Ltd and Doubleday and Company Ltd.

Scripture quotations marked TLB taken from The Living Bible, copyright © 1971 by Tyndale House Foundation. Used by permission of Tyndale House Publishers Inc., Carol Stream, Illinois 60188. All rights reserved. The Living Bible, TLB, and the The Living Bible logo are registered trademarks of Tyndale House Publishers.

All rights reserved. No portion of this book may be reproduced, stored in a retrieval system, or transmitted in any form or by any means—electronic, mechanical, photocopy, recording, scanning, or other—except for brief quotations in critical reviews or articles, without the prior written consent of the publisher.

First Printing July 2024 / Printed in the United States of America

CONTENTS

INTRODUCTION

THE CAST

The ten men of the Bible we're going to focus on in this study weren't exactly all what you'd call a list of "Who's Who in Purity and Sainthood." In fact, some of their antics and attitudes would make you think of the Saturday night crowd at the county jail. What few halos there are among this cast of characters could probably use a bit of straightening and polishing.

Their stories are marked by scandal, stumble, and intrigue. Yet they are also marked by remarkable faith.

Noah, who built an ark but then drank a bit too much wine from his vineyard.

Job, who thought he knew more about God than God did until God showed up and set him straight.

Jacob, who hijacked his brother's birthright and stole his blessing.

Moses, who murdered an Egyptian and fled to the wilderness.

David, the giant-killer who couldn't corral his testosterone.

Joseph, the man who went out on a shaky limb.

Matthew, the tax collector who left it all to follow Christ.

Lazarus, who . . . well, died.

Peter, who betrayed Jesus three times and then fled the scene.

And Paul, the killer of Christians who did a 180-degree-turn when he met Jesus on the Damascus Road.

We find our stories in theirs. We find our hope where they found theirs. And in the midst of them all . . . hovering over them all . . . we find the hero of it all: God. Maker. Shaper. Rescuer of sinking hearts. God. Passing out high callings, second chances, and moral compasses to all comers and takers.

So if you ever wonder how in the world God could use you to change the world, just look at these men. This ragbag group of down-and-outs, has-beens, failed followers, and despairing church leaders found hope not in their performance but in God's proverbially open arms.

Each of us should do the same.

HOW TO USE THIS STUDY

This study guide is designed to help you delve into God's Word and learn more about these ten fascinating men in the Bible. Each lesson contains the following elements:

OPENING INSIGHTS: To help you get to know more about these ten men, each lesson opens with an insight and a retelling of the character's story as drawn from Max's books. Two reflection questions will then get you thinking about how each person's story relates to your own.

DAILY BIBLE STUDY: Each lesson contains five days of Bible study with insights drawn from Max's books and leading questions to help you navigate the stories in Scripture.

POINTS TO REMEMBER: Each day's lesson concludes with a summary of the main points in the study. These serve as reminders of the key points of Max's teaching and a review at the close of your study time.

PRAYER FOR THE DAY: Each day's lesson includes a prayer to help you focus your thoughts on God and move into your quiet time with him.

WEEKLY MEMORY VERSES: Our lives are changed when we encounter Jesus, and our hearts are changed by what is kept there. The weekly memory verse will relate to the main theme of the lesson and help you hide God's Word in your heart.

SCRIPTURE QUOTATIONS: Many Scripture quotes have been provided in the margins to help you follow the retelling of the story in your Bible. (Note: All of these quotes are from the *New International Version*.)

During the daily Bible study portions, in addition to answering the questions that have been provided, you will also want to make notes of what comes to mind when you read the selected passage of Scripture. So, be sure to have pen and paper. Commit this time to the Lord, and ask him to reveal himself to you as you work through each of the lessons in this study guide.

FOR LEADERS

If you would like to lead a group through the material in this study guide, please see the section at the end of the guide for a basic design of how to set up your group time, navigate problems and opportunites that may come up during your discussion, and get the most out of the study as a group.

LESSON 1

Noah

WATER. ALL NOAH CAN SEE IS WATER. The evening sun sinks into it. The clouds are reflected in it. His boat is surrounded by it.

Water. Water to the north. Water to the south. Water to the east. Water to the west. Water.

All Noah can see is water.

He can't remember when he's seen anything but. He and the boys had barely pushed the last hippo up the ramp when heaven opened a thousand fire hydrants. Within moments the boat was rocking, and for days the rain was pouring, and for weeks Noah has been wondering, *How long is this going to last?* For forty days it rained. For months they have floated. For months they have eaten the same food, smelled the same smell, and looked at the same faces. After a certain point you run out of things to say to each other.

Finally the boat bumped, and the rocking stopped. Mrs. Noah gave Mr. Noah a look, and Noah gave the hatch a shove and poked his head through. The hull of the ark was resting on ground, but the ground was still surrounded by water. "Noah," she yelled up at him, "what do you see?"

"Water."

He sent a raven on a scouting mission; it never returned. He sent a dove. It came back shivering and spent, having found no place to roost. Then, just this morning, he tried again. He pulled a dove out of the bowels of the ark and ascended the ladder. The morning sun caused them both to squint. As he kissed the breast of the bird, he felt a pounding heart. Had he put a hand on his chest, he would have felt another. With a prayer he let it go and watched until the bird was no bigger than a speck on a window.

All day he looked for the dove's return. In between chores he opened the hatch and searched. The boys wanted him to play a little pin the tail on the donkey, but he passed. He chose instead to climb into the crow's nest and look. The wind lifted his gray hair. The sun warmed his weather-beaten face. But nothing lifted his heavy heart. He had seen nothing. Not in the morning. Not after lunch. Not later.

God said to Noah, "I am going to put an end to all people, for the earth is filled with violence. . . . So make yourself an ark of cypress wood" (Genesis 6:13–14).

For forty days the flood kept coming on the earth, and as the waters increased they lifted the ark high above the earth (7:17).

After forty days Noah opened a window he had made in the ark and sent out a raven, and it kept flying back and forth until the water had dried up from the earth (8:6–7).

Then he sent out a dove to see if the water had receded from the surface of the ground (v. 8).

Now the sun is setting, and the sky is darkening, and he has come to look one final time, but all he sees is water. Water to the north. Water to the south. Water to the east. Water to the . . .

You know the feeling. You've stood where Noah stood. You've known your share of floods. Flooded by sorrow at the cemetery, stress at the office, anger at the disability in your body or the inability of your spouse. You've seen the floodwater rise, and you've likely seen the sun set on your hopes as well. You've been on Noah's boat.

And you've needed what Noah needed; you've needed some hope. You're not asking for a helicopter rescue, but the sound of one would be nice. Hope doesn't promise an instant solution but rather the possibility of an eventual one. Sometimes all we need is a little hope.

That's all Noah needed. And that's all Noah received.

But now, Lord, what do I look for? My hope is in you (Psalm 39:7).

1. Think of your life as an ark. What conditions are you facing right now? Are you docked in a port, feeling safe, secure, and full of hope? Are you drifting a little? Are you feeling the water level around you start to rise? Or are you, like Noah, riding out a massive flood with no dry ground—and very little hope—in sight?

   _____
   _____
   _____
   _____

2. What affects the "water level" in your life? What things can make you lose sight of hope? List them in the order they affect you.

   _____
   _____
   _____
   _____
   _____

Noah faced a literal extinction-level threat. The world as he knew it was gone, yet his hope could not be destroyed. He sent out the raven and the doves to get a sense of *when*—not *if*—God would ease the flood. In the first study, we'll see how God rewarded Noah's hope in a small but profound way.

⌒ PRAYER FOR THE WEEK ⌒

Heavenly Father, thank you for making yourself known to us through your Word. Thank you for filling its pages with stories of hope. Thank you for keeping the spark of hope alive in us, no matter how dark our world becomes. Bless our efforts to understand better the incredible hope you offer. In Jesus' name, amen.

$\mathcal{D}$ay One: Olive Leaves

THE PROMISE

The old sailor stares at the sun bisected by the horizon. He could hardly imagine a more beautiful sight. But he'd give this one and a hundred more for an acre of dry ground and a grove of grapes. Mrs. Noah's voice reminds him that dinner is on the table and he should lock the hatch, and he's just about to call it a day when he hears the cooing of the dove. Here is how the Bible describes the moment: "When the dove returned to him in the evening, there in its beak was a freshly plucked olive leaf!" (Genesis 8:11 NIV).

An olive leaf. Noah would have been happy to have the bird but to have the leaf! This leaf was more than foliage; this was promise. The bird brought more than a piece of a tree; it brought hope. For isn't that what hope is? Hope is an olive leaf—evidence of dry land after a flood. Proof to the dreamer that dreaming is worth the risk.

He waited seven more days and again sent out the dove from the ark (Genesis 8:10).

When the dove returned to him in the evening, there in its beak was a freshly plucked olive leaf! (v. 11).

1. When the dove delivered the olive leaf, it brought hope to Noah of a new world to come. Read Genesis 6:9–21. What was the problem with the old world of Noah's day? How would you summarize the events that led up to the Flood?

   _____

   _____

   _____

   _____

   _____

2. How would you summarize Noah's role in those events? Why did God choose him and his family to be rescued from the Flood?

   _____

   _____

   _____

3. Read Genesis 7:17–24. What emotions do you imagine Noah experienced when he saw the waters rise? What thoughts were running through his mind?

   _____

   _____

   _____

   _____

   _____

4. Notice the waters "flooded the earth for a hundred and fifty days" (verse 24). How would that have affected Noah's hope? How do you think his attitude toward God helped him as he waited for the waters to recede?

_____

_____

_____

_____

GIVING AN OLIVE LEAF

Don't we love the olive leaves of life?

"It appears the cancer may be in remission." "I can help you with those finances." "We'll get through this together."

What's more, don't we love the doves that bring them? When the father walks his son through his first broken heart, he gives him an olive leaf. When the wife of many years consoles the wife of a few months, when she tells her that conflicts come and all husbands are moody and these storms pass, you know what she is doing? She is giving an olive leaf.

There is surely a future hope for you, and your hope will not be cut off (Proverbs 23:18).

5. To be able to give an olive leaf is a hard-earned privilege. Hope doesn't always come easily. In Noah's story, we know his first attempt at avian exploration ended in disappointment when the raven didn't come back. Read Genesis 8:1–12. Based on what does—or doesn't—happen with each bird release, what can we learn about the way God chooses to work in certain situations?

_____

_____

_____

_____

_____

_____

6. The olive leaf was good news, but not necessarily *miraculously* good news. God hadn't caused the floodwaters to vanish overnight, even though that's probably what more than one person in the ark had been hoping. What does that tell us about hope and expectations?

_____

_____

_____

_____

_____

_____

7. Noah and his family knew the conditions outside were improving, but they had no idea how much longer they would have to stay in the ark. Read Jeremiah 29:11. What's the secret to maintaining hope for an indefinite period of time?

_____

_____

_____

_____

_____

_____

8. What are some "olive leaves of life" that you would like to receive right now? What are some leaves you could give to others?

_____

_____

_____

_____

_____

The thread of hope—regardless of circumstances—that runs through the story of Noah weaves its way throughout the rest of Scripture. That hope found its personification in Jesus. As we'll see in the next study, no one brought hope like Christ.

❧ POINTS TO REMEMBER ❧

❖ During trying times, God sends an olive leaf of hope to assure us there is dry land after a flood.
❖ The olive leaves of life—and those who bring them—prove to the dreamer that the dream is worth the risk.
❖ We make a tremendous impact on another person's life when we offer them an olive leaf of hope.

❧ PRAYER FOR THE WEEK ❧

Father, we praise you for making all things happen in your perfect, perfect time. We thank you for your loving concern. Even in the midst of your judgment of the world, you kept Noah and his family safe. You gave them reason to hope, just as you give us reason to hope. May we never forget that.
In Jesus' name, amen.

𝒟ay Two: The Hope We Need

THE DOVE OF HEAVEN

At dawn [Jesus] appeared again in the temple courts. . . . The teachers of the law and the Pharisees brought in a woman caught in adultery. They made her stand before the group (John 8:2–3).

[Jesus] straightened up and said to them, "Let any one of you who is without sin be the first to throw a stone at her" (v. 7).

At this, those who heard began to go away one at a time (v. 9).

"Go now and leave your life of sin" (v. 11).

We love olive leaves. And we love those who give them. Perhaps that's the reason so many loved Jesus.

He stands near a woman who was yanked from a bed of promiscuity. She's still dizzy from the raid. A door slammed open, covers were pulled back, and the fraternity of moral police barged in. And now here she stands. Noah could see nothing but water. She can see nothing but anger. She has no hope.

But then Jesus speaks, "If any one of you is without sin, let him be the first to throw a stone at her" (John 8:7 NIV). Silence. Both the eyes and the rocks of the accusers hit the ground. Within moments they have left, and Jesus is alone with the woman. The dove of heaven offers her a leaf.

"Woman, where are they? Has no one condemned you?"

"No one, sir," she said.

"Then neither do I condemn you," Jesus declared. "Go now and leave your life of sin" (verses 10–11 NIV).

Into her shame-flooded world he brings a leaf of hope.

1. Hope can be given and hope can be taken. Read John 8:1–11. In this story, the "moral police" put the woman in a seemingly hopeless position. In what other ways do people tend to rob other people of hope?

   _____

   _____

   _____

   _____

   _____

   _____

2. Who in the past has robbed—or attempted to rob—you of hope? How did they do it? How successful were they?

   _____

   _____

   _____

   _____

   _____

   _____

   _____

3. What did you learn from those experiences?

_____

_____

_____

_____

4. Based on what you read in John 8, what do you think Jesus would say to the people who attempted to rob you? What do you think he would say to you about those encounters?

_____

_____

_____

THE HOPE JESUS GIVES

Jesus also brings a leaf of hope to Martha. She is bobbing in a sea of sorrow. Her brother is dead. His body has been buried. And Jesus, well, Jesus is late. "If you had been here, my brother would not have died." Then I think she might have paused. "But I know that even now God will give you whatever you ask" (John 11:21–22 NIV). As Noah opened his hatch, so Martha opens her heart. As the dove brought a leaf, so Christ brings the same.

"I am the resurrection and the life. He who believes in me will live, even though he dies; and whoever lives and believes in me will never die. Do you believe this?"

"Yes, Lord," she told him, "I believe that you are the Christ, the Son of God, who was to come into the world" (verses 25–27 NIV).

How could he get by with such words? Who was he to make such a claim? What qualified him to offer grace to one woman and a promise of resurrection to another? Simple. He had done what the dove did. He'd crossed the shoreline of the future land and journeyed among the trees. And from the grove of grace he plucked a leaf for the woman. And from the tree of life he pulled a sprig for Martha.

And from both he brings leaves to you. Grace and life. Forgiveness of sin. The defeat of death. This is the hope he gives. This is the hope we need.

On his arrival, Jesus found that Lazarus had already been in the tomb for four days (John 11:17).

Martha said . . . "I know that even now God will give you whatever you ask" (vv. 21–22).

Jesus said . . . "I am the resurrection and the life" (v. 25).

"Yes, Lord," she replied, "I believe that you are the Messiah" (v. 27).

The sting of death is sin. . . . But thanks be to God! He gives us the victory through our Lord Jesus Christ (1 Corinthians 15:56–57).

5. Martha essentially told Jesus, "If you had been here when my brother was sick, we would have had reason to hope." In light of what Jesus did minutes later—raise her brother from the dead—her words seem shortsighted. In what other ways do people tend to be shortsighted when it comes to hope?

_____

_____

_____

_____

6. Earlier in the story, it's revealed Jesus *could* have arrived in Bethany while Martha's brother, Lazarus, was still alive. Instead, he delayed his visit. Why do you suppose Jesus allowed Mary and Martha to endure such a seemingly hopeless situation?

_____

_____

_____

_____

7. Has Jesus ever done something similar in your life? In what ways has he allowed you to endure seemingly hopeless situations to cause you to rethink your definition of *hopeless*?

_____

_____

_____

8. Jesus' defeat of death and forgiveness of sins gives us hope for eternal life, but what about in the meantime? What present hope does his salvation give us?

_____

_____

_____

Jesus' raising of Lazarus opens the door for all kinds of hope for those who believe in him. In many instances, holding on to hope may not seem logical. However, as the next study will make clear, the Lord has a perspective—a vision of the here and now as well as of what's to come—that we do not. And that perspective makes all the difference in the world.

❦ POINTS TO REMEMBER ❧

❖ Jesus enters our shame-flooded world when everything seems the most hopeless and offers us a leaf from the grove of grace.

❖ Jesus comforts us in our sorrow and assures us he is "the way and the truth and the life" (John 14:6 NIV).

❖ Jesus promises all who believe in him will one day have the ultimate hope of eternal life.

❦ PRAYER FOR THE DAY ❧

Father, thank you for sending your Son. Thank you for sacrificing that which was most precious to you in order to give us hope. May that hope burn so brightly in us that it inspires others to hope—and to claim the gift of salvation that you offer. In Jesus' name, amen.

*D*ay Three: Bobby Pins and Rubber Bands

IS THERE ANY HOPE?

In his book *The Grand Essentials*, Ben Patterson tells of an S–4 submarine that sank off the coast of Massachusetts. The entire crew was trapped. Every effort was made to rescue the sailors, but every effort failed. Near the end of the ordeal, a deep-sea diver heard tapping on the steel wall of the sunken sub. As he placed his helmet against the vessel, he realized he was hearing a sailor tap out this question in Morse code: "Is there any hope?"[1]

To the guilty who ask that question, Jesus says, "Yes!"

To the death-struck who ask that question, Jesus answers, "Yes!"

To all the Noahs of the world, to all who search the horizon for a fleck of hope, he proclaims, "Yes!" And he comes. He comes as a dove. He comes bearing fruit from a distant land, from our future home. He comes with a leaf of hope.

Have you received yours? Don't think your ark is too isolated. Don't think your flood is too wide. Your toughest challenge is nothing more than bobby pins and rubber bands to God.

"Peace I leave with you; my peace I give you. I do not give to you as the world gives. Do not let your hearts be troubled and do not be afraid" (John 14:27).

1. The question the submarine crew posed was desperate and simple: "Is there hope?" How many people in your circle of acquaintances do you suppose are asking the same question—if not aloud, then alone in a quiet, desperate panic? How can you spot those who need an answer?

   _____

   _____

   _____

   _____

2. What makes people assume their "ark is too isolated" or their "flood is too wide" to allow for any hope?

   _____

   _____

   _____

   _____

3. How can we counter that way of thinking without sounding delusional?

   _____

   _____

   _____

   _____

4. Whatever hope the crew of the sunken S-4 submarine may have had, it ended with their deaths. But death is not the only cause of hopes being left unfulfilled. What would you say to someone who's been scarred by hopes that never came to fruition?

_____

_____

_____

_____

_____

A BETTER PERSPECTIVE

Bobby pins and rubber bands? My older sister used to give them to me when I was a child. I would ride my tricycle up and down the sidewalk, pretending that the bobby pins were keys and my trike was a truck. But one day I lost the "keys." Crisis! What was I going to do? My search yielded nothing but tears and fear. But when I confessed my mistake to my sister, she just smiled. Being a decade older, she had a better perspective.

God has a better perspective as well. With all due respect, our severest struggles are, in his view, nothing worse than lost bobby pins and rubber bands. He is not confounded, confused, or discouraged.

Receive his hope, won't you? Receive it because you need it. Receive it so you can share it.

What do you suppose Noah did with his? What do you think he did with the leaf? Did he throw it overboard and forget about it? Do you suppose he stuck it in his pocket and saved it for a scrapbook? Or do you think he let out a whoop and assembled the troops and passed it around?

Certainly he whooped. That's what you do with hope. What do you do with olive leaves? You pass them around. You don't stick them in your pocket. You give them to the ones you love. Love always hopes. "Love . . . bears all things, believes all things, *hopes* all things, endures all things" (1 Corinthians 13:4–7 NKJV, emphasis added).

Love has hope in you.

"For my thoughts are not your thoughts, neither are your ways my ways," declares the LORD. "As the heavens are higher than the earth, so are my ways higher than your ways and my thoughts than your thoughts" (Isaiah 55:8–9).

5. Noah wasn't the only one to receive an olive leaf the day the dove came back bearing the twig in its talons. His whole family was fervently hoping for something to happen. From your own perspective, why is it easier to maintain hope when you are not going through tough times alone?

_____

_____

_____

_____

_____

6. What happens when a community of people experience hope? How does that shape their lives and the lives of generations to come?

_____

_____

_____

_____

7. As believers in Christ, we have hope because we know God has a greater perspective on our troubles than we do. What do the following verses say about why we can always trust in God's plans for our lives?

Proverbs 3:5–6: "Trust in the Lord with all your heart and lean not on your own understanding; in all your ways submit to him, and he will make your paths straight" (NIV).

_____

_____

_____

_____

_____

Jeremiah 1:5: "Before I made you in your mother's womb, I chose you. Before you were born, I set you apart for a special work. I appointed you as a prophet to the nations" (NCV).

_____

_____

_____

_____

Matthew 6:25–27: "Therefore I tell you, do not worry about your life, what you will eat or drink; or about your body, what you will wear. Is not life more than food, and the body more than clothes? Look at the birds of the air; they do not sow or reap or store away in barns, and yet your heavenly Father feeds them. Are you not much more valuable than they? Can any one of you by worrying add a single hour to your life?" (NIV).

_____

_____

_____

_____

Romans 8:28: "We know that in everything God works for the good of those who love him. They are the people he called, because that was his plan" (NCV).

_____

_____

_____

_____

8. Hope is meant to be shared and given out to the ones you love. What is the most memorable "olive leaf" you've ever offered to someone?

_____

_____

_____

Perspective is the key to maintaining hope. We can't see things from God's perspective, but we can trust that his vision will see us through any circumstance and bring ultimate good from any situation.

❧ POINTS TO REMEMBER ☙

❖ Jesus offers the promise to those caught in the floodwaters and storms of life that there *is* hope.
❖ Even our severest struggles and most difficult trials are nothing that God, in his infinite power and grace, cannot handle.
❖ When we receive olive leaves of hope, we are not to keep them to ourselves but share them with others who are also in need.

❧ PRAYER FOR THE DAY ☙

Father, we humbly acknowledge that you are all-powerful. No situation and no circumstance in this world are beyond your ability to change. Because of that, we know that hope always exists—even when we can't see it. Open our eyes to the potential for good in everything that happens.
In Jesus' name, amen.

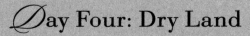

Day Four: Dry Land

THE GIFT OF HOPE

The aspiring young author was in need of hope. More than one person had told him to give up. "Getting published is impossible," one mentor said. "Unless you are a national celebrity, publishers won't talk to you." Another warned, "Writing takes too much time. Besides, you don't want all your thoughts on paper."

Initially he listened. He agreed that writing was a waste of effort and turned his attention to other projects. But somehow the pen and pad were bourbon and Coke to the wordaholic. He'd rather write than read. So he wrote. How many nights did he pass on that couch in the corner of the apartment reshuffling his deck of verbs and nouns? And how many hours did his wife sit with him? He wordsmithing. She cross-stitching. Finally a manuscript was finished. Crude and laden with mistakes but finished.

She gave him the shove. "Send it out. What's the harm?"

So out it went. Mailed to fifteen different publishers. While the couple waited, he wrote. While he wrote, she stitched. Neither expecting much, both hoping everything. Responses began to fill the mailbox. "I'm sorry, but we don't accept unsolicited manuscripts." "We must return your work. Best of luck." "Our catalog doesn't have room for unpublished authors."

I still have those letters. Somewhere in a file. Finding them would take some time. Finding Denalyn's cross-stitch, however, would take none. To see it, all I do is lift my eyes from this monitor and look on the wall. "Of all those arts in which the wise excel, nature's chief masterpiece is writing well."

She gave it to me about the time the fifteenth letter arrived. A publisher had said yes. That letter is also framed. Which of the two is more meaningful? The gift from my wife or the letter from the publisher? The gift, hands down. For in giving the gift, Denalyn gave hope.

Love does that. Love extends an olive leaf to the loved one and says, "I have hope in you."

Be joyful in hope, patient in affliction, faithful in prayer (Romans 12:12).

1. Think about a seemingly hopeless situation that you faced in the past. Put yourself back in that situation and back in that mindset. How did you feel? What emotions were you experiencing? What kinds of thoughts were going through your head? Why did the situation seem so hopeless to you?

   _____

   _____

   _____

2. What gifts of hope did you receive during that time? Who or what did God use to give you hope?

   _____

   _____

   _____

3. What did that hope do for you? How did it affect your outlook?

   _____

   _____

   _____

4. How have the gifts of hope you have received affected your ability to dream?

   _____

   _____

   _____

HOPE TO THE ARKBOUND

By faith Noah, when warned about things not yet seen, in holy fear built an ark to save his family. By his faith he condemned the world and became heir of the righteousness that is in keeping with faith (Hebrews 11:7).

Love is just as quick to say, "I have hope *for* you."

You can say those words. You are a flood survivor. By God's grace you have found your way to dry land. You know what it's like to see the waters subside. And since you do, since you passed through a flood and lived to tell about it, you are qualified to give hope to someone else.

What? Can't think of any floods in your past? Let me jog your memory.

How about adolescence? Remember the torrent of the teenage years? Remember the hormones and hemlines? The puberty and pimples? Those were tough times. *Yeah,* you're thinking, *but you get through them.* That's exactly what teenagers need to hear you say. They need an olive leaf from a survivor.

So do young couples. It happens in every marriage. The honeymoon ends, and the river of romance becomes the river of reality, and they wonder if they will survive. You can tell them they will. You've been through it. Wasn't easy, but you survived. You and your spouse found dry land. Why don't you pluck an olive leaf and take it to an ark?

Therefore encourage one another and build each other up (1 Thessalonians 5:11).

Are you a cancer survivor? Someone in the cancer ward needs to hear from you. Have you buried a spouse and lived to smile again? Then find the recently widowed and walk with them. Your experiences have deputized you into the dove brigade. You have an opportunity—yea, verily, an obligation—to give hope to the arkbound.

5. How can you tell if someone is "arkbound" and in need of hope? What clues would you look for in the way he or she talks and acts?

_____
_____
_____

6. What role does empathy play in giving people hope?

_____
_____
_____

7. How can you develop or sharpen your empathy skills?

_____
_____
_____

8. Why is it vital that with every olive leaf you distribute, you also deflect all credit and glory to the One who made the leaf?

_____
_____
_____
_____

Each of us has a powerful story of hope to tell. We may not recognize just how powerful our story is, however, until we see it resonate in the life of someone else. Noah's story still resonates thousands of years after it happened. In fact, as we'll see in the next study, Jesus himself used Noah's story to give hope to people concerning his own return.

⟶ POINTS TO REMEMBER ⟵

❖ Love extends encouragement to our loved ones and communicates that we have hope in them.
❖ We are all survivors who have been through the floods of life and seen the waters subside, and this qualifies us to offer hope to others.
❖ We have an incredible opportunity—even an obligation—to bring hope to those who are in need of it.

⟶ PRAYER FOR THE DAY ⟵

Father, thank you for creating in us an interconnectedness—common ground, similar experiences, and shared emotions that we can draw on to give hope to one another. Help us to be mindful of the hope we have been given. Bless our efforts to share that hope with others. In Jesus' name, amen.

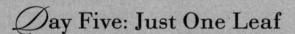

Day Five: Just One Leaf

HIDDEN IN CHRIST

As Jesus sought for a way to explain his return, he hearkened back to the flood of Noah. "In those days before the flood," he said, "people were eating and drinking, marrying and giving their children to be married, until the day Noah entered the boat. They knew nothing about what was happening until the flood came and destroyed them. It will be the same when the Son of Man comes" (Matthew 24:38–39 NCV).

The parallels are obvious. A message of judgment was proclaimed then. It is proclaimed still. People didn't listen then. They refuse to listen today. Noah was sent to save the faithful. Christ was sent to do the same. A flood of water came then. A flood of fire will come next. Noah built a safe place out of wood. Jesus made a safe place with the cross. Those who believed hid in the ark. Those who believe are hidden in Christ.

"But about that day or hour no one knows . . . only the Father. As it was in the days of Noah, so it will be at the coming of the Son of Man (Matthew 24:36–37).

"So you also must be ready, because the Son of Man will come at an hour when you do not expect him" (v. 44).

1. To the grief-stricken, God says, "Never will I leave you; never will I forsake you" (Hebrews 13:5 NIV). Do you know anyone who has recently lost a loved one, gone through a divorce, or experienced an estrangement from a family member? If so, how can you explain God's assurance to that person in a hope-giving way?

   _____

   _____

   _____

2. To the guilt-ridden, Paul writes, "There is now no condemnation for those who are in Christ Jesus" (Romans 8:1 NIV). Do you know anyone with an unquiet conscience? If so, how can you translate the words of the apostle Paul into hope for that person?

   _____

   _____

   _____

3. To the jobless, the Bible says, "In all things God works for the good of those who love him" (Romans 8:28 NIV). Do you know anyone who's struggling with job security at the moment? If so, how can you use the promise of this verse to offer hope to that person?

   _____

   _____

   _____

   _____

4. To those who feel beyond God's grace, John writes, "For God so loved the world that he gave his one and only Son, that whoever believes in him shall not perish but have eternal life" (John 3:16 NIV). Do you know anyone who feels too far gone to receive God's grace? If so, how can you use Jesus' words to bring hope into that person's life?

   _____

   _____

   _____

   _____

A BASKET OF LEAVES

God sends a safe place for the faithful today: his Son. So encourage those who are lost and struggling. Don't know what to say? Open your Bible. The olive leaf for the Christian is a verse of Scripture. "For everything that was written in the past was written to teach us, so that through endurance and the encouragement of the Scriptures we might have hope" (Romans 15:4 NIV).

Do you have a Bible? Then start passing out the leaves.

Your Bible is a basket of leaves. Won't you share one? They have amazing impact. After receiving his, Noah was a changed man. "Then Noah knew that the water had receded from the earth" (Genesis 8:11 NIV). He went up the ladder with questions and came down the ladder with confidence. What a difference one leaf makes.

Then Noah knew that the water had receded from the earth. . . . Noah then removed the covering from the ark and saw that the surface of the ground was dry (Genesis 8:11,13).

5. What do the following passages—your "olive leaves"—say about hope?

Zephaniah 3:17: "For the LORD your God is living among you. He is a mighty savior. He will take delight in you with gladness. With his love, he will calm all your fears. He will rejoice over you with joyful songs" (NLT).

_____

_____

_____

_____

Psalm 3:2-6: "Many are saying about me, 'God won't rescue him.' But, LORD, you are my shield, my wonderful God who gives me courage. I will pray to the LORD, and he will answer me from his holy mountain. I can lie down and go to sleep, and I will wake up again, because the LORD gives me strength. Thousands of troops may surround me, but I am not afraid" (NCV).

_____

_____

_____

_____

John 14:1-3: "Do not let your hearts be troubled. You believe in God; believe also in me. My Father's house has many rooms; if that were not so, would I have told you that I am going there to prepare a place for you? And if I go and prepare a place for you, I will come back and take you to be with me that you also may be where I am" (NIV).

_____

_____

_____

_____

1 Peter 1:4-6: "Now we hope for the blessings God has for his children. These blessings, which cannot be destroyed or be spoiled or lose their beauty, are kept in heaven for you. God's power protects you through your faith until salvation is shown to you at the end of time. This makes you very happy, even though now for a short time different kinds of troubles may make you sad" (NCV).

_____

_____

6. In 1 Peter 3:15 we read, "Always be prepared to give an answer to everyone who asks you to give the reason for the hope that you have" (NIV). What is the hope that you have? How would you summarize it in one sentence?

_____

_____

_____

_____

_____

_____

_____

7. How prepared are you to follow Peter's instructions? What reasons would you give for your hope?

_____

_____

_____

_____

_____

_____

_____

8. Of all the people you know, who would benefit most from hearing about the hope you have?

_____

_____

_____

_____

_____

_____

_____

_____

God said to Noah . . . "I now establish my covenant with you and with your descendants after you" (Genesis 9:8–9).

At the end of the story of the Flood, God says to Noah, "I establish my covenant with you: Never again will all life be cut off by the waters of a flood; never again will there be a flood to destroy the earth . . . This is the sign of the covenant I am making between me and you and every living creature with you, a covenant for all generations to come: I have set my rainbow in the clouds, and it will be the sign of the covenant between me and the earth" (Genesis 9:11–13 NIV).

The Hebrew word for covenant, *beriyth*, means a solemn agreement with binding force. God makes and never breaks his promises. His irrevocable covenant runs like a scarlet thread through the tapestry of Scripture. Every rainbow reminds us of God's covenant. Curiously, astronauts who've seen rainbows from outer space tell us they form a complete circle. God's promises are equally unbroken and unending.

"This is the sign of the covenant I have established between me and all life on the earth" (v. 17).

⤚✥ POINTS TO REMEMBER ✥⤚

❖ Jesus made a safe place for us with the cross, but we must accept his gift of hope and get on board the ark of salvation.

❖ Whenever we are struggling and need encouragement, we can open the pages of the Bible—our olive leaves of hope.

❖ God's promises, like the rainbow at the end of the Flood, are eternally unbroken and unending.

⤚✥ PRAYER FOR THE DAY ✥⤚

Jesus, help us to not be stubborn or set in our ways. Help us to listen for your voice and follow your call as we extend the hope you have given us to others. Thank you, Lord, for making a safe place for each of us through your ark of salvation. In your name, amen.

⤚✥ WEEKLY MEMORY VERSE ✥⤚

May the God of hope fill you with all joy and peace as you trust in him, so that you may overflow with hope by the power of the Holy Spirit.
ROMANS 15:13 (NIV)

For Further Reading

Selections throughout this lesson were taken from *A Love Worth Giving* (Nashville: Thomas Nelson, 2002); *When Christ Comes* (Nashville: Thomas Nelson, 1999); and *Facing Your Giants* (Nashville: Thomas Nelson, 2006).

Note

1. Charles Swindoll, *The Tale of the Tardy Oxcart and 1,501 Other Stories* (Nashville: Word Publishing, 1998), p. 275.

LESSON 2

JOB

GOD'S PRESENCE IN THE STORM

WHEN I LIVED IN BRAZIL, I took my mom and her friend to see Iguacu Falls, the largest waterfalls in the world. Some weeks earlier I'd become an expert on the cataracts by reading an article in *National Geographic* magazine. Surely, I thought, my guests would appreciate their good fortune in having me as a guide.

To reach the lookout point, tourists must walk a winding trail that leads them through a forest. I took advantage of the hike to give an Iguacu nature report to my mom and her friend. So full of information I was, I chattered the entire time. After some minutes, however, I caught myself speaking louder and louder. A sound in the distance forced me to raise my voice. With each turn in the trail, my volume increased. Finally, I was shouting above a roar which was proving to be quite irritating. *Whatever that noise is, I wish they'd shut it off so I could complete my lecture.*

Only after reaching the clearing did I realize that the noise we heard was the waterfalls. My words were drowned out by the force and fury of what I was trying to describe. I could no longer be heard. Even if I could, I no longer had an audience. Even my mother would rather see the splendor than hear my description. I shut my mouth.

There are times when to speak is to violate the moment . . . when silence represents the highest respect. The word for such times is reverence. The prayer for such times is, "Hallowed be thy name." Only you and God are here, and you can surmise who occupies the throne.

This was a lesson Job learned. If he had a fault, it was his tongue. He talked too much. Not that anyone could blame him. Calamity pounced on the man like a lioness on a herd of gazelles, and by the time the rampage passed, there was hardly a wall standing or a loved one living. And it all happened in *one day*. One moment Job could choose his tee time at the nicest golf course in the country; the next he couldn't even be the caddie. One moment he could jet across the country to see a heavyweight bout in Las Vegas. The next he couldn't afford a city bus across town.

Talk about calm becoming chaos . . .

"Our Father in heaven, hallowed by your name" (Matthew 6:9)

In the land of Uz there lived a man whose name was Job. . . . He was the greatest man among all the people of the East (Job 1:1,3).

"The oxen were plowing and the donkeys were grazing nearby, and the Sabeans attacked and made off with them. . . . The fire of God fell from the heavens and burned up the sheep and the servants. . . . The Chaldeans formed three raiding parties and swept down on your camels. . . . Your sons and daughters were feasting and drinking wine at the oldest brother's house . . . it collapsed on them and they are dead" (Job 1:13–19).

The first thing to go is his empire. The market crashes; his assets tumble. What is liquid goes dry. What has been up goes down. Stocks go flat, and Job goes broke. There he sits in his leather chair at his soon-to-be-auctioned-off mahogany desk when the phone rings with news of calamity number two: the kids were at a resort for the holidays when a storm blew in and took them with it.

Shell-shocked and dumbfounded, Job looks out the window into the sky that seems to be getting darker by the minute. He starts praying, telling God that things can't get any worse . . . and that's exactly what happens.

1. Read Job 1:13–22 and think about all the calamities that affected Job in that one day. What do you think his thoughts would have been when each messenger arrived? What does his ultimate response to the crisis say about his character?

   _____

   _____

   _____

   _____

2. What circumstances and situations are darkening your sky right now? What is your reaction to those events? What questions are you asking? What are your thoughts about and emotions toward God?

   _____

   _____

   _____

   _____

If indeed there is such a thing as the "school of hard knocks," Job may well have been its founder. At the very least, he was its star pupil. This man of God received a doctorate-level education in theology, counseling, and a host of other subjects in the midst of the most devastating circumstances imaginable. And one of the first things Job learned—as you'll discover in the first study—is that where there is tragedy, there are always people who claim to understand why it is happening.

⤳ PRAYER FOR THE WEEK ⤲

Heavenly Father, thank you for the life-changing lessons found in the story of Job. Thank you for revealing yourself to be patient, gracious, and understanding even when we are at our worst. Please bless our efforts to understand you better in the midst of our suffering. Help us learn from Job's experience so we may honor you. In Jesus' name, amen.

*D*ay One: Why Is This Happening?

SOME LESS-THAN-HELPFUL ADVICE

Job hasn't even had time to call his insurance company before he sees the leprosy on his hands and the boils on his skin. His wife, compassionate soul that she is, tells him to "curse God and die." Who could blame her for being upset at the week's calamities? Who could blame her for telling Job to curse God? But to curse God *and die*? If Job doesn't already feel abandoned, he does the minute his wife tells him to pull the plug and be done with it.

Next come his four friends with the bedside manner of drill sergeants and the compassion of chainsaw killers. A revised version of their theology might read like this: "Boy, you must have done something really bad! We know that God is good, so if bad things are happening to you, then you have been bad. Period." As sure as two-plus-two equals four, Job must have some criminal record in his past to suffer so.

Each friend has his own interpretation of God, and each speaks long and loud about who God is and why God did what he has done. They aren't the only ones talking about God. When his accusers pause, Job gives his response.

"Job cried out . . ." (Job 3:1 NCV).
"Then Eliphaz the Temanite answered . . ." (4:1 NCV).
"Then Job answered . . ." (6:1 NCV).
"Then Bildad the Shuhite answered . . ." (8:1 NCV).
"Then Job answered . . ." (9:1 NCV).
"Then Zophath the Naamathite answered . . ." (11:1 NCV).

Back and forth they go. Finally, Job says, "You are doctors who don't know what they are doing. Oh, please be quiet! That would be your highest wisdom" (Job 13:4–5 TLB). Translation? "Why don't you take your philosophy back to the pigpen where you learned it."

1. In Proverbs 15:22 we read, "Without counsel, plans go awry, but in the multitude of counselors they are established" (NKJV). Job certainly had a "multitude of counselors," but they proved to be of no help to him in this situation. What nuggets of advice do Job's three friends give in the following verses?

Eliphaz the Temanite: Job 4:7; 5:8; 15:20; 22:21–22

_____

_____

_____

_____

Satan . . . afflicted Job with painful sores from the soles of his feet to the crown of his head. . . . His wife said to him, "Are you still maintaining your integrity? Curse God and die!" (Job 2:7–9).

When Job's three friends . . . heard about all the troubles that had come upon him, they set out from their homes . . . to go and sympathize with him and comfort him (v. 11).

"You, however, smear me with lies; you are worthless physicians, all of you! If only you would be altogether silent!" (13:4–5).

Bildad the Shuhite: Job 8:5–6; 18:2–3; 25:4

_____

_____

_____

_____

Zophath the Naamathite: Job 11:13–15; 20:6–7

_____

_____

_____

_____

2. Every counselor has an agenda. Most have a genuine desire to help; others have a genuine desire to be seen as wise; and some have ulterior motives. How can a suffering person like Job discern the motives of his or her would-be counselors? What makes a person a good counselor in times of need?

_____

_____

_____

_____

_____

_____

3. Who would likely offer you counsel when your sky grows dark? What would that person say? Whose counsel would be most welcome to you? Why?

_____

_____

_____

_____

4. Who might turn to _you_ for comfort or advice when his or her sky grows dark? What would you say?

_____

_____

_____

_____

A GOOD MAN IN HIS OWN EYES

"Though he slay me, yet will I hope in him; I will surely defend my ways to his face" (Job 13:15).

Job is, in his eyes, a good man. "I paid my taxes. I'm active in civic duties. I'm a major contributor to charitable causes and a volunteer at the hospital bazaar." And, a good man, he reasons, deserves a good answer.

"Your suffering is for your own good," states Elihu, a young minister fresh out of seminary who hasn't lived long enough to be cynical and hasn't hurt enough to be quiet. He paces back and forth in the hospital room, with his Bible under his arm and his finger punching the air.

"God does all these things to a man—twice, even three times—to turn back his soul from the pit, that the light of life may shine on him" (Job 33:29–30 NLV).

Job follows his pacing like you'd follow a tennis player, head turning from side to side. What the young man says isn't bad theology, but it isn't much comfort either. Job steadily tunes him out and slides lower and lower under the covers. His head hurts. His eyes burn. His legs ache. And he can't stomach any more hollow homilies.

Yet his question still hasn't been answered: "God, why is this happening to me?"

Elihu had waited before speaking to Job because they were older than he (Job 33:4).

"God does all these things to a person . . . to turn them back from the pit" (vv. 29–30).

5. Read Job 32:1–5. Why did Elihu feel compelled to speak up and state his opinions at this point in the story?

_____

_____

_____

_____

_____

_____

6. Why is Elihu angry with Job? Why is he angry with Job's three friends? Do think his anger was justified?

_____

_____

_____

_____

7. Homilies and platitudes are as popular today as they were in Job's day. Put yourself in Job's position. How would you respond to someone who said . . .

"God never gives you more than you can handle"?

_____

_____

_____

_____

"Everything happens for a reason"?

_____

_____

_____

_____

"What doesn't kill you makes you stronger"?

_____

_____

_____

_____

"There are other people in this world who have it worse than you do"?

_____

_____

_____

_____

8. Read Job 36:2–4. From what authority does Elihu say he derives his knowledge? What is the danger in claiming to speak on "God's behalf"?

_____

_____

_____

_____

The longer Job's friends spoke, the more frustrated he grew. Their words certainly gave the appearance of being profound, but ultimately for Job they were empty. His friends didn't know what he was going through. Not really. They couldn't empathize with his situation, so Job decided to set them straight. And, as we'll see in the next study, in so doing Job spoke for all those whose pain and suffering has ever caused them to question God.

➴ POINTS TO REMEMBER ➴

❖ Many people have interpretations of God, but we have to remember that God's ways are always higher than our own (see Isaiah 55:8).
❖ Job was a good man, but even good men have no right to demand anything of God.
❖ While what Job's friends said to him might have represented good theology, it was of no comfort to him—and of little use to him.

➴ PRAYER FOR THE DAY ➴

Father, thank you for your faithfulness. Thank you for never deserting us in our time of need, even when we push you away. Thank you for your Word, which is never empty or shallow but always capable of giving us comfort and insight into your work. Help us recognize your presence and keep our minds free of teachings that do not represent your truth. In Jesus' name, amen.

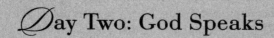

Day Two: God Speaks

JOB TAKES THE STAND

The verbal Ping-Pong between Job and his friends continues for twenty-three chapters. Finally Job has enough of this "answering." He will have no more discussion-group chitchat. It's time for the keynote address. He grips the microphone with one hand and the pulpit with the other and launches forth. For six chapters Job gives his opinions on God. This time the chapter headings read: "And Job continued," "And Job continued," "And Job continued." He defines God, explains God, and reviews God. One gets the impression that Job knows more about God than God does!

We are thirty-seven chapters into the book before God clears his throat to speak. Job 38 begins with these words: "Then the Lord answered Job" (NCV). If your Bible is like mine, there is a mistake in this verse. The words are fine, but the printer uses the wrong size type. The words should look like this:

Then the LORD Answered Job!

God speaks. Faces turn toward the sky. Winds bend the trees. Neighbors plunge into the storm shelters. Cats scurry up the trees and dogs duck into the bushes. "Somethin's a-blowin' in, honey. Best take cover inside." God has no more than opened his mouth before Job knows he should have kept his sore one shut.

"As surely as God lives, who has denied me justice, the Almighty, who has made my life bitter . . . my lips will not say anything wicked, and my tongue will not utter lies. I will never admit you are in the right" (Job 27:2, 4–5).

Then the LORD spoke to Job out of the storm (38:1).

1. In Psalm 22:1, David wrote, "My God, my God, why have you forsaken me? Why are you so far from saving me, so far from my cries of anguish?" (NIV). Job, like David, was a righteous man. What do you think would cause them to give voice to such thoughts about God?

_____

_____

_____

_____

2. What impact does suffering have on our outlook and our feelings about God? Why do we often feel the need to blame God for the things that go wrong?

_____

_____

_____

3. "Then the LORD spoke to Job out of the storm" (Job 38:1 NIV). What did Job recognize in that moment? How has your life been impacted when you recognized God was speaking into your situation?

_____

_____

_____

_____

_____

4. What conclusions can we draw from the fact that God chose to answer Job out of the storm instead of punishing Job for questioning him?

_____

_____

_____

_____

THE THUNDER OF GOD

Out of the thunder, God speaks. Out of the sky, he speaks. For all of us who would put ditto marks under Job's question and sign our names to it, he speaks.

For the father who holds a rose taken off his son's coffin, he speaks.

For the wife who holds the flag taken off her husband's casket, he speaks.

For the couple with the barren womb and the fervent prayers, he speaks.

For any person who has tried to see God through shattered glass, he speaks.

For those of us who have dared to say, "If God is God, then . . ." God speaks.

He speaks out of the storm and into the storm, for that is where Job is. That is where God is best heard.

God's voice thunders in the room. Elihu sits down. Job sits up. And the two will never be the same again.

"I will instruct you and teach you in the way you should go; I will counsel you with my loving eye on you. Do not be like the horse or the mule, which have no understanding" (Psalm 32:8–9).

5. In the midst of suffering and doubt, would the audible voice of God be more comforting or frightening to you? Explain.

_____

_____

_____

_____

6. Read Mark 4:35–41. How did Jesus speak into the storm in this situation?

_____

_____

_____

_____

7. Notice that Jesus wasn't angry with his disciples for being scared—he was more disappointed they didn't yet fully recognize and trust his power. How is that similar to Job's encounter with God?

_____

_____

_____

_____

_____

8. How might Job have reacted to his circumstances if he had possessed a deeper understanding of who God is?

_____

_____

_____

_____

_____

_____

God gave Job and his friends time to question, misrepresent, and accuse him. He allowed them to pour out their feelings and conjectures. He remained silent while they vented and pontificated. And then, when they were finished, *he spoke.* We'll find out what he said in the next study, but suffice it to say, his words were exactly what anyone who faces trials or suffering needs to hear.

❧ POINTS TO REMEMBER ❧

❖ An encounter with God—whether or not it is as dramatic as Job's encounter—will forever change our outlook on life.
❖ God allows us to pour out our concerns, questions, and emotions to him, and then extends his mercy to us.
❖ Just as God spoke out of the storm and into the storm of Job's life, he meets us where we are in whatever situation we are facing.

❧ PRAYER FOR THE DAY ❧

Father, we praise you for your sovereignty and power. Thank you for patiently enduring our questions about you and hearing us when we cry out to you in our pain. Remind us, as you did with Job, who it is we are talking to in the midst of our struggles. Guide our thoughts and attitudes.
In Jesus' name, amen.

Day Three: Who Is God Here?

GOD'S QUESTIONS

"Who is this that obscures my plans with words without knowledge? Brace yourself like a man; I will question you, and you shall answer me" (Job 38:2–3).

"Who is this that darkens my counsel with words without knowledge?" God says (Job 38:2 NLV). Job doesn't respond.

"Brace yourself like a man;" God continues. "I will question you, and you shall answer me" (verse 3 NLV).

One question would have been enough for Job, but it isn't enough for God.

"Where were you when I laid the foundations of the earth? Tell me, if you know so much" (verse 4 TLB).

"Do you know how its dimensions were determined, and who did the surveying?" (verse 5 TLB).

"What supports its foundations, and who laid its cornerstone, as the morning stars sang together and all the angels shouted for joy?" (verses 6–7 TLB).

"Have you ever gone to where the sea begins or walked the valleys under the sea?" (verse 16 NCV).

"Have you ever gone to the storehouse for snow or seen the storehouses for hail?" (verse 22 NCV).

"Are you the one who gives the horse his strength or puts the flowing mane on its neck? (39:19 NCV).

"Do you make the horse jump like a locust? " (verse 20 NCV).

"Is it through your wisdom that the hawk flies and spreads its wings toward the south?" (verse 26 NCV).

Job barely has time to shake his head at one question before he is asked another. They pour like sheets of rain out of the clouds. They splatter in the chambers of Job's heart with a wildness and a beauty and a terror that leave every Job who has ever lived drenched and speechless, watching the Master redefine who is who in the universe.

1. Why is it so easy to lose sight of who God is?

_____

_____

_____

_____

2. What role does the Bible play in helping us maintain a proper sense of awe toward God? What stories and passages of Scripture have been especially effective for you in this regard?

_____

_____

_____

3. What role does prayer play? How do you maintain a sense of awe in your conversations with God?

_____

_____

_____

4. What role does the natural world around us play? How have you been awed by God's handiwork?

_____

_____

_____

SILENCED BY THE TORRENT

God's questions aren't intended to teach; they are intended to stun. They aren't intended to enlighten; they are intended to awaken. They aren't intended to stir the mind; they are intended to bend the knees.

"Has the location of the gates of Death been revealed to you? Do you realize the extent of the earth? Tell me about it if you know! Where does the light come from, and how do you get there? Or tell me about the darkness. Where does it come from? Can you find its boundaries, or go to its source? But of course you know all this! For you were born before it was all created, and you are so very experienced!" (Job 38:17–21 TLB).

The Father's implication is clear: "As soon as you are able to handle these simple matters of storing stars and stretching the neck of the ostrich, then we'll have a talk about pain and suffering. But until then, we can do without your commentary." Job cannot help but get the point: Only God defines God. You've got to know the alphabet before you can read, and God tells Job, "You don't even know the ABCs of heaven, much less the vocabulary."

Job is quiet. Silenced by a torrent of questions.

5. In Job 1–2 we saw the calamities in Job's life had fallen on him as a result of Satan's challenge to God. How do you think Job would have reacted if he had known his misery was the result of this cosmic challenge?

_____

_____

_____

6. What was God trying to get across to Job in asking him all these questions? Why do you think God chose not to directly answer Job's question about suffering?

_____

_____

_____

The LORD said to Job: "Will the one who contends with the Almighty correct him? Let him who accuses God answer him!" (Job 40:1–2).

Then Job answered the LORD: "I am unworthy—how can I reply to you?" (v. 3).

7. How does God's response to Job nevertheless provide us with an answer as to why we go through trials? What can we be sure of as we face adversity?

_____

_____

_____

8. Trying to figure out *why* bad things happen to us isn't necessarily the most effective way of dealing with trials and tragedy. What better strategy is found in the following verses?

"Take delight in the LORD, and he will give you your heart's desires. Commit everything you do to the LORD. Trust him, and he will help you" (Psalm 37:4–5 NLT).

_____

_____

_____

_____

"Surely the righteous will never be shaken; they will be remembered forever. They will have no fear of bad news; their hearts are steadfast, trusting in the LORD" (Psalm 112:6–7 NCV).

_____

_____

_____

_____

_____

"You will keep in perfect peace those whose minds are steadfast, because they trust in you" (Isaiah 26:3 NIV).

_____

_____

_____

_____

"Blessed is the man who trusts in the LORD, whose trust is the LORD. He is like a tree planted by water, that sends out its roots by the stream, and does not fear when heat comes, for its leaves remain green, and is not anxious in the year of drought, for it does not cease to bear fruit" (Jeremiah 17:7–8 ESV).

_____

_____

_____

_____

God has made it clear that he is in charge of *everything* that happens. Yet perhaps what is most striking about this exchange is that God chose to respond to Job at all. He was certainly under no obligation to do so, yet he desired to reach down and speak into Job's life. As we will see in the next study, while God's questions were intended to stun Job and shake him up a bit, the Lord wasn't punishing his servant for asking questions. Instead, he was putting Job in the proper frame of mind to receive the peace and comfort he sought. He was moving Job to a place of quiet contemplation.

⌁ POINTS TO REMEMBER ⌁

❖ God's knowledge is perfect, and we only get glimpses into the way things really work when God chooses to reveals his plans to us.
❖ God will get our attention when he needs to correct us or rebuke us, but he always does so with love.
❖ Sometimes the best thing we can do is be silent in reverence before an all-powerful and all-holy God.

⌁ PRAYER FOR THE DAY ⌁

Father, thank you for your loving concern and patience when we have questions about your intentions or why we have to endure trials. Thank you for looking beyond our words to the fear and uncertainty that drive them. Thank you for engaging us at the heart of our suffering. Give us wisdom and help us to remember that all things are under your control.
In Jesus' name, amen.

$\mathcal{D}$ay Four: The Proper Response

SPEECHLESS

Does Job get the message? I think so. Finally, his feeble hand lifts, and God stops long enough for him to respond. "I am nothing—how could I ever find the answers? I lay my hand upon my mouth in silence. I have said too much already" (Job 40:4–5 TLB).

Notice the change. Before he heard God, Job couldn't speak enough. After he heard God, he couldn't speak at all.

"I put my hand over my mouth. I spoke once, but I have no answer—twice, but I will say no more" (Job 40:4–5).

Be still before the LORD and wait patiently for him (Psalm 37:7).

Silence was the only proper response. There was a time in the life of Thomas à Kempis (1380–1471), author of the famous work *The Imitation of Christ*, when he, too, covered his mouth. He had written profusely about the character of God. But one day God confronted him with such holy grace that, from that moment on, all Kempis's words "seemed like straw." He put down his pen and never wrote another line. He put his hand over his mouth.

The word for such moments is reverence: "Hallowed be thy name."

This phrase is a petition, not a proclamation. A request, not an announcement. Hallowed *be* your name. Do whatever it takes to be holy in my life. Take your rightful place on the throne. Exalt yourself. Magnify yourself. Glorify yourself. You be Lord, and I'll be quiet.

1. God got Job's attention, and Job finally realized he was nothing before the almighty Creator of the world. How has God gotten your attention in the past and revealed his holiness to you? How did you react?

_____

_____

_____

_____

_____

2. God made himself known to Job through a "storm" (NIV) or "whirlwind" (NKJV). Read 1 Kings 19:1–18. How did God make himself known to Elijah? Why do you think he chose to speak to Elijah in this way? What are some other ways that God chooses to communicate to us today?

_____

_____

_____

_____

3. When Job was faced with God's holiness, his only response was silence. How easily does silence come to you? What percent of your prayer time is spent talking to God and what percent is spent listening?

_____

_____

_____

4. Based on God's words to Job, do you think God is satisfied with those percentages? If not, what changes do you need to make?

_____

_____

_____

BE STILL

The word *hallowed* comes from the word *holy*, and the word *holy* means "to separate." The ancestry of the term can be traced back to an ancient word which means "to cut." To be holy, then, is to be a cut above the norm, superior, extraordinary. The Holy One dwells on a different level from the rest of us. What frightens us does not frighten him. What troubles us does not trouble him.

There is no one holy like the LORD; there is no one besides you (1 Samuel 2:2).

I'm more a landlubber than a sailor, but I've puttered around in a bass boat enough to know the secret for finding land in a storm . . . you don't aim at another boat. You certainly don't stare at the waves. You set your sights on an object unaffected by the wind—a light on the shore—and go straight toward it. The light is unaffected by the storm.

When you set your sights on our God, you focus on One "a cut above" any storm life may bring.

Like Job, you find peace in the pain.

Like Job, you cover your mouth and sit still.

"Be still and know that I am God" (Psalm 46:10 NCV). This verse contains a command with a promise.

The command?

Be still.

Cover your mouth. Bend your knees.

The promise? You will *know that I am God.*

The vessel of faith journeys on soft waters. Belief rides on the wings of waiting.

5. Why is it important to "be still" before God to experience his holiness? In what ways does silence and stillness set the stage for entering into God's presence?

_____

_____

_____

_____

_____

_____

_____

6. Read Matthew 14:28–31. Why is it important to always keep our focus on the Lord in the midst of a storm?

_____

_____

_____

_____

_____

_____

_____

_____

7. One of the ways we stay anchored during seasons of storms is to have the Word of God hidden in our hearts. What promises would the following passages allow us to draw on in the midst of trying times?

"I have told you all this so that you may have peace in me. Here on earth you will have many trials and sorrows. But take heart, because I have overcome the world" (John 16:33 NLT).

_____
_____
_____
_____

"We have troubles all around us, but we are not defeated. We do not know what to do, but we do not give up the hope of living. We are persecuted, but God does not leave us. We are hurt sometimes, but we are not destroyed" (2 Corinthians 4:8–9 NCV).

_____
_____
_____
_____

"And the God of all grace, who called you to his eternal glory in Christ, after you have suffered a little while, will himself restore you and make you strong, firm and steadfast" (1 Peter 5:10 NIV).

_____
_____
_____
_____
_____

"'He will wipe every tear from their eyes. There will be no more death' or mourning or crying or pain, for the old order of things has passed away" (Revelation 21:4 NIV).

_____
_____
_____
_____
_____

Part of the meditative process is coming to grips with God's sovereignty. He answers to no one, least of all the work of his creation. Yet in his mercy, God accommodates our questioning. What's more, as we'll see in the next study, he allows us to see him in the midst of our suffering.

—◦ POINTS TO REMEMBER ◦—

❖ When God confronts us with his holy grace, we begin to understand that our knowledge of him is "like straw."
❖ When we comprehend the true nature of God, we will invite him to take his rightful place on the throne of our lives.
❖ Focusing our sights on God in the midst of a storm will enable us to see above the wind and the waves and find peace in the pain.

—◦ PRAYER FOR THE DAY ◦—

Father, thank you for giving us a fixed point to aim for when the storms of life threaten us. Thank you for understanding our frailties and weaknesses. Still our hearts and quiet our tongues. Help us meditate on your Word so we may find comfort and direction in our time of need. In Jesus' name, amen.

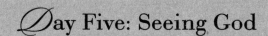

Day Five: Seeing God

GOD OWES NOTHING

In the end, God's message reveals the fact that Job is a peasant, telling the King how to run the kingdom. That he is an illiterate, telling e. e. cummings to capitalize his personal pronouns. That he is the clay, telling the potter not to press so hard.

"I owe no one anything," God declares in the crescendo of the wind. "Everything under the heaven is mine" (Job 41:11 TLB). Job couldn't argue. God owes no one anything. No explanations. No excuses. No help. God has no debt, no outstanding balance, no favors to return. God owes no man anything.

Which makes the fact that he gave us everything even more astounding.

How you interpret this holy presentation is key. You can interpret God's hammering speech as a divine in-your-face tirade if you want. You can use the list of unanswerable questions to prove that God is harsh, cruel, and distant. You can use the book of Job as evidence that God gives us questions

"Who has a claim against me that I must pay? Everything under heaven belongs to me" (Job 41:11).

and no answers. But to do so, you need some scissors. To do so, you need to cut out the rest of the book of Job.

For that is not how Job heard it. All his life, Job had been a good man. All his life, he had believed in God. All his life, he had discussed God, had notions about him, and had prayed to him. *But in the storm Job sees him!*

He sees Hope. Lover. Destroyer. Giver. Taker. Dreamer. Deliverer. Job sees the tender anger of a God whose unending love is often received with peculiar mistrust. Job stands as a blade of grass against the consuming fire of God's splendor. Job's demands melt like wax as God pulls back the curtain and heaven's light falls uneclipsed across the earth.

Job sees God.

Then Job replied to the LORD: "I know that you can do all things.... Surely I spoke of things I did not understand, things too wonderful for me to know" (Job 42:1–3).

1. In Romans 5:3–5, Paul outlines the process by which Job was able to find hope. First, "suffering produces endurance" (verse 3 NIV). Why is endurance such a valuable commodity?

_____

_____

_____

_____

_____

_____

2. Second, perseverance "develops strength of character" (verse 4 NLT). How does our ability to endure a storm build our character?

_____

_____

_____

_____

_____

_____

3. Third, "character strengthens our confident hope of salvation" (verse 4 NLT). How does our strength of character produce hope within us?

_____

_____

_____

_____

_____

_____

4. Finally, "Hope does not disappoint, because the love of God has been poured out in our hearts by the Holy Spirit" (verse 5 NKJV). How did Job experience the love of God? How did his interaction with God lead to hope?

_____

_____

_____

_____

JOB SEES GOD

God could turn away at this point. The gavel has been slammed; the verdict has been rendered. The Eternal Judge has spoken.

Ah, but God is not angry with Job. Firm? Yes. Direct? No doubt.

Clear and convincing? Absolutely. But angry? No.

God is never irritated by the candle of an honest seeker.

If you underline any passage in the book of Job, underline this one: "I had heard about you before, but now I have seen you" (Job 42:5 TLB).

Job sees God—and that is enough. But it isn't enough for God.

The years to come find Job once again sitting behind his mahogany desk with health restored and profits up. His lap is once again full of children and grandchildren and great-grandchildren—for four generations! If Job ever wonders why God doesn't bring back the children he had taken away, he doesn't ask. Maybe he doesn't ask because he knows that his children could never be happier than they are in the presence of this One he has seen so briefly.

Something tells me that Job would do it all again, if that's what it took to hear God's voice and stand in the Presence. Even if God left him with his bedsores and bills, Job would do it again.

For God gave Job more than Job ever dreamed. God gave Job himself.

> "You said, 'Listen now, and I will speak; I will question you, and you shall answer me.' My ears had heard of you but now my eyes have seen you" (Job 42:4–5).

> The LORD restored [Job's] fortunes and gave him twice as much as he had before. . . . And [Job] also had seven sons and three daughters (vv. 10, 13).

5. What's the difference between *hearing* about God and *seeing* him?

_____

_____

_____

6. Why do we often see God more clearly in the midst of suffering and tragedy than in the midst of happiness and prosperity?

_____

_____

_____

_____

7. What difference might it have made to Job if he had been convinced from the start that God would bring ultimate good from his situation?

_____

_____

_____

_____

_____

8. Not everyone who suffers a devastating loss receives a new family, restored wealth, or a clean bill of health. In what other ways might God bring ultimate good from tragic or painful circumstances?

_____

_____

_____

_____

_____

_____

Job lived a hundred and forty years; he saw his children and their children to the fourth generation. And so Job died, an old man and full of years (Job 42:16–17).

The devil had dared to question the stability of Job's faith, and God had given him permission to test Job. "All right," the Lord God had said. "Everything Job has is in your power, but you must not touch Job himself" (Job 1:12 NCV).

God set both the permission and parameters of the struggle, and Job passed the test. Then Satan complained again, stating that Job would have fallen had he been forced to face pain. Again, God gave permission, and again, God set the parameters. "Job is in your power," he told Satan, "but you may not take his life" (2:6 NCV).

Although the pain and the questions were abundant, in the end Job's faith and health were greater than ever. The family of Job "comforted him and made him feel better about the trouble the Lord had brought on him" (42:11 NCV). Satan had no power except that which God gave to him.

When crises come, you may lose the sense of God's presence. Job certainly did. "But if I go to the east, he is not there; if I go to the west, I do not find him. When he is at work in the north, I do not see him; when he turns to the south, I catch no glimpse of him" (23:8–9 NIV). Job felt far from God. Yet in spite of his inability to feel God, Job resolved, "But he knows the way that I take; when he has tested me, I will come forth as gold" (verse 10 NIV). Difficult days demand decisions of faith.

In the midst of your daily storms, make it a point to be still and set your sights on God. Let God bathe you in his glory so that both your breath and your troubles are sucked from your soul. Be still. Be quiet. Be open and willing. Then you will know that God is God, and you can't help but confess, "Hallowed be thy name."

❧ POINTS TO REMEMBER ☙

❖ It is often during the storms of life that we truly see God and begin to understand how he is working in our situation.

❖ We may think we know all about God, but we will never truly understand him if we do not experience his presence.

❖ God is in the business of restoration—our homes, our families, our friendships, and our very lives.

❧ PRAYER FOR THE DAY ☙

*Father, thank you for the promise that you will never leave us
or forsake us. We know that while the enemy will scheme against us, ultimately
you are in control and will use all things for your glory.
Help us during times of difficulty to always set our sights on you
so we will never be blown off course. In Jesus' name, amen.*

❧ WEEKLY MEMORY VERSE ☙

*Blessed is the one who perseveres under trial because,
having stood the test, that person will receive the crown of life that
the Lord has promised to those who love him.*
JAMES 1:12 (NIV)

For Further Reading

Selections throughout this lesson were taken from *The Great House of God* (Nashville: Thomas Nelson, 1997); *In the Eye of the Storm* (Nashville: Thomas Nelson, 1991); and *You'll Get Through This* (Nashville: Thomas Nelson, 2013).

LESSON 3

JACOB

WRESTLING WITH THE PAST

BETWEEN 1854 AND 1929 about 200,000 orphans and abandoned children in eastern cities were placed on westbound trains and shipped across the United States in search of homes and families. Many of the children had lost their parents in epidemics. Others were children of down-on-their-luck immigrants. Some were orphaned by the Civil War, others by alcohol.

But they all needed homes. Loaded on trains in groups of thirty to forty, they stopped in rural areas for viewings. The children were lined on the platform like livestock at an auction. Potential parents asked questions, evaluated health, and even examined teeth. If selected, the children went to their homes. If not, they got back on the train.

The Orphan Train.

Lee Nailling remembers the experience. He had been living at the Jefferson County Orphan Home for two years when he, as an eight-year-old, was taken with his two younger brothers to a train station in New York City. The day before, his biological father had handed him a pink envelope that bore the father's name and address. He told the boy to write him as soon as he reached his destination. The boy placed the envelope within his coat pocket so no one would take it. The train embarked for Texas. Lee and his brothers fell asleep. When he awoke, the pink envelope was gone.

He never saw it again.

What I'd love to tell you is that Lee's father found him. That the man, unwilling to pass another second without his sons, sold every possession so he could reunite his family. I'd love to describe the moment when Lee heard his father say, "Son, it's me! I came for you." Lee Nailling's biography, however, contains no such event.

But yours does.

Long ago, even before he made the world, God loved us and chose us in Christ to be holy and without fault in his eyes. His unchanging plan

He chose us in him before the creation of the world to be holy and blameless in his sight. In love he predestined us for adoption to sonship through Jesus Christ, in accordance with his pleasure and will (Ephesians 1:4–5).

has always been to adopt us into his own family by bringing us to himself through Jesus Christ. And this gave him great pleasure (see Ephesians 1:4–5).

There is something in you that God loves. Not just appreciates or approves but loves. You cause his eyes to widen, his heart to beat faster. He loves you. And he accepts you.

Don't we yearn to know this? Jacob did. The Old Testament relates the story of this cunning, slippery, sly soul. He spent his early years collecting wives, money, and livestock the way some men today collect wives, money, and livestock. But Jacob grew restless. By midlife he had an ache in his heart that caravans and concubines couldn't comfort, so he loaded up his family and struck out for the home country.

1. How easy is it for you to agree that God approves of you, accepts you, and loves you? If it is difficult, why do think that is the case?

_____

_____

_____

_____

_____

_____

_____

2. What causes you to feel restless or dissatisfied in life, as Jacob did?

_____

_____

_____

_____

_____

_____

_____

Restlessness was part of Jacob's personality. Not satisfied with the cards life had dealt him, he tried to rig the game. He played fast and loose with the concepts of truth, integrity, and honor. He cheated and scammed anyone who stood in his way. Through it all, though, God loved him and never stopped pursuing him.

❧ PRAYER FOR THE WEEK ❧

Father, thank you for loving us, for pursuing us, for adopting us into your family. Thank you for seeing in us what no one else could. Guide us through this study of your servant Jacob. Help us understand what it means to wrestle with you. In Jesus' name, amen.

$\mathscr{D}$ay One: Showdown at Jabbok

JACOB THE CONNIVER

Jacob was the riverboat gambler of the patriarchs. A master of sleight-of-hand and fancy footwork. He had gained a seamy reputation of getting what he wanted by hook or by crook—or both.

Twice he dealt hidden cards to his dull-witted brother, Esau, in order to climb the family tree. He once pulled the wool over the eyes of his own father, a trick especially dirty since his father's eyes were rather dim, and the wool he pulled ensured him a gift he would never have received otherwise.

He later conned his father-in-law out of his best livestock and, when no one was looking, he took the kids and the cattle and skedaddled.

Yes, Jacob had a salty reputation, and deservedly so. For him the ends always justified the means. His cleverness was outranked only by his audacity. His conscience was calloused just enough to let him sleep, and his feet were just fast enough to keep him one step ahead of the consequences.

That is, until he reached a river called Jabbok. At Jabbok his own cunning caught up with him.

1. The book of Genesis gives us many accounts of Jacob's cunning and deceit. Look at the verses below and describe how he deceived each person.

Esau, his brother: Genesis 25:27–34

_____

_____

_____

_____

_____

Isaac, his father: Genesis 27:14–29

_____

_____

_____

_____

Laban, his father-in-law: Genesis 30:29–43

_____

_____

_____

_____

Jacob gave Esau some bread and some lentil stew. . . . Esau despised his birthright (Genesis 25:34).

Esau said, "Isn't he rightly named Jacob? This is the second time he has taken advantage of me: He took my birthright, and now he's taken my blessing!" (27:36).

So the weak animals went to Laban and the strong ones to Jacob. In this way the man grew exceedingly prosperous (30:42–43).

2. How do you think Jacob rationalized his behavior? How is it possible for people today to be so oblivious—or so indifferent—to the consequences of their actions?

_____

_____

_____

3. In 1 Samuel 16:7 we read, "People look at the outward appearance, but the LORD looks at the heart" (NIV). Given this, why did God choose a person like Jacob to play such a prominent role in his plan?

_____

_____

_____

4. What hope does this give to us who may have more in common with Jacob than we care to admit?

_____

_____

_____

NO MORE RUNNING

When the messengers returned to Jacob, they said, "We went to your brother Esau, and now he is coming to meet you, and four hundred men are with him" (Genesis 32:6).

Jacob was camped near the river when word reached him that big, hairy Esau was coming to see him. It had been twenty years since Jacob had tricked his brother. More than enough time, Jacob realized, for Esau to stir up a boiling pot of revenge. Jacob was in trouble. This time he had no more tricks up his sleeve. He was finally forced to face up to himself and to God.

To Jacob's credit, he didn't run away from the problem. One has to wonder why. Maybe he was sick of running. Or maybe he was tired of looking at the shady character he saw every morning in the mirror. Or maybe he simply knew that he'd dealt from the bottom of the deck one too many times.

Jacob's gifts went on ahead of him, but he himself spent the night in the camp (v. 21).

Whatever the motivation, it was enough to cause him to come out of the shadows, cross Jabbok Creek alone, and face the facts.

The word *Jabbok* in Hebrew means "wrestle," and wrestle is what Jacob did. He wrestled with his past: all the white lies, scheming, and scandalizing. He wrestled with his situation: a spider trapped in his own web of deceit and craftiness. But more than anything, he wrestled with God.

5. Read Genesis 32:3–6. What tactic did Jacob try to pave the way for his meeting with Esau? What was the result?

_____

_____

_____

_____

6. Up until this point, Jacob's preferred strategy for dealing with his past was to run away. Why does it often seem so much easier to run from our problems than face them? What does Jacob's story show us about the long-term consequences of continually running?

_____

_____

_____

7. When was a time you were forced to confront something ugly from your past? What compelled you to stay and face it instead of run from it?

_____

_____

_____

8. When you consider your past, what other potential wrestling matches do you see? What unresolved issues or broken relationships need to be tackled?

_____

_____

_____

When Jacob crossed Jabbok Creek, he did more than make peace with his past: He embarked on the journey of creating a better future for himself. It is quite likely he finally understood his old habits were unsustainable and he needed to aspire to something new—something more fulfilling. First, however, he needed to know whether he had value in the grand scheme of things. He needed to know that he mattered.

━☙ POINTS TO REMEMBER ☙━

❖ We can rationalize our misdeeds and convince ourselves we are getting away with our sins, but ultimately we all have to confront our pasts at our own Jabbok.
❖ God has a way of orchestrating events to cause us to confront our past and deal with it.
❖ Jacob ultimately realized he couldn't spend his life running from his problems—and the same is true of us today.

━☙ PRAYER FOR THE DAY ☙━

Father, thank you for standing ready to engage with us when we are ready to confront our past and make positive changes in our lives. Guide our search. Give us a sense of the future you have in store for us. In Jesus' name, amen.

Day Two: Do We Matter?

WRESTLING MATCH

Jacob got up and took his two wives, his two female servants and his eleven sons and crossed the ford of the Jabbok. . . . So Jacob was left alone (Genesis 32:22,24).

Jacob's first move was to send his wives, his servants, and his eleven sons across the River Jabbok without him. He needed to be alone. With his fears? Perhaps to gather his courage. With his thoughts? A break from the kids and camels would be nice. Again, we aren't told why he stayed alone at the river. But we are told that "a Man wrestled with him until the breaking of day" (Genesis 32:24 NKJV).

When the man saw that he could not overpower him, he touched the socket of Jacob's hip so that his hip was wrenched as he wrestled with the man (v. 25).

Yes, Man with a capital *M*, for this was no common man. Out of the dark he pounced. Through the night the two fought, flopping and plopping in Jabbok's mud. At one point Jacob had the best of the Man until the Man decided to settle the matter once and for all. With a deft jab to the hip, he left Jacob writhing like a gored matador. The jolt cleared Jacob's vision, and he realized, *I'm tangling with God.* He grabbed hold of the Man and then held on for dear life. "I will not let You go unless You bless me!" he insisted (verse 26 NKJV).

Jacob replied, "I will not let you go unless you bless me" (v. 26).

1. In Ephesians 3:12, Paul writes, "Because of Christ and our faith in him, we can now come boldly and confidently into God's presence" (NLT). Jacob demonstrated this kind of boldness when he wrestled with God. Why does God reward our boldness when we come to him?

   _____

   _____

   _____

2. Why did God leave Jacob with an injury to remember the encounter?

   _____

   _____

   _____

3. What do you suppose Jacob thought every time he felt a twinge in his hip?

   _____

   _____

   _____

4. What methods has God used to remind you of your encounters with him?

   _____

   _____

   _____

CHOSEN CHILDREN

What are we to make of this? God in the mud. A tooth-and-nail fight to the finish. Jacob clinging, and then limping. Sounds more like a bootlegger brawl than a Bible story. Bizarre. But the blessing request? I get that part. Distill it down to our language, and Jacob was asking, "God, do I matter to you?"

I would ask the same question. Given a face-to-face encounter with the Man, I'd venture, "Do you know who I am? In the great scheme of things, do I count for anything?"

So many messages tell us we don't. We get laid off at work, turned away by the school. Everything from acne to Alzheimer's leaves us feeling like the girl or the guy with no date to the prom.

We react. We validate our existence with a flurry of activity. We do more, buy more, achieve more. Like Jacob, we wrestle. All our wrestlings, I suppose, are merely asking this question: "Do I matter?"

All of grace, I believe, is God's definitive reply: "Be blessed, my child. I accept you. I have adopted you into my family."

Adopted children are chosen children.

Your eyes saw my unformed body; all the days ordained for me were written in your book before one of them came to be (Psalm 139:16).

You, LORD, are our Father, our Redeemer from of old is your name (Isaiah 63:16).

5. Throughout the Bible we are reminded God has accepted us and adopted us into his family. Read the following passages and write down what God is saying to you about being his chosen son or daughter.

"But to all who did accept him and believe in him he gave the right to become children of God" (John 1:12 NCV).

_____
_____
_____

"The Spirit you received does not make you slaves, so that you live in fear again; rather, the Spirit you received brought about your adoption to sonship. And by him we cry, 'Abba, Father.' The Spirit himself testifies with our spirit that we are God's children" (Romans 8:15–16 NIV).

_____
_____
_____
_____

"See how very much our Father loves us, for he calls us his children, and that is what we are! But the people who belong to this world don't recognize that we are God's children because they don't know him" (1 John 3:1 NLT).

_____
_____
_____

"From now on you are not strangers and people who are not citizens. You are citizens together with those who belong to God. You belong in God's family" (Ephesians 2:19 NLV).

_____
_____
_____
_____

"So you are no longer a slave, but God's child; and since you are his child, God has made you also an heir" (Galatians 4:7 NIV).

_____
_____
_____
_____

6. What messages from others or circumstances in your life have caused you to doubt that you matter to God?

_____
_____
_____

7. In Isaiah 49:16, God states, "See, I have engraved you on the palms of my hands; your walls are ever before me" (NIV). What does this tell you about your true importance to God?

_____
_____
_____
_____

8. Why is it essential for God's adopted children to believe that he has a future and a hope for them?

_____
_____
_____

9. What do you suspect God's plan for you involves? Why?

_____
_____
_____

First-responders will tell you that one of the hazards of their job is the threat of injury at the hands of the victims they are rescuing. A certain reflex causes some people to struggle with those who are trying to help them. As we'll see in the next study, that reflex may have been at work in Jacob. Perhaps his years of guilt, frustration, unfulfillment, and fear caused him to push back against the One who could save him.

❧ POINTS TO REMEMBER ❧

❖ God invites us to come boldly into his presence and even wrestle difficult matters with him.

❖ Just as Jacob left his wrestling match with God with a limp, our encounters with God will always profoundly change us in some way.

❖ To all our questions as to whether we matter to God, he answers with a definitive yes.

❧ PRAYER FOR THE DAY ❧

Father, thank you for being the ultimate first-responder—on the spot even before we realize we need you. Thank you for looking past our self-defeating instincts as you work with us. Guide our struggles as you see fit to produce the kind of peace of mind and fulfillment that Jacob experienced after his match with you. In Jesus' name, amen.

Day Three: What's in a Name?

A NEW NAME AND A NEW PROMISE

Jacob wrestled with the same God who had descended the ladder at Bethel to assure him that he wasn't alone (although he deserved to be). He met the same God who had earlier guaranteed him that he would never break his promise (though one could hardly fault God if he did). He confronted the same God who had reminded him that the land prepared for him was still his. (Proof again that God blesses us *in spite* of our lives and not *because of* our lives.)

Jacob wrestled with God the entire night. On the banks of Jabbok he rolled in the mud of his mistakes. He met God face-to-face, sick of his past and in desperate need of a fresh start. And because Jacob wanted it so badly, God honored his determination. God gave him a new name and a new promise. But he also gave a wrenched hip as a reminder of that mysterious night at the river.

The fact that God gave Jacob a new name is important, because names tell a lot about a person. In Genesis 25, we find that when Jacob was born, he was grasping the heel of his twin brother. So his mother, Rebekah, named him "Jacob," which in Hebrew sounds like the word for "heel." The phrase "grabbing someone's heel" is a Hebrew saying for tricking someone, and it described Jacob's character well.

There above it stood the LORD, and he said . . . "I will give you and your descendants the land on which you are lying. . . . I am with you and will watch over you wherever you go, and I will bring you back to this land" (Genesis 28:13,15).

The man said, "Your name will no longer be Jacob, but Israel" (32:28).

The socket of Jacob's hip was touched near the tendon (v. 32).

After this, his brother came out, with his hand grasping Esau's heel; so he was named Jacob (25:26).

Now God was saying, "Your name will no longer be Jacob. Your name will now be Israel, because you have wrestled with God and with people, and you have won" (Genesis 32:28 NCV). The name Israel can mean "prince of God."

1. Why did Jacob refuse to let go of the Man? What does his determination in wrestling with God tell us about what was going on in his life at this moment?

_____

_____

_____

_____

_____

2. What was the significance of the new name God was giving to Jacob? How did it communicate God's blessing on his life?

_____

_____

_____

_____

3. What does your name mean? What is its significance? What does it mean to other people? When they hear it, what do they think of?

_____

_____

_____

_____

4. If God were to wrestle with you and give you a new name as he did with Jacob, what would you want it to mean? Why?

_____

_____

_____

_____

_____

THE NAMES OF GOD

[The man] replied, "Why do you ask my name?" Then he blessed him there (Genesis 32:29).

Immediately after God gives Jacob a new name, he says to the Lord, "Please tell me your name" (verse 29 NCV).

It's interesting that Jacob asked this question, because the names of God in the Bible give us an understanding of his character. Let me explain.

Imagine that you and I are having a conversation in 1978. You approach me on the college campus where I was a student and ask, "Do you know Denalyn Preston?" I would have answered, "Let me think. Oh, I know Denalyn. She's an acquaintance of mine. She's that cute girl who likes to ride bikes and wear overalls to class." That's all I knew about her.

But go forward a year. Now we are in Miami, Florida, where I am a minister and Denalyn is a schoolteacher. "Do you know Denalyn Preston?" "Of course, I do. She's a friend. I see her every Sunday."

Ask me again a year later, "Denalyn Preston? Sure I know her. She can't take her eyes off of me." (Just kidding, honey.)

Fast-forward twelve months. "Who doesn't know Denalyn Preston?" I would answer. "You think she might be willing to go out on a date with me?"

Six months later, "Of course I know her—I can't quit thinking about her. We're going out again next week."

Two months later, "Do I know Denalyn Preston? I'm going to marry her next August!"

Now it's August of 1981. "Do I know Denalyn Preston? No, but I do know Denalyn Lucado. She's my wife, and quit bugging us—we're on our honeymoon."

In three years my relationship with Denalyn evolved. And with each change came a new name. She went from acquaintance to friend to eye-popping beauty to date to fiancée and wife. Of course the names have only continued. Now she is confidante, mother of my children, lifelong partner, boss (just kidding, again). The more I know her, the more names I give her.

The more God's people came to know him, the more names they gave him. Initially, God was known as Elohim. "In the beginning God [Elohim] created" (Genesis 1:1 NCV). The Hebrew word *Elohim* carries with it the meaning "strong one or creator" and appears 31 times in the first chapter of Genesis, where we see his creative power. As God revealed himself to his children, however, they saw him as more than a mighty force. They saw him as a loving Father who met them at every crossroad of their lives.

Jacob, for his part, came to see God as Jehovah-raah, a caring shepherd. "Like a shepherd," Jacob told his family, "God has led me all my life" (Genesis 48:15 NCV). The phrase was surely a compliment to God, for as we have seen, Jacob was never a candidate for the most well-behaved sheep award. Yet God never forgot him. He gave him food in the famine, forgiveness in his failures, and faith in his final years. Ask Jacob to describe God in a word, and his word would be Jehovah-raah, the caring shepherd.

5. Chart the progression of how you might have described God at various times in your life. What was your earliest image of him?

_____

_____

_____

_____

_____

A good name is more desirable than great riches (Proverbs 22:1).

"I am the LORD [Yahweh], the God [Elohim] of all mankind. Is anything too hard for me?" (Jeremiah 32:27).

God is love (1 John 4:8).

The LORD is my shepherd, I lack nothing. He makes me lie down in green pastures (Psalm 23:1–2).

6. What was your image of him when you suffered a loss or personal tragedy?

_____

_____

_____

_____

7. What was your image of him when other things—your job, your family, your pursuit of happiness—took precedence in your life?

_____

_____

_____

_____

8. How did God prove to be Jehovah-raah—the caring shepherd—in Jacob's life? How has he proven to be a caring shepherd in your life?

_____

_____

_____

_____

_____

_____

Jacob uncovered an amazing secret at Jabbok. It was one all heroes of the faith learned at some point in their spiritual development: every encounter with God—every prayer, every sincere effort to understand him—reveals a new, exciting, and life-changing aspect of his nature. As we'll see in the next study, Jacob's life was transformed when he recognized God as his caring shepherd.

❧ POINTS TO REMEMBER ❧

❖ God honors our determination when we come before his throne in prayer.
❖ Just like Jacob, God gives us a new name and a new purpose when we give our lives to him.
❖ God will never forget us, in spite of our misbehavior, and he will prove himself to be our caring shepherd.

❧ PRAYER FOR THE DAY ❧

Father, thank you for the opportunity to deepen our relationship with you. We praise you that what we know of you today is just a fraction of what we will know of you at the end of our lives. Reveal yourself to us according to your perfect timing. Give us, as you gave Jacob, the glimpses of your nature that we need to sustain us. In Jesus' name, amen.

Day Four: All in a Night's Work

TIME AT THE RIVERBANK

Jacob wouldn't be the only man in the Bible to wrestle with self and God because of past antics. David would later do the same after his rendezvous with Bathsheba. Samson would wrestle, blind and bald, after Delilah's seduction. Elijah would be at his own Jabbok when he heard the "still small voice" (1 Kings 19:12 NKJV). Peter would wrestle with his guilt with echoes of a crowing cock still ringing in his ears.

I imagine that most of us have spent some time on the riverbanks as well. Our scandalous deeds have a way of finding us. Want some examples? Consider these scenes.

The unfaithful husband standing at the table with a note from his wife in his hands: "I couldn't take it anymore. I've taken the kids with me."

The twenty-year-old single woman in the doctor's office. The words are still fresh on her mind: "The test was positive. You are pregnant."

The businessman squirming in the IRS office: "Your audit shows that you took some loopholes that weren't yours to take."

The red-faced student who got caught red-handed copying the test answers of someone else: "We'll have to notify your parents."

All of us at one time or another come face-to-face with our past. And it's always an awkward encounter. When our sins catch up with us we can do one of two things: run or wrestle.

Many choose to run. They brush it off with a shrug of rationalization. "I was a victim of circumstances." Or, "It was his fault." Or, "There are many who do worse things." The problem with this escape is that it's no escape at all. It's only a shallow camouflage. No matter how many layers of makeup you put over a black eye, underneath it is still black. And down deep it still hurts.

Have mercy on me, O God, according to your unfailing love; according to your great compassion blot out my transgressions. Wash away all my iniquity and cleanse me from my sin (Psalm 51:1–2).

Whoever conceals their sins does not prosper, but the one who confesses and renounces them finds mercy (Proverbs 28:13).

1. Of the four Bible characters mentioned, whose wrestling experience resonates mostly strongly with you?

❑ Samson, who fell under the spell of an especially persuasive person
❑ David, whose lust and cowardice drove him to commit a heinous betrayal
❑ Elijah, the faithful prophet who needed encouragement and strength
❑ Peter, the well-meaning disciple who folded under pressure

Why does this character's experience resonate with you? Explain.

_____

_____

_____

2. Think about a time when you came face-to-face with your past. How did you feel about it at the time? How do you feel about it now? Can you see God's fingerprints on it? Explain.

_____

_____

_____

_____

3. In 1 John 1:9 we read, "If we confess our sins, he will forgive our sins, because we can trust God to do what is right. He will cleanse us from all the wrongs we have done" (NCV). What promises does God give to us in this verse if we choose to own up to our mistakes instead of run from them? Given this, why is it still tempting to try to run from our sins?

_____

_____

_____

_____

4. What does it mean to _repent_? What's the difference between tossing out a quick "my bad" and genuinely repenting for what we've done?

_____

_____

_____

_____

FROM GAMBLER TO MAN OF FAITH

Jacob finally figured out he couldn't run from his past. As a result, his example is one worthy of imitation. The best way to deal with our past is to hitch up our pants, roll up our sleeves, and face it head-on. No more shifting the blame to others or scapegoating. No more glossing over or covering up. No more games. We need a confrontation with our Master.

We, too, should cross the creek alone and struggle with God over ourselves. We, too, should stand eyeball to eyeball with him and be reminded that left alone we fail. We, too, should unmask our stained hearts and grimy souls and be honest with the One who knows our most secret sins.

The result could be refreshing. We know it was for Jacob. After his encounter with God, Jacob was a new man. He crossed the river in the dawn of a new day and faced Esau with newfound courage.

Each step he took, however, was a painful one. His stiff hip was a reminder of the lesson he had learned at Jabbok: Shady dealings bring pain. Mark it down: play today, and tomorrow you'll pay.

And for you who wonder if you've played too long to change, take courage from Jacob's legacy. No one is too bad for God. To transform a lifelong

Jacob looked up and there was Esau, coming with his four hundred men. . . . He himself went on ahead and bowed down to the ground seven times as he approached his brother (Genesis 33:1, 3).

conniver into a man of faith would be no easy task. But for God, it was all in a night's work.

5. What are some of the things that prevent or interfere with a one-on-one encounter with God?

_____

_____

_____

_____

_____

6. After Jacob's encounter with God, he was a new man. Read the following passages from Psalm 32. What does each state about the benefits of confessing our sins before God?

"Blessed is the one whose transgressions are forgiven, whose sins are covered. Blessed is the one whose sin the LORD does not count against them and in whose spirit is no deceit" (verses 1–2 NIV).

_____

_____

_____

_____

_____

"I acknowledged my sin to you and did not cover up my iniquity. I said, 'I will confess my transgressions to the LORD.' And you forgave the guilt of my sin" (verse 5 NIV).

_____

_____

_____

_____

_____

"Therefore let all the faithful pray to you while you may be found; surely the rising of the mighty waters will not reach them. You are my hiding place; you will protect me from trouble and surround me with songs of deliverance" (verses 6–7 NIV).

_____

_____

_____

_____

_____

"Many are the woes of the wicked, but the LORD'S unfailing love surrounds the one who trusts in him" (verse 10 NIV).

_____

_____

_____

_____

7. "As far as the east is from the west, so far has he removed our transgressions from us" (Psalm 103:12 NIV). What does this tell us that God does with our past after we've wrestled with it and confessed our sins?

_____

_____

_____

_____

_____

8. God changed Jacob from lifelong conniver to man of faith in the span of one night. What does that say about his ability to change our lives? Is there any person who is "too far gone" to change? Why or why not?

_____

_____

_____

_____

_____

Unfortunately, as we'll see in the next study, a clean slate stays clean for only so long. The potential for making poor decisions—even staggeringly awful decisions—never really goes away. Jacob had grown immeasurably since his callow younger days, but he still had much more growing to do.

❧ POINTS TO REMEMBER ❧

❖ When we are confronted with our past at our own "riverbank," we can either choose to stand up and face it or run away.
❖ The problem with escape is that it is no escape at all.
❖ It is never too late for us to change and transform into the people God wants us to be.

❧ PRAYER FOR THE DAY ❧

Father, thank you for the clean slate you offer, regardless of what we've done. Help us recognize the wisdom of staying close to you— of seeking your counsel and input—in the good times and in bad. Guide our steps, O Lord. In Jesus' name, amen.

Day Five: Family Reunion

TROUBLE AT HOME

It would be nice if the story of Jacob ended with the wrestling match at Jabbok and everyone ended up living "happily ever after." But the truth is there were a lot of problems in Jacob's family. And Jacob was the cause of much of it.

With all due respect, the patriarch could have used a course on marriage and family life. Mistake number one: he married Leah, a woman he didn't love, so he could marry Rachel, one he did. Mistake number two: the two wives were sisters. (Might as well toss a lit match into a fireworks stand.) Leah bore him sons. Rachel bore him none. So to expand his clan, he slept with an assortment of handmaidens and concubines until he had a covey of kids.

Rachel, his favorite wife, finally gave birth to Joseph, who became his favorite son. But some time later—right after God reaffirmed Jacob's "new name will be Israel" (Genesis 35:10 NCV)—Rachel died giving birth to a second son, Benjamin. Jacob was left with a contentious household and a broken heart.

To keep Rachel's memory alive, Jacob fawned over their first son. The brothers worked all day. Joseph played all day. They wore clothes from a secondhand store. Jacob gave Joseph a hand-stitched, multicolored cloak with embroidered sleeves. They slept in the bunkhouse. He had a queen-sized bed in his own room. While they ran the family herd, Joseph, Daddy's little darling, stayed home. Jacob treated the eleventh-born like a firstborn. The brothers spat at the sight of Joseph.

Jacob coped by checking out. When Joseph later bragged to his brothers about their bowing to him, Jacob stayed silent. When Jacob got wind that his sons had taken the sheep to graze near Shechem, the spot of prior conflict, did he spring into action to correct them? No, he sent Joseph to get a report. He sent a son to do a father's job.

Obstinate sons. Oblivious dad. The brothers needed a father. The father needed a wake-up call. And Joseph needed a protector. But he wasn't protected; he was neglected. As a result, Joseph ended up in a distant, dark place.

1. How did Jacob cope with his family situation? What problems did that create? How do people tend to do the same today?

_____

_____

_____

_____

Jacob had twelve sons: The sons of Leah: Reuben the firstborn of Jacob, Simeon, Levi, Judah, Issachar and Zebulun. The sons of Rachel: Joseph and Benjamin. The sons of Rachel's servant Bilhah: Dan and Naphtali. The sons of Leah's servant Zilpah: Gad and Asher (Genesis 35:22–26).

Now Israel loved Joseph more than any of his other sons . . . and he made an ornate robe for him (37:3).

Israel said to Joseph . . . "Your brothers are grazing the flocks near Shechem. Come, I am going to send you to them" (v. 13).

When the Midianite merchants came by, his brothers pulled Joseph up out of the cistern and sold him for twenty shekels of silver to the Ishmaelites (v. 28).

2. Sibling rivalry was rampant in Jacob's household, and his sons ultimately decided to sell Joseph to a caravan of traders. Read Genesis 37:17–35. What was Jacob feeling when he heard his favorite son was dead? How do you suppose Joseph's disappearance affected his feelings about and relationship toward God?

_____

_____

_____

_____

3. What similarities can you find between Jacob's family situation and your own? Why do you think Jacob allowed these rifts in his household to develop?

_____

_____

_____

_____

4. In Psalm 119:105 we read, "Your word is a lamp to my feet and a light to my path" (ESV). What role does God's Word play in preventing us from making the kind of mistakes Jacob made after his wrestling match with God?

_____

_____

_____

RESTORATION MATTERS

Pharaoh said to Joseph, "I hereby put you in charge of the whole land of Egypt" (Genesis 41:41).

Pharaoh said to Joseph . . . "Bring your father and your families back to me. I will give you the best of the land of Egypt and you can enjoy the fat of the land" (45:17–18).

Jacob was stunned; he did not believe them (v. 26).

This could have been the end of the story for Jacob. After all, Joseph went on to do well for himself in Egypt and become second in power only to Pharaoh. The family could have remained divided, content to leave the past in the past. But God had other plans, because restoration matters to him. So God shook things up.

Ultimately, God led Jacob's sons not borne by Rachel to Egypt, and then orchestrated a family reunion with Joseph. Jacob's boys returned back home to Canaan in style. Gone were the shabby robes and emaciated donkeys. They drove brand-new pickup trucks packed with gifts. They wore leather jackets and alligator skin boots.

Jacob emerged from a tent. A rush of hair, long and silver, reached his shoulders. Stooped back. Face leathery, like rawhide. He squinted at the sun-kissed sight of his sons and all the plunder. He was just about to ask where they stole the stuff when one of them blurted, "'Joseph is still alive, and he is governor over all the land of Egypt.' And Jacob's heart stood still, because he did not believe them" (Genesis 45:26 NKJV).

The old man grabbed his chest. He had to sit down. Leah brought him some water and glared at the sons as if to say they had better not be playing a joke on their father. But this was no trick. "When they told him all the words which Joseph had said to them, and when he saw the carts which Joseph had sent to carry him, the spirit of Jacob their father revived" (verse 27 NKJV).

Sadness had sapped the last drop of joy out of Jacob. Yet when the sons told him what Joseph had said, how he had asked about Jacob, how he had called them to Egypt, Jacob's spirit revived. He looked at the preliminary evidence of carts and clothes. He looked at the confirming smiles and nods of his sons, and for the first time in more than twenty years, the old patriarch began to believe he would see his son again.

His eyes began to sparkle, and his shoulders straightened. "Then Israel said, 'It is enough. Joseph my son is still alive. I will go and see him before I die'" (verse 28 NKJV). Yes, the narrator calls Jacob by his other name. The promise of a family reunion can do this. It changes us. From sad to seeking. From lonely to longing. From hermit to pilgrim. From Jacob, the heel-grabber, to Israel, prince of God.

The spirit of their father Jacob revived (Genesis 45:27).

Israel said . . . "My son Joseph is still alive. I will go and see him before I die" (v. 28).

5. Ultimately, Jacob was responsible for his separation from Joseph. Can you empathize? Have you experienced a separation—or perhaps an emotional distance—from a loved one for which you were at least partially responsible? If so, what were (or are) the circumstances?

_____

_____

_____

6. What comfort or wisdom can you find in Jacob's story?

_____

_____

_____

7. For all of the heartache and guilt Joseph's disappearance caused, in God's big picture he ended up exactly where he needed to be in order to save his family from the famine that devastated the region. If you could see the big picture of God's plan for your life, what might it reveal?

_____

_____

_____

8. Few people have seen God bring good from bad in the way Jacob did. If Jacob were surveying the "bad" areas of your life (self-inflicted or otherwise) with you, what advice do you think he would offer?

_____

_____

_____

Then Jacob left Beersheba, and Israel's sons took their father Jacob and their children and their wives in the carts that Pharaoh had sent to transport him (Genesis 46:5).

Joseph had his chariot made ready and went to Goshen to meet his father Israel (v. 29).

Joseph settled his father and his brothers in Egypt and gave them property in the best part of the land, the district of Rameses, as Pharaoh directed. Joseph also provided his father and his brothers and all his father's household with food, according to the number of their children (47:11–12).

"So Israel took his journey with all that he had, and came to Beersheba, and offered sacrifices to the God of his father Isaac" (Genesis 46:1 NKJV). Jacob was 130 years old by this point. Hardly a spring chicken. He had a hitch in his walk, an ache in his joints. But nothing was going to keep him from his son. He took his staff in hand and issued the command: "Load 'em up! We are headed to Egypt."

And what a trip it was. Pyramids. Palaces. Irrigated farms. Silos. They had never seen such sights. Then the moment they'd been waiting for: A wide flank of royalty appeared on the horizon. Chariots, horses, and the Imperial Guard.

As the entourage drew near, Jacob leaned forward to get a better glimpse of the man in the center chariot. When he saw his face, Jacob whispered, "Joseph, my son."

Across the distance Joseph leaned forward in his chariot. He told his driver to slap the horse. When the two groups met on the flat of the plain, the prince didn't hesitate. He bounded out of his chariot and ran in the direction of his father. "The moment Joseph saw him, he threw himself on his neck and wept" (verse 29 MSG).

Gone were the formalities. Forgotten were the proprieties. Joseph buried his face in the crook of his father's shoulder. "He wept a long time" (verse 29 MSG). As tears moistened the robe of his father, both men resolved that they would never say goodbye to each other again.

Goodbye. For some of you this word is the challenge of your life. To get through this is to get through raging loneliness, strength-draining grief. You sleep alone in a double bed. You walk the hallways of a silent house. You catch yourself calling out his name or reaching for her hand. As with Jacob, the separation has exhausted your spirit. You feel quarantined, isolated. The rest of the world has moved on; you ache to do the same. But you can't; you can't say goodbye.

If you can't, take heart. God has served notice. All farewells are on the clock. They are filtering like grains of sand through an hourglass. Our final home will hear no goodbyes. We will speak of the Good Book and remember good faith, but goodbye? Gone forever. Let the promise change you. From sagging to seeking, from mournful to hopeful. From dwellers in the land of goodbye to a heaven of hellos. The Prince has decreed a homecoming.

Let's take our staffs and travel in his direction.

❧ POINTS TO REMEMBER ❧

❖ We need to continually listen to God's instruction so we don't fall into patterns of sin and repeat the mistakes of our past.
❖ Restoration matters to God, and he will shake things up to bring that healing into our lives.
❖ No matter what evil others intend for us, God can always use our situation to accomplish his good purposes.

➘ PRAYER FOR THE DAY ➚

Lord, thank you that no matter how often we fall, you are always there to pick us up again. You are a God of restoration, and we want to be restored to you today. Help us to follow your instruction and to continually draw closer to you. In Jesus' name, amen.

➘ WEEKLY MEMORY VERSES ➚

You were taught, with regard to your former way of life, to put off your old self, which is being corrupted by its deceitful desires; to be made new in the attitude of your minds; and to put on the new self, created to be like God in true righteousness and holiness.

EPHESIANS 4:22–24 (NIV)

For Further Reading

Selections throughout this lesson were taken from *Grace* (Nashville: Thomas Nelson, 2013); *God Came Near* (Nashville: Thomas Nelson, 1986); *Great House of God* (Nashville: Thomas Nelson, 1997); and *You'll Get Through This* (Nashville: Thomas Nelson, 2013).

LESSON 4

THE HALLWAY IS SILENT except for the wheels of the mop bucket and the shuffle of the old man's feet. Both sound tired. Both know these floors. How many nights has Hank cleaned them? Always careful to get in the corners. Always careful to set up his yellow caution sign warning of wet floors. Always chuckling as he does. "Be careful everyone," he laughs to himself, knowing no one is near. Not at 3:00 AM.

Hank's health isn't what it used to be. Gout keeps him awake. Arthritis makes him limp. His glasses are so thick that his eyeballs look twice their size. Shoulders stoop. But he does his work. Slopping soapy water on linoleum. Scrubbing the heel marks left by the well-heeled lawyers. He'll be finished an hour before quitting time. Always finishes early. Has for twenty years.

When finished he'll put away his bucket and take a seat outside the office of the senior partner and wait. Never leaves early. Could. No one would know. But he doesn't. He broke the rules once. Never again.

Sometimes, if the door is open, he'll enter the office. The suite is larger than his apartment. He'll run his finger over the desk. He'll stroke the soft leather couch. He'll stand at the window and watch the gray sky turn gold. And he'll remember. He once had such an office. Back when Hank was Henry. Back when the custodian was an executive. Long ago. Before the scandal.

It's his secret.

Hank's story, by the way, is true. I changed the name and a detail or two. I gave him a different job and put him in a different century. But the story is factual. You've heard it. But more than a true story, it's a common story. It's a story of a derailed dream. It's a story of high hopes colliding with harsh realities.

In Hank's case, it was a mistake he could never forget. A grave mistake. Hank killed someone. He came upon a thug beating up an innocent man, and Hank lost control. He killed the mugger. When word got out, Hank ran away. Hank would rather hide than go to jail. So he ran. The executive became a fugitive.

Most stories aren't as extreme as Hank's. Few spend their lives running from the law. Many, however, live with regrets. Some dreams have come true, but many haven't. Not that all should, mind you. I hope the little guy who dreamed of being a sumo wrestler came to his senses. And I hope he didn't lose his passion in the process. Changing direction in life is not tragic. Losing passion in life is.

Something happens to us along the way. Convictions to change the world downgrade to commitments to pay the bills. Rather than make a difference, we make a salary. Rather than look forward, we look back. Rather than look outward, we look inward. And we don't like what we see.

Hank didn't. Hank saw a man who'd settled for the mediocre. Trained in the finest institutions of the world, yet working the night shift in a minimum-wage job so he wouldn't be seen in the day. But all that changed when he heard the voice from the mop bucket. (Did I mention that his story is true?)

At first he thought the voice was a joke. Some of the fellows on the third floor played these kinds of tricks.

"Henry, Henry," the voice called.

Hank turned. No one called him Henry anymore. "Henry, Henry."

He turned toward the pail. It was glowing. Bright red. Hot red. He could feel the heat ten feet away. He stepped closer and looked in. The water wasn't boiling.

"This is strange," Hank mumbled to himself as he took another step to get a closer look. But the voice stopped him.

"Don't come any closer. Take off your shoes. You are on holy tile." Suddenly Hank knew who was speaking. "God?"

Sounds crazy. Almost irreverent. God speaking from a hot mop bucket to a janitor named Hank? Would it be believable if I said God was speaking from a burning bush to a shepherd named Moses?

Maybe that one's easier to handle—because you've heard it before. But just because it's Moses and a bush rather than Hank and a bucket, it's no less spectacular.

1. Think of a time when God spoke to you—perhaps not audibly, but unmistakably. What was that experience like for you? Explain.

   _____

   _____

   _____

2. What were the results of your encounter? Did you talk about it with anyone else? If so, what reactions did you get?

   _____

   _____

   _____

Some encounters with God are more dramatic than others, as Moses' run-in with the burning bush in the desert demonstrates. Moses was not what you would call an obvious choice to receive a message from God. What could the Lord possibly have to say to him? What indeed. That single encounter would eventually shift the balance of power in the ancient world and set into motion events that still reverberate today. It would also give Moses the remarkable opportunity to witness God's glory firsthand.

❧ PRAYER FOR THE WEEK ❧

Father, thank you for speaking to us—through prayer, through our consciences, through the work of your creation, and through other more mysterious ways. Thank you for your exciting unpredictability and for the prospect that you will one day call us to do something far beyond our comfort zone and seemingly beyond our capabilities. Bless our efforts to approach your work with confidence and humility. In Jesus' name, amen.

Day One: School's Out

A SUDDEN CAREER SHIFT

The encounter in the desert sure shocked the sandals off Moses. We wonder what amazed the old fellow more: that God spoke in a bush or that God spoke at all.

Moses, like Hank, had made a mistake.

You remember his story. Adopted nobility. An Israelite reared in an Egyptian palace. His countrymen were slaves, but Moses was privileged. Ate at the royal table. Educated in the finest schools.

But his most influential teacher had no degree. She was his mother. A Jewess who was hired to be his nanny. "Moses," you can almost hear her whisper to her young son, "God has put you here on purpose. Someday you will set your people free. Never forget, Moses. Never forget."

Moses didn't. The flame of justice grew hotter until it blazed. Moses saw an Egyptian beating a Hebrew slave. Just like Hank killed the mugger, Moses killed the Egyptian. The next day Moses saw the Hebrew. You'd think the slave would say thanks. He didn't. Rather than express gratitude, he expressed anger. "Are you going to kill me as you killed the Egyptian?" he asked (Exodus 2:14 NCV).

When the child grew older, she took him to Pharaoh's daughter and he became her son (Exodus 2:10).

Seeing no one, he killed the Egyptian and hid him in the sand (v. 12).

The man said, "Who made you ruler and judge over us?" (v. 14).

Moses fled from Pharaoh and went to live in Midian (Exodus 2:15).

Moses was tending the flock of Jethro his father-in-law (3:1).

Moses knew he was in trouble. He fled Egypt and hid in the wilderness. Call it a career shift. He went from dining with the heads of state to counting heads of sheep.

Hardly an upward move.

And so it happened that a bright, promising Hebrew began herding sheep in the hills.

Moses thought the move was permanent. There is no indication he ever intended to go back to Egypt. In fact, there is every indication he wanted to stay with his sheep. Standing barefoot before the bush, he confessed, "I am not a great man! How can I go to the king and lead the Israelites out of Egypt?" (3:11 NCV).

I'm glad Moses asked that question. It's a good one. Why Moses? Or, more specifically, why eighty-year-old Moses? The forty-year-old version was more appealing. The Moses we saw in Egypt was brash and confident. But the Moses we find four decades later is reluctant and weather-beaten.

1. In Genesis 47:11, Pharaoh had said to Joseph, "The land of Egypt is before you; settle your father and your brothers in the best part of the land. Let them live in Goshen. And if you know of any among them with special ability, put them in charge of my own livestock" (NIV). Read Exodus 1:1–14. What changes in the Israelites' status in Egypt had taken place since the time of Joseph?

_____

_____

_____

_____

_____

2. Read Exodus 2:1–15. Where did Moses fit in Egyptian society? Where did he fit in Hebrew society?

_____

_____

_____

_____

3. Forty-year-old Moses fled his privileged place in Egyptian society with a manslaughter charge hanging over his head. How do you think he viewed himself? How did he view his life? How did he view his future?

_____

_____

_____

4. Read Exodus 3:1–6. Eighty-year-old Moses now encountered God out in the wilderness in the form of a burning bush. How do you think forty years in the desert had changed him? How do you think he viewed himself, his life, and his future at this point?

_____

_____

_____

THE RIGHT MAN FOR THE JOB?

Had you or I looked at Moses back in Egypt, we would have said, "This man is ready for battle." Educated in the finest system in the world. Trained by the ablest soldiers. Instant access to the inner circle of the Pharaoh. Moses spoke their language and knew their habits. He was the perfect man for the job.

Moses at forty we like. But Moses at eighty? No way. Too old. Too tired. Smells like a shepherd. Speaks like a foreigner. What impact would he have on Pharaoh? He's the wrong man for the job.

And Moses would have agreed. "Tried that once before," he would say. "Those people don't want to be helped. Just leave me here to tend my sheep. They're easier to lead." Moses wouldn't have gone. You wouldn't have sent him. I wouldn't have sent him. But God did.

How do you figure? Would you choose a wanted murderer to lead a nation out of bondage? Would you call on a fugitive to carry the Ten Commandments? But God did. He called him, of all places, right out of the sheep pasture. Called his name through a burning bush. Scared old Moses right out of his shoes!

Why? What did Moses know now that he didn't know before? What did Moses learn in the desert that he didn't learn in Egypt? The ways of the desert, for one. Forty-year-old Moses was a city boy. Octogenarian Moses knows the name of every snake and the location of every watering hole. If he's going to lead thousands of Hebrews into the wilderness, he better know the basics of Desert Life 101.

Family dynamics, for another. If he's going to be traveling with families for forty years, it might help to understand how they work. He marries a woman of faith, the daughter of a Midianite priest, and establishes his own family.

But more than the ways of the desert and the people, Moses needed to learn something about himself.

Apparently he has learned it. God says Moses is ready.

And to convince him, God speaks through a bush. (Had to do something dramatic to get Moses' attention.)

"School's out," God tells him. "Now it's time to get to work." Poor Moses. He didn't even know he was enrolled.

But he was. And, guess what? So are you. The voice from the bush is the voice that whispers to you. It reminds you that God is not finished with you

Moses was educated in all the wisdom of the Egyptians and was powerful in speech and action (Acts 7:22).

Moses said to God, "Who am I that I should go to Pharaoh and bring the Israelites out of Egypt?" (Exodus 3:11).

After forty years had passed, an angel appeared to Moses in the flames of a burning bush in the desert (Acts 7:30).

Moses agreed to stay with the man, who gave his daughter Zipporah to Moses in marriage (Exodus 2:21).

yet. Oh, you may think he is. You may think you've peaked. You may think he's got someone else to do the job. If so, think again.

5. How had God shaped, trained, and equipped Moses during his time in the wilderness without Moses even realizing it?

_____

_____

_____

_____

_____

6. Think of a wilderness period in your own life—a time when it seemed nothing was going right. How might God have been preparing you as he did Moses?

_____

_____

_____

_____

_____

7. Read Exodus 3:7–12. What reason did God give as to why he had appeared to Moses? What did he instruct Moses to do? What was Moses' response?

_____

_____

_____

_____

_____

8. Why do you think so many people today are resistant to God's message? What challenges does that present for those of us who desire to follow God's call?

_____

_____

_____

_____

_____

School was out for Moses. God had deemed him to be *the* right person to lead the Hebrew people out of slavery in Egypt, across the wilderness, and into the Promised Land. Moses' unique strengths and character traits, combined with his background and eighty years' worth of life experiences, had made him custom-fit for the task at hand. Unfortunately, Moses couldn't yet see it. So God would have to broaden his perspective and give him a glimpse of the big picture—and how he fit into it.

⤳ POINTS TO REMEMBER ⤶

❖ Our setbacks and "time in the wilderness" may seem permanent to us, but they are never permanent to God.
❖ God uses our wilderness experiences to shape us and mold us into people who can accomplish his purposes on earth.
❖ God can use us at any stage of our lives—we are never too old or too young to fulfill God's will.

⤳ PRAYER FOR THE DAY ⤶

Father, thank you for entrusting us with a role in your plan. Thank you for seeing in us what no one else can see. Maximize our potential and give us the wisdom and perseverance to recognize our "desert experiences" as training for the work that is to come. In Jesus' name, amen.

Day Two: Throw It Down

GOD'S NAME

When the Lord said to Moses, "Go . . . you must lead my people Israel out of Egypt" (Exodus 3:10 NLT), Moses responded by raising more excuses than a kid at bedtime. God patiently trumped each one. Finally Moses asked, "Suppose I go to the Israelites and say to them, 'The God of your fathers has sent me to you,' and they ask me, 'What is his name?' Then what shall I tell them?" (verse 13 NIV).

God said to Moses, "I AM WHO I AM. When you go to the people of Israel, tell them, 'I AM sent me to you'" (verse 14 NCV). He would later remind Moses, "I am Yahweh. To Abraham and Isaac and Jacob I appeared as El Shaddai; I did not make myself known to them by my name Yahweh" (Exodus 6:2–3 TJB).

Why Yahweh? Because Yahweh is God's name. You can call me preacher or writer or half-baked golfer—these are accurate descriptions, but these aren't my names. I might call you dad, mom, doctor, or student, and those terms may describe you, but they aren't your name. If you want to call me by my name, say Max. If I call you by your name, I say it. And if you want to call God by his name, say Yahweh.

The Israelites would later consider the name too holy to be spoken by human lips. Whenever they needed to say Yahweh, they substituted

"Go. I am sending you to Pharaoh to bring my people the Israelites out of Egypt" (Exodus 3:10).

"Suppose . . . they ask me, 'What is his name?' Then what shall I tell them?" (v. 13).

God said to Moses, "I AM WHO I AM" (v. 14).

Let them praise your great and awesome name—he is holy
(Psalm 99:3).

the word *Adonai*, which means "Lord." If the name needed to be written, the scribes would take a bath before they wrote it and destroy the pen afterward.

God never gave a definition of the word *Yahweh*, and Moses never requested one. The name I AM sounds strikingly close to the Hebrew verb "to be"—*havah*. It's quite possibly a combination of the present tense form (I am) and the causative tense (I cause to be). Yahweh, then, seems to mean "I am" and "I cause." God is the "One who is" and the "One who causes."

God simply stated "I AM" to Moses and added nothing else. He needed no further descriptive word because he never changes. God is what he is. He is what he has always been. Yahweh is an unchanging God, an uncaused God, and an ungoverned God.

In him all things were created: things in heaven and on earth
(Colossians 1:16).

1. Read Exodus 3:13–22. What did God tell Moses to say to the people? Of what past promises was Moses to remind them? What future promises did God make?

   _____

   _____

   _____

   _____

2. Moses' reluctance to assume leadership is understandable given his past history. How did God help him see the bigger picture from his eternal perspective rather than from Moses' own human perspective? Why is our human point of view a bad perspective when it comes to our potential for accomplishing God's will?

   _____

   _____

   _____

   _____

3. If someone were looking critically at you, your background, and your likelihood of accomplishing something remarkable in God's service, what flaws and shortcomings might they see?

   _____

   _____

   _____

   _____

4. In what ways might those flaws and shortcomings be of particular interest to God?

   _____

   _____

   _____

THE ONLY CREDENTIALS THAT MATTER

Poor Moses is still not convinced. "Suppose they will not believe me or listen to my voice?" he says. "Suppose they say you haven't appeared to me?"

"What's that in your hand?" speaks the voice from the bush.

"This?" replies Moses. "It's just my walking stick."

"Throw it down."

Moses, who has walked this mountain for forty years, is not comfortable with the command. "God, you know a lot about a lot of things, but you may not know that out here . . . well, you just don't go around throwing down your staff. After all, you never know when . . ."

"Throw it down, Moses."

So Moses throws it down. The rod becomes a snake, and Moses begins to run.

"Moses!"

The old shepherd stops.

"Pick up the snake."

Moses peers over his shoulder, first at the snake and then the bush, and then he gives the most courageous response he can muster.

"What?"

"Pick up the snake . . . by the tail." (God had to be smiling at this point.)

"God, I don't mean to object. I mean, as I said, you know a lot of things, but out here in the desert . . . well, you don't pick up snakes too often, and you never pick up snakes by the tail."

"Moses!"

"Yessir."

Just as Moses' hand touches the squirmy scales of the snake, it hardens. And Moses lifts up the rod. The same rod he would lift up in Pharaoh's court. The same rod he would lift up to divide the water and guide two million people through a desert. The rod that would remind Moses that if God can make a stick become a snake, then become a stick again—then perhaps he can do something with stubborn hearts and a stiff-necked people. Perhaps he can do something with the common.

Our achievements, however noble they may be, are not important. Our credentials, as starry as they may be, are of no concern. God is the foundation of this house. The key question in life is not "How strong am I?" but rather "How strong is God?" The focus is on his strength, not ours.

That's what Moses did. Or at least that's what God told Moses to do. As we read further, we discover God spent no time convincing Moses what Moses could do, but much time explaining to Moses what God could do.

You and I would do the opposite. We would explain to Moses how he is ideally suited to return to Egypt. (Who better understands the culture than a former prince?) Then we'd remind Moses how perfect he is for wilderness travel. (Who knows the desert better than a shepherd?) We'd spend time reviewing with Moses his résumé and strengths. (Come on, Moses, you can do it. Give it a try.)

Moses answered, "What if they do not believe me?" (Exodus 4:1).

Moses threw [the staff] on the ground and it became a snake, and he ran from it (v. 3).

The LORD said to him, "Reach out your hand and take it" (v. 4).

Moses reached out and took hold of the snake and it turned back into a staff in his hand (v. 5).

"With man this is impossible, but with God all things are possible" (Matthew 19:26).

"I form the light and create darkness, I bring prosperity and create disaster; I, the LORD, do all these things" (Isaiah 45:7).

But God doesn't. He never considers Moses' strength. No pep talk is given; no pats on the backs are offered. Not one word is spoken to recruit Moses. But many words are used to reveal God. The strength of Moses is not the issue; the strength of God is.

5. Read Exodus 4:1–17. Why didn't God chastise Moses for his doubt and reluctance? Why did he indulge him with a few miracles for reassurance?

_____

_____

_____

_____

6. How is doubt a reflection of our attitude toward God?

_____

_____

_____

_____

7. Read Daniel 3:16–18. In this passage, three Hebrew men are facing the prospect of being thrown into a blazing furnace for not bowing down and worshiping the king of Babylon. How is their response different from Moses' response to God?

_____

_____

_____

_____

8. Moses had lots of excuses, but ultimately he obeyed God and went before Pharaoh. What did people like Moses, Shadrach, Meshach, and Abednego understand about God that made them so valuable in his service?

_____

_____

_____

_____

Moses' doubts eased when he realized whose work he was doing. He, like Shadrach, Meshach, and Abednego, understood the consequences of obeying God—no matter how intimidating or dangerous they may seem—are infinitely preferable to the consequences of disobeying or being excluded from his work.

‿❧ POINTS TO REMEMBER ❧‿

- ❖ When God said his name was "I AM," he was revealing he is an unchanging God, an uncaused God, and an ungoverned God.
- ❖ God is patient and is not put off by our doubts, questions, and excuses—but he does require our obedience.
- ❖ The key question is never how strong or capable we are but how strong and capable God is to do his work through us.

‿❧ PRAYER FOR THE DAY ❧‿

Father, thank you for the examples of obedience and faithfulness found in your Word. Help us understand the same courage that drove Moses and Shadrach, Meshach, and Abednego is available to us. Guide our thoughts and calm our fears. Make us ready for your service. In Jesus' name, amen.

*D*ay Three: What God Can Do

GOD IS PRESENT

Satan and his horde had howled with delight the day the young prince Moses was run out of Egypt by the very people he wanted to deliver. They thought they had derailed God's plan, when actually they had played into God's hand. God had used the defeat to humble his servant, and the wilderness to train him. Now, some forty years later, Moses stood with his brother, Aaron, before Pharaoh. This was a seasoned Moses who had learned to listen to God and survive in the desert.

Moses and Aaron went to Pharaoh and said, "This is what the LORD, the God of Israel, says: 'Let my people go'" (Exodus 5:1).

"Let my people go," Moses said to Pharaoh. But the king of Egypt refused. So God gave him a front-row seat in the arena of divine devotion. The entire Ancient East soon knew what God could do. Aaron's staff became a snake and the Nile became blood. The air was filled so thick with gnats the people breathed them. The ground so layered with locusts they crunched them. Noonday blackness. Hail-pounded crops. Flesh landscaped with boils. Funerals for the firstborn.

He led them out of Egypt and performed wonders and signs in Egypt (Acts 7:36).

Pharaoh let the people go, but then changed his mind. He chased the Israelites to the Red Sea, which God turned into a red carpet. The Egyptian army drowned. All this was not lost on Moses. Listen to these impassioned words he speaks to the Israelites:

The water flowed back and covered . . . the entire army of Pharaoh that had followed the Israelites (Exodus 14:28).

Nothing like this has ever happened before! Look at the past, long before you were even born. Go all the way back to when God made humans on the earth, and look from one end of heaven to the other. Nothing like this has ever been heard of! No other people have ever heard God speak from a fire and have still lived. But you have. No other god has ever taken for himself one nation out of another. But the LORD your God did this for you in Egypt, right before your own eyes. He did it with tests, signs, miracles, war, and great sights, by his great power and strength (Deuteronomy 4:32–34 NCV).

Moses' message? God will change the world to reach the world. God is tireless, relentless. He refuses to quit. Listen as God articulates his passion: "My heart beats for you, and my love for you stirs up my pity. I won't punish you in my anger, and I won't destroy Israel again. I am God and not a human; I am the Holy One, and I am among you" (Hosea 11:8–9 NCV). God wants you to know he is in the midst of your world. He is present. In your car. On the plane. In your office, your bedroom, your den. He's near.

1. Moses had grown up in Pharaoh's household, and now, forty years later, was returning to the people who had known him in his prime. What do you suppose was their reaction to him?

_____

_____

_____

_____

2. God had used the setbacks in Moses' life to humble him and the wilderness to train him for service. Why is humility a necessary quality for any servant of God? How do we learn from failure without being destroyed by it?

_____

_____

_____

_____

3. Read Exodus 14:1–4. After God freed the Israelites, the king of Egypt had second thoughts about losing his workforce and went in pursuit of them. Why did God instruct Moses to lead the people to a place where they would be trapped?

_____

_____

_____

_____

4. Read Exodus 14:10–14. What does Moses' response to the people reveal he had learned about God? What had caused his faith and trust in God to grow?

_____

_____

_____

_____

_____

_____

_____

FORGETFULNESS SIRES FRETFULNESS

God had freed the Israelites from their Egyptian oppressors. Given everything God had done in their midst, you'd think they would have given seminars on faith. They had beheld one miracle after another. But instead, the freed slaves took anxiety to a new art form. "The whole community of Israel complained about Moses and Aaron. 'If only the LORD had killed us back in Egypt,' they moaned. 'There we sat around pots filled with meat and ate all the bread we wanted. But now you have brought us into this wilderness to starve us all to death'" (Exodus 16:2–3 NLT).

Wait a minute. Weren't these the same people the Egyptians had beat and overworked? The same Hebrews who had cried to God for deliverance? Now, just a month into freedom, they spoke as if Egypt were a paid vacation. They had the miracles they saw and the misery they knew. Forgetfulness sires fretfulness.

God, patient as he is with memory loss, sent reminders. "Then the LORD said to Moses, 'Look, I'm going to rain down food from heaven for you. Each day the people can go out and pick up as much food as they need for that day. I will test them in this to see whether or not they will follow my instructions. On the sixth day they will gather food, and when they prepare it, there will be twice as much as usual'" (verses 4–5 NLT).

Note the details of God's provision plan. He met daily needs *daily*. Quail covered the compound in the evenings; manna glistened like fine frost in the mornings. Meat for dinner. Bread for breakfast. The food fell every day. Not annually, monthly, or hourly, but daily. And there was more.

He met daily needs *miraculously*. When the people first saw the wafers on the ground, "the Israelites took one look and said to one another, *man-hu* (What is it?). They had no idea what it was" (verse 15 MSG). The stunned people named the wafers *man-hu*, Hebrew for "What in the world is this?" God had resources they knew nothing about, solutions outside their reality, provisions outside their possibility. They saw the scorched earth; God saw heaven's breadbasket. They saw dry land; God saw a covey of quail behind every bush. They saw problems; God saw provision.

And the people were reminded of exactly what God can do.

In the desert the whole community grumbled against Moses and Aaron (Exodus 16:2).

"The people are to . . . gather enough for that day" (v. 4).

When the dew was gone, thin flakes like frost on the ground appeared on the desert floor (v. 14).

5. God could have fed the Hebrew people in any number of ways. Why do you suppose he chose a daily collection process?

_____
_____
_____
_____
_____
_____

6. Why were God's miraculous daily provisions ultimately not enough to keep the Hebrews' faith from wavering?

_____
_____
_____
_____
_____

7. We often see problems where God sees provision. In the following verses, what do you see God promising to you as you choose to rely on him completely?

Psalm 23:1–4: "The LORD is my shepherd, I lack nothing. He makes me lie down in green pastures, he leads me beside quiet waters, he refreshes my soul. He guides me along the right paths for his name's sake. Even though I walk through the darkest valley, I will fear no evil, for you are with me" (NIV).

_____
_____
_____
_____
_____
_____

Malachi 3:10: "'Bring the whole tithe into the storehouse, that there may be food in my house. Test me in this,' says the LORD Almighty, 'and see if I will not throw open the floodgates of heaven and pour out so much blessing that there will not be room enough to store it'" (NIV).

_____
_____
_____
_____
_____

2 Corinthians 9:10–11: "Now he who supplies seed to the sower and bread for food will also supply and increase your store of seed and will enlarge the harvest of your righteousness. You will be enriched in every way so that you can be generous on every occasion, and through us your generosity will result in thanksgiving to God" (NIV).

_____

_____

_____

Philippians 4:19: "My God will meet all your needs according to the riches of his glory in Christ Jesus" (NIV).

_____

_____

_____

8. What daily miracles do we overlook or take for granted? How do we prevent our emotions and circumstances from blinding us to these miracles around us?

_____

_____

_____

The Hebrew people were happy to be fed and protected by God—the more miraculous the means, the better. However, their understanding of their benefactor was shaky at best. The slightest bump in the road could send them into a panic, certain that God had abandoned them and left them for dead in the wilderness. That kind of panic can cause people to make extremely regrettable decisions.

❧ POINTS TO REMEMBER ❧

❖ God is always present in the midst of our world—wherever we are, we can be sure that he is near.
❖ God meets our needs _daily_, and he often meets them miraculously.
❖ Where we see insurmountable problems, God sees an opportunity to show his provision to us.

❧ PRAYER FOR THE DAY ❧

Father, thank you for your daily protection and care. Open our eyes to the many ways you provide for us. Give us your vision so we may see a breadbasket instead of scorched earth, nourishment instead of dryness, provision instead of problems. Bless our efforts to maintain trust in you when road bumps arise. In Jesus' name, amen.

Day Four: The Promise of Prayer

COW-WORSHIPING FOLLY

On the morning of the third day there was thunder and lightning, with a thick cloud over the mountain (Exodus 19:16).

The sight was so terrifying that Moses said, "I am trembling with fear" (Hebrews 12:21).

When Moses approached the camp and saw the calf . . . his anger burned and he threw the tablets out of his hands (Exodus 33:19).

The LORD said to Moses, "Go down, because your people, whom you brought up out of Egypt, have become corrupt" (v. 7).

Moses knew God could move mountains. He knew this because God was now moving the very mountain of Sinai on which he was standing. When God spoke, Sinai shook, and Moses' knees followed suit. Yes, Moses certainly knew what God could do. Worse, he knew what the people were prone to do.

When Moses came down from Sinai, he found them dancing around a golden calf. He was carrying the handwriting of God on a stone, and here the Israelites were worshiping a heartless farm animal. It was more than Moses could take. It was more than God could take. The Lord had given the people a mayor's-seat perch at his Exodus extravaganza. He had earned their trust. The former slaves had witnessed a millennium of miracles in a matter of days.

And yet, when God had called Moses to a summit meeting, the people had panicked like hen-less chicks. "They rallied around Aaron and said, 'Do something. Make gods for us who will lead us. That Moses, the man who got us out of Egypt—who knows what's happened to him?'" (Exodus 32:1 MSG).

The scurvy of fear infected everyone in the camp. They crafted a metal cow and talked to it. God, shocked at the calf-praising service, commanded Moses, "Go! Get down there! . . . In no time at all they've turned away from the way I commanded them . . . Oh! what a stubborn, hard-headed people!" (verses 7–9 MSG).

The presence of fear in the Hebrews didn't bother God; their response to it did. Nothing persuaded the people to trust him. Plagues didn't. Liberation from slavery didn't. God shed light on their path and dropped food in their laps, and still they didn't believe him. Nothing penetrated their hearts. They were flinty. Stiff.

Mount Rushmore is more pliable, an anvil more tender. The people were as responsive as the gold statue they worshiped. More than three thousand years removed, we understand God's frustration. Turn to a statue for help? How stupid. Face your fears by facing a cow? Udderly foolish!

We opt for more sophisticated therapies: belly-stretching food binges or budget-busting shopping sprees. We bow before a whiskey bottle or lose ourselves in an eighty-hour workweek. Progress? Hardly. We still face fears without facing God. He sends Exodus-level demonstrations of power: sunsets, starry nights, immeasurable oceans. He solves Red Sea-caliber problems and air-drops blessings like morning manna.

But let one crisis surface, let Moses disappear for a few hours, and we tornado into chaos. Rather than turn *to* God, we turn *from* him, hardening our hearts. The result? Cow-worshiping folly.

1. Put yourself in the sandals of one of the Hebrew refugees. You've been uprooted from the only life you've ever known—that of a slave. You're in the middle of a desert wilderness. The man who has led you every step of the way on your treacherous journey has disappeared into a lightning storm on top of a mountain. This is especially bad news because not only is he the only one who knows where you're going, but he is also your only conduit to God. How does this help you understand the Israelites' decision to worship a golden calf—something that would have been familiar to them from their time in Egypt?

_____

_____

_____

2. Still imagining yourself as an ancient Hebrew, what instinct would cause you to abandon God in that moment? Why would you reject the One who had obviously done so much for you and turn to an idol of your own making?

_____

_____

_____

3. Think of a time when you felt abandoned by God or his people. What created a hardened heart in you?

_____

_____

_____

4. What did you turn to in lieu of a golden calf? Why? What were the results?

_____

_____

_____

CHANGING GOD'S MIND

When God saw the golden calf stunt, he was ready to wipe out the nation of Israel. They were eyewitnesses to ten plagues and one Red Sea opening. Their bellies were full of God-given manna and heaven-sent quail, but did they remember their Deliverer? No, they danced the night away in front of a homemade statue.

God was not happy.

Then the Lord said to Moses, "Go down from this mountain, because your people, the people you brought out of the land of Egypt, have ruined themselves. They have quickly turned away from the things I commanded them to do . . . I have seen these people, and I know that they are

"They have been quick to turn away from what I commanded them" (Exodus 32:8).

The LORD said to Moses . . . "Leave me alone so that my anger may burn against them and that I may destroy them" (Exodus 32:10).

very stubborn. So now do not stop me. I am so angry with them that I am going to destroy them. Then I will make you and your descendants a great nation" (Exodus 32:7–10 NCV).

Dry grass on an erupting volcano stood a better chance of survival. Their only hope was their octogenarian leader, who'd met God, possibly on this same mountain, some years earlier. If Moses had any clout, this was the time to use it. He did.

But Moses sought the favor of the LORD his God (v. 11).

[Moses] begged the LORD his God and said, "LORD, don't let your anger destroy your people, whom you brought out of Egypt with your great power and strength. Don't let the people of Egypt say, 'The LORD brought the Israelites out of Egypt for an evil purpose. He planned to kill them in the mountains and destroy them from the earth.' So stop being angry, and don't destroy your people" (verses 11–12 NCV).

Look at the passion of Moses on Mount Sinai. He is not calm and quiet, with folded hands and a serene expression. He's on his face one minute, in God's face the next. He's on his knees, pointing his finger, lifting his hands. Shedding tears. Shredding his cloak. Wrestling like Jacob at Jabbok for the lives of his people.

Then the LORD relented (v. 14).

And how did God react? "So the LORD changed his mind and did not destroy the people as he had said he might" (verse 14 NCV).

"Therefore I tell you, whatever you ask for in prayer, believe that you have received it, and it will be yours" (Mark 11:24).

This is the promise of prayer! We can change God's mind! His ultimate will is inflexible, but the implementation of his will is not. He does not change in his character and purpose, but he does alter his strategy because of the appeals of his children. We do not change his intention, but we can influence his actions.

5. What do you suppose would have happened if someone other than Moses had made this request to God? Why was Moses able to boldly go before God and ask him to spare the people? How does a person like Moses gain clout with God?

_____

_____

_____

_____

6. Abraham was another man who boldly interceded with God on someone else's behalf. Read Genesis 18:16–33. What do Abraham's intervention for Sodom and Gomorrah and Moses' intervention for the Hebrew people have in common? What differences do you see between the two accounts?

_____

_____

_____

_____

7. What do we learn about God from these two stories?

_____

_____

_____

8. What do the following verses tell you about the power of prayer in your life?

2 Chronicles 7:14: "If my people, who are called by my name, will humble themselves, if they will pray and seek me and stop their evil ways, I will hear them from heaven. I will forgive their sin, and I will heal their land" (NCV).

_____

_____

_____

_____

Psalm 34:17: "The righteous cry out, and the LORD hears them; he delivers them from all their troubles" (NIV).

_____

_____

_____

Jeremiah 33:3: "Call to me and I will answer you, and will tell you great and hidden things that you have not known" (ESV).

_____

_____

_____

Luke 11:9: "So I tell you, ask, and God will give to you. Search, and you will find. Knock, and the door will open for you" (NCV).

_____

_____

John 15:7: "If you remain in me and follow my teachings, you can ask anything you want, and it will be given to you" (NCV).

_____

_____

The boldness and humility with which Moses negotiated with God suggest an extraordinary spiritual strength and maturity. Yet the beloved Hebrew leader was not immune to doubts and struggles in his relationship with Yahweh. Occasionally he needed booster shots for his faith and reminders of whom he was serving.

∽ POINTS TO REMEMBER ∾

❖ God isn't bothered by our fears, but he is bothered when we seek comfort from those fears in anything other than him.
❖ When we are in the midst of a crisis, it is important for us to remember all the ways God has come through in the past—and then trust in him.
❖ The promise of prayer is that we can actually change the mind of God!

∽ PRAYER FOR THE DAY ∾

Father, thank you for being with us during our mountaintop experiences as well the valleys of our faith. Thank you for patience and understanding. Thank you for giving us glimpses of your glory—for equipping, encouraging, and inspiring us in our daily journey. May your work, your deeds, and your glory never be far from our memory. In Jesus' name, amen.

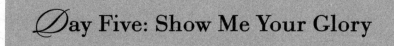

$\mathscr{D}$ay Five: Show Me Your Glory

A BOLD REQUEST

Moses said . . . "How will anyone know that you are pleased with me and with your people unless you go with us?" (Exodus 33:15–16).

It's little wonder that as Moses led the people, he needed reminders of God's presence from time to time. "Look," he said at one point, "you tell me, 'Lead this people,' but you don't let me know whom you're going to send with me . . . Are you traveling with us or not?" (Exodus 33:12, 16 MSG).

You can hardly fault his fears. Encircled first by Israelites who long for Egypt, and second by a desert of hot winds and blazing boulders, the ex-shepherd needs assurance. His Maker offers it. "I myself will go with you . . . I will do what you ask, because I know you very well, and I am pleased with you" (verses 14, 17 NCV).

You'd think that would have been enough for Moses, but he lingers. Thinking, perhaps, of that last sentence, "I will do what you ask . . ." Perhaps God will indulge one more request. So he swallows, sighs, and asks . . .

So many requests he could make. How about a million requests? That's how many adults are in Moses' rearview mirror. A million stiff-necked, unappreciative ex-slaves who are grumbling with every step. Had Moses prayed,

"Could you turn these people into sheep?" who would have blamed him? And what about Israel's enemies? Battlefields lie ahead. Combat with Hittites, Jebusites . . . Termites and Cellulites. They infest the land. Can Moses mold an army out of pyramid-building Hebrews?

I will do what you ask . . .

God had been ready to be done with the people and start over with Moses as he had with Noah. But Moses had pleaded for mercy, and mercy had been extended. God, touched by Moses' heart, had heard Moses' prayer and answered it. But Moses needs more. One more request. Glory. "Now, please show me your glory" (verse 18 NCV).

Then Moses said, "Now show me your glory" (Exodus 33:18).

We cross a line when we make such a request. When our deepest desire is not the things of God, or a favor from God, but God himself, we cross a threshold. Less self-focus, more God-focus. Less about me, more about him.

"Show me your radiance," Moses is praying. "Flex your biceps. Let me see your preeminence. Your heart-stopping, ground-shaking extra-spectacularness. Forget the money and the power. Bypass the youth. I can live with an aging body, but I can't live without you. I want more God, please. I'd like to see more of your glory."

Why did Moses want to see God's greatness?

Ask yourself a similar question. Why do you stare at sunsets and ponder the summer night sky? Why do you search for a rainbow in the mist or gaze at the Grand Canyon? Why do you allow the Pacific surf to mesmerize and Niagara to hypnotize? How do we explain our fascination with such sights?

Beauty? Yes. But doesn't the beauty point to a beautiful Someone? Doesn't the immensity of the ocean suggest an immense Creator? Doesn't the rhythm of migrating cranes and beluga whales hint of a brilliant mind? And isn't that what we desire? A beautiful Maker? An immense Creator? A God so mighty that he can commission the birds and command the fish?

One thing I ask from the LORD, this only do I seek: that I may dwell in the house of the LORD all the days of my life, to gaze on the beauty of the LORD and to seek him in his temple (Psalm 27:4).

1. Like most of us, Moses needed reminders of God's presence from time to time. What are some instances in your life when you needed to be reassured God was near? How did God answer your request?

_____

_____

_____

_____

_____

2. What situations have caused you to make the kind of request Moses made? What has caused you to say, "God, show me your glory. Help me understand who you are and what you're capable of doing"?

_____

_____

_____

_____

_____

3. How do you recognize God's glory? What happens when you experience it?

_____

_____

_____

_____

4. In Psalm 19:1, David wrote, "The heavens declare the glory of God, and the skies announce what his hands have made" (NCV). In this world, what declares the glory of God more clearly to you than anything else? Why?

_____

_____

_____

_____

_____

TRANSFORMED BY GOD'S GLORY

"Show me your glory, God," Moses begs. Forget a bank; he wants to see the gold reserve. He needs a walk in the vault of God's wealth. *Would you stun me with your strength? Numb me with your wisdom? Steal my breath with a brush of yours? A moment in the spray of the cataract of grace, a glimpse of your glory, God.* This is the prayer of Moses.

And God answers it. He places his servant in the cleft of a rock, telling Moses: "You cannot see My face; for no man shall see Me, and live . . . I . . . will cover you with My hand while I pass by. Then I will take away My hand, and you shall see My back; but My face shall not be seen" (Exodus 33:20, 22–23 NKJV).

And so Moses, cowering beneath the umbrella of God's palm, waits, surely with face bowed, eyes covered, and pulse racing, until God gives the signal. When the hand lifts, Moses' eyes do the same and catch a distant, disappearing glance of the back parts of God. The heart and center of the Maker is too much for Moses to bear. A fading glimpse will have to do.

I see the long gray hair of Moses wind-whipped forward and his leathery hand grabbing a rock in the wall lest he fall. And as the gust settles and his locks rest again on his shoulders, we see the impact. His face. Gleaming. Bright as if backlit by a thousand torches. Unknown to Moses, but undeniable to the Hebrews, is his shimmering face. When he descended the mountain, "the children of Israel could not look steadily at the face of Moses because of the glory of his countenance" (2 Corinthians 3:7 NKJV).

The LORD said, "I will cause all my goodness to pass in front of you" (Exodus 33:19).

Then the LORD said, "There is a place near me where you may stand on a rock" (v. 21).

When Moses came down from Mount Sinai . . . he was not aware that his face was radiant because he had spoken with the LORD (34:29).

Witnesses saw not anger in his jaw, or worry in his eyes, or a scowl on his lips; they saw God's glory in his face.

Did he have reason for anger? Cause for worry? Of course. Challenges await him. A desert and forty years of great challenges. But now, having seen God's face, he can face them.

Forgive my effrontery, but shouldn't Moses' request be yours? You've got problems. Look at you. Living in a dying body, walking on a decaying planet, surrounded by a self-centered society. Some saved by grace; others fueled by narcissism. Many of us by both. Cancer. War. Disease.

These are no small issues. A small god? No thanks. You and I need what Moses needed—a glimpse of God's glory. Such a sighting can change you forever.

The Israelites could not look steadily at the face of Moses because of its glory (2 Corinthians 3:7).

5. Read Exodus 34:29–35. What was the peoples' reaction to Moses after his encounter with God? What effects did God's presence have on Moses?

_____

_____

_____

_____

6. By this point in Moses' life, he had seen more miraculous events than most people will ever see. God had spoken to him from a burning bush. His walking stick had turned into a snake—and back again. He had seen God inflict nine plagues against Egypt, lead the Israelites safely through the Red Sea, bring water from a rock . . . and on and on. What does it say about Moses that even with all the miracles he had witnessed, he still needed more from God? What does it say about God that he gave Moses what he needed?

_____

_____

_____

_____

_____

7. Not even Moses could see God revealed in all his glory. However, in John 1:1, we read, "The Word became flesh and made his dwelling among us. We have seen his glory, the glory of the one and only Son, who came from the Father, full of grace and truth" (NIV). How are we able to see God's glory through Jesus?

_____

_____

_____

_____

8. In John 20:29, Jesus said to his disciple Thomas, "You believe because you've seen with your own eyes. Even better blessings are in store for those who believe without seeing" (MSG). What are some of the blessings Jesus offers to those who believe in him? How does God still show glimpses of his glory?

_____

_____

_____

_____

By faith Moses ... refused to be known as the son of Pharaoh's daughter. He chose to be mistreated along with the people of God rather than to enjoy the fleeting pleasures of sin (Hebrews 11:24–25).

As a young man, Moses excelled in the ways of the court. He mastered the laws of the ancient land. He studied at the feet of the world's finest astronomers, mathematicians, and lawyers. Fifteen hundred years later he was remembered as "learned in all the wisdom of the Egyptians" and "mighty in words and deeds" (Acts 7:22 NKJV).

What little we know of Moses' upbringing tells us he displayed an affinity for higher learning and an allergy to injustice. When he saw an Egyptian beating a Hebrew slave, he killed the Egyptian. When the next day he saw two Hebrews fighting, he intervened again. This time one of the Hebrews asked, "Who made you a prince and a judge over us?" (Exodus 2:14 NKJV).

A *prince* and a *judge*. How accurate is the description? Turn to the second act. To avoid arrest, Moses scampered into the badlands, where he encountered more injustice. "Now the priest of Midian had seven daughters. And they came and drew water, and they filled the troughs to water their father's flock. Then the shepherds came and drove them away; but Moses stood up and helped them, and watered their flock" (verses 16–17 NKJV).

What drove Moses to protect these young women? Their beauty? His thirst? Maybe both or maybe more. Maybe irrepressible seeds of fairness grew in his soul. When he decked a cruel Egyptian or scattered chauvinistic shepherds, was he acting out his God-given bent toward justice?

By faith the people passed through the Red Sea as on dry land; but when the Egyptians tried to do so, they were drowned (v. 29).

The rest of his life would say so. Forty years after he fled Egypt, Moses returned, this time with God's burning-bush blessing and power. He dismantled Pharaoh and unshackled the Hebrews. Moses the prince escorted his people into a new kingdom. Moses the judge framed the Torah and midwifed the Hebrew law.

The strengths of his youth unveiled the passions of his life, and God began doing a good work in him. The same is true of you. "God began doing a good work in you, and I am sure he will continue it until it is finished when Jesus Christ comes again" (Philippians 1:6 NCV).

Did you see what God is doing? *A good work in you.*

Did you see when he will be finished? *When Jesus comes again.*

May I spell out the message? *God ain't finished with you yet.*

Moses the servant of the LORD died there in Moab.... Since then, no prophet has risen in Israel like Moses, whom the LORD knew face to face (Deuteronomy 34:5, 10).

Your Father wants you to know that. And to convince you, he may surprise you. He may speak through a bush, a mop bucket, or stranger still, he may speak through this book.

⁓ POINTS TO REMEMBER ⁓

❖ God honors bold requests when we seek his glory and ask him to reveal his presence in our lives.

❖ We all desire to know we serve a beautiful Maker, an immense Creator, and a God so mighty there is nothing he cannot do.

❖ We need a glimpse of God's glory, for such a sighting can change us forever.

⁓ PRAYER FOR THE DAY ⁓

Dear God, as we go through our day, we ask that you give us little glimpses of your glory. Reveal your presence to us and transform us more and more into the likeness of your son, Jesus. Thank you for the promise that you always hear our prayers and for the continual work you are doing within us. In Jesus' name, amen.

⁓ WEEKLY MEMORY VERSE ⁓

The Word became flesh and made his dwelling among us. We have seen his glory, the glory of the one and only Son, who came from the Father, full of grace and truth.
JOHN 1:14 (NIV)

For Further Reading

Selections throughout this lesson were taken from *When God Whispers Your Name* (Nashville: Thomas Nelson, 1999); *And the Angels Were Silent* (Nashville: Thomas Nelson, 1987); *The Applause of Heaven* (Nashville: Thomas Nelson, 1990); *Great House of God* (Nashville: Thomas Nelson, 1997); *Traveling Light* (Nashville: Thomas Nelson, 2001); *It's Not About Me* (Nashville: Thomas Nelson, 2004); *Cure for the Common Life* (Nashville: Thomas Nelson, 2006); *3:16, The Numbers of Hope* (Nashville: Thomas Nelson, 2007); *Great Day Every Day* (Nashville: Thomas Nelson, 2007); and *Before Amen* (Nashville: Thomas Nelson, 2014).

DAVID

GIANT PROBLEMS AND COLOSSAL COLLAPSES

THE SLENDER, BEARDLESS BOY kneels by the brook. Mud moistens his knees. Bubbling water cools his hand. Were he to notice, he could study his handsome features in the water. Hair the color of copper. Tanned, sanguine skin and eyes that steal the breath of Hebrew maidens. He searches not for his reflection, however, but for rocks. Stones. Smooth stones. The kind that stack neatly in a shepherd's pouch, rest flush against a shepherd's leather sling. Flat rocks that balance heavy on the palm and missile with comet-crashing force into the head of a lion, a bear, or, in this case, a giant.

Goliath stares down from the hillside. Only disbelief keeps him from laughing. He and his Philistine herd have rendered their half of the valley into a forest of spears; a growling, bloodthirsty gang of hoodlums.

Goliath towers above them all: nine feet, nine inches tall in his stocking feet, wearing 125 pounds of armor, and snarling like the main contender at the World Wrestling Federation championship night. He wears a size–20 collar, a 10½ hat, and a 56-inch belt. His biceps burst, thigh muscles ripple, and boasts belch through the canyon. "This day I defy the ranks of Israel! Give me a man and let us fight each other" (1 Samuel 17:10 NIV). *Who will go mano a mano conmigo? Give me your best shot.*

No Hebrew volunteers. Until today. Until David.

David just showed up this morning. He clocked out of sheep watching to deliver bread and cheese to his brothers on the battlefront. That's where David hears Goliath defying God, and that's when David makes his decision. Then he takes his staff and sling in his hand, and he chooses for himself five smooth stones from the brook, putting them in a shepherd's bag.

Goliath scoffs at the kid, nicknames him Twiggy. "Am I a dog, that you come to me with sticks?" (verse 43 NASB). Skinny, scrawny David. Bulky, brutish Goliath. The toothpick versus the tornado. The mini-bike attacking the eighteen-wheeler. The toy poodle taking on the Rottweiler. What odds do you give David against his giant?

A champion named Goliath, who was from Gath, came out of the Philistine camp. His height was six cubits and a span (1 Samuel 17:4).

The Philistine said, "This day I defy the armies of Israel!" (v. 10).

David left the flock. . . . He reached the camp as the army was going out to its battle positions, shouting the war cry (v. 20).

He looked David over and saw that he was little more than a boy . . . and he despised him (v. 42).

Our struggle is not against flesh and blood, but against . . . the spiritual forces of evil in the heavenly realms (Ephesians 6:12).

Better odds, perhaps, than you give yourself against yours.

Your Goliath doesn't carry sword or shield; he brandishes blades of unemployment, abandonment, sexual abuse, or depression. Your giant doesn't parade up and down the hills of Elah; he prances through your office, your bedroom, your classroom. He brings bills you can't pay, grades you can't make, people you can't please, whiskey you can't resist, pornography you can't refuse, a career you can't escape, a past you can't shake, and a future you can't face.

You know well the roar of Goliath.

David faced one who foghorned his challenges morning and night. "For forty days, twice a day, morning and evening, the Philistine giant strutted in front of the Israelite army" (verse 16 NLT). Yours does the same. First thought of the morning, last worry of the night—your Goliath dominates your day and infiltrates your joy.

1. David's reflection revealed a young, determined warrior—overmatched in everyone's eyes but his own. What does *your* reflection reveal?

_____

_____

_____

_____

_____

_____

2. What weapons have you reached for in the past to do battle with your giant(s)? How effective were they?

_____

_____

_____

_____

_____

_____

David appeared to be all wrong for the job. No more than a boy, really. No formal military training. No skills to speak of with a sword and shield. What he *did* have, however, was an Ally he trusted with his life. In the first study, we'll see how David's reliance on his Ally tilted the battle in his favor.

─ᴄ⦿ PRAYER FOR THE WEEK ⦿ɔ─

Father, thank you for giving us a fighting chance against the giants in our lives. Thank you for ensuring human might doesn't always make right. Guide our thoughts and direct our focus when battles arise. Help us look to you for the strength we need. In Jesus' name, amen.

Day One: Challenging the Giant

THE LONG-STANDING BULLY

Goliath's family was an ancient foe of the Israelites. Joshua had driven them out of the Promised Land 300 years earlier. He destroyed everyone except the residents of three cities: Gaza, Gath, and Ashdod. Gath bred giants like Yosemite grows sequoias. Guess where Goliath was raised. See the *G* on his letter jacket? Gath High School.

Saul's soldiers saw Goliath and mumbled, "Not again. My dad fought his dad. My granddad fought his granddad."

You've groaned similar words. "I'm becoming a workaholic, just like my father." "Divorce streaks through our family tree like oak wilt." "My mom couldn't keep a friend either. Is this ever going to stop?"

Goliath: the long-standing bully of the valley. Tougher than a two-dollar steak. More snarls than twin Dobermans. He awaits you in the morning, torments you at night. He stalked your ancestors and now looms over you. He blocks the sun and leaves you standing in the shadow of doubt. "When Saul and his troops heard the Philistine's challenge, they were terrified and lost all hope" (1 Samuel 17:11 MSG).

But what am I telling you? You know Goliath. You recognize his walk and wince at his talk. You've seen your giant. The question is: *Is he all you see?* You know his voice—but is it all you hear? David saw and heard more. Read the first words he spoke, not just in the battle, but in the Bible: "David asked the men standing near him, 'What will be done for the man who kills this Philistine and removes this disgrace from Israel? Who is this uncircumcised Philistine that he should defy the armies of the living God?'" (verse 26 NIV).

David shows up discussing God. The soldiers mentioned nothing about him, the brothers never spoke his name, but David takes one step onto the stage and raises the subject of the living God. He does the same with King Saul: no chitchat about the battle or questions about the odds. Just a God-birthed announcement: "The LORD, who delivered me from the paw of the lion and from the paw of the bear, He will deliver me from the hand of this Philistine" (verse 37 NKJV). No one else discusses God. David discusses no one else *but* God.

1. Read Psalm 121. David seems to outline his battle strategy in these verses. How would you summarize the mindset that helped him approach Goliath with confidence? What did he trust God to do in each battle?

_____
_____
_____
_____

At that time Joshua went and destroyed the Anakites from the hill country. . . . No Anakites were left in Israelite territory; only in Gaza, Gath and Ashdod did any survive (Joshua 11:21–22).

All the Israelites were dismayed and terrified (1 Samuel 17:11).

For forty days the Philistine came forward every morning and evening and took his stand (v. 16).

"Who is this uncircumcised Philistine that he should defy the armies of the living God?" (v. 26).

David said to Saul, "Let no one lose heart on account of this Philistine; your servant will go and fight him" (v. 32).

2. Read 1 Samuel 17:1–37. Why couldn't King Saul and the rest of the Israelite army see the Ally that David saw?

_____

_____

_____

3. What giants in your life are big enough to make you temporarily lose sight of God and fear for your well-being? What do you learn from the story of David and Goliath on how to confront these giants?

_____

_____

_____

4. As a shepherd, David had protected his flock from attacks by a lion and a bear. He was able to draw on those experiences to build his confidence for the showdown with Goliath. What experiences can you draw on to build your confidence for your battles?

_____

_____

_____

FIVE SMOOTH STONES

Saul replied, "You are not able to go out against this Philistine and fight him; you are only a young man, and he has been a warrior from his youth" (1 Samuel 17:33).

Saul dressed David in his own tunic. He put a coat of armor on him and a bronze helmet on his head (v. 38).

[Goliath] said to David, "Am I a dog, that you come at me with sticks?" (v. 43).

The stone sank into [Goliath's] forehead, and he fell facedown on the ground (v. 49).

There are certain things anyone knows not to do. You don't try to lasso a tornado. You don't fight a lion with a toothpick. You don't sneeze into the wind. You don't go bear hunting with a cork gun. And you don't send a shepherd boy to battle a giant. You don't, that is, unless you are out of options. Saul was. And it is when we are out of options that we are most ready for God's surprises.

The king tried to give David some equipment. "What do you want, boy? Shield? Sword? Grenades? Rifles? A helicopter? We'll make a fighting soldier out of you." David had something else in mind. Five smooth stones and an ordinary leather sling.

David's brothers cover their eyes, both in fear and embarrassment. Saul sighs as the young Hebrew races to certain death. Goliath throws back his head in laughter, just enough to shift his helmet and expose a square inch of forehead flesh. David spots the target and seizes the moment. The sound of the swirling sling is the only sound in the valley. Ssshhhww. Ssshhhww. Ssshhhww. The stone torpedoes through the air and into the skull; Goliath's eyes cross and legs buckle. He crumples to the ground and dies. David runs over and yanks Goliath's sword from its sheath, shish-kebabs the Philistine, and cuts off his head.

You might say that David knew how to get *a head* of his giant.

When was the last time you did the same? How long since you ran toward your challenge? We tend to retreat, duck behind a desk of work, or crawl into a nightclub of distraction or a bed of forbidden love. For a moment, a day, or a year, we feel safe, insulated, anesthetized, but then the work runs out, the liquor wears off, or the lover leaves, and we hear Goliath again. Booming. Bombastic.

Try a different tack. Rush your giant with a God-saturated soul. *Giant of divorce, you aren't entering my home! Giant of depression? It may take a lifetime, but you won't conquer me. Giant of alcohol, bigotry, child abuse, insecurity . . . you're going down.* How long since you loaded your sling and took a swing at your giant?

So David triumphed over the Philistine with a sling and a stone (1 Samuel 17:50).

5. In 2 Corinthians 10:3–5, Paul wrote, "For though we live in the world, we do not wage war as the world does. The weapons we fight with are not the weapons of the world. On the contrary, they have divine power to demolish strongholds. We demolish arguments and every pretension that sets itself up against the knowledge of God, and we take captive every thought to make it obedient to Christ" (NIV). What did David understand about the weapons he had been given that enabled him to refuse Saul's armor?

_____

_____

_____

6. Think of a time when you relied on the weapons of God instead of your own strength. What circumstances were you facing? How did God equip you to fight the battle? What did you learn from the experience?

_____

_____

_____

7. Read 1 Samuel 17:38–51. How did Goliath taunt David? What was David's response to his challenges?

_____

_____

_____

8. Think of a giant that looms large right now. How does that giant taunt you? Are you at an impasse? Avoiding the battle? Licking your wounds after a recent defeat? What can you learn from David's story on how best to proceed?

_____

_____

_____

David's victory should have put him in good stead with the powers-that-be in Israel. After all, his defeat of Goliath dealt a crushing blow to the hated Philistines. David soon learned, however, that one person's success is another person's cause for jealousy. As we'll see in the next study, when the person feeling threatened is the king of Israel, there are few places to turn for refuge.

⟶◠ POINTS TO REMEMBER ◠⟵

❖ Like David, we need to see past our Goliaths and realize we serve a God who can bring down our toughest foe.
❖ It is when we are out of options that we are most ready for God's surprises.
❖ Retreating from our Goliaths might make us feel safe in the short run, but the only way to real victory is by rushing our giants with a God-saturated soul.

⟶◠ PRAYER FOR THE DAY ◠⟵

Father, thank you for siding with the underdog and for tilting the balance of power in our confrontations with our giants. Please guide our decisions and help us to look to you as our source of strength. Give us the confidence and courage David had when he faced Goliath. May our victories be as decisive as his. In Jesus' name, amen.

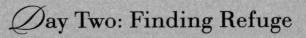

$\mathcal{D}$ay Two: Finding Refuge

SAUL'S ANGER

What ogres roam your world? Controlling moms. Brutal coaches. The pit-bull math teacher. The self-appointed cubicle commandant. The king who resolves to spear the shepherd boy to the wall.

Whatever mission Saul sent him on, David was . . . successful (1 Samuel 18:5).

That last one comes after David. Poor David. The Valley of Elah proved to be boot camp for the king's court. When Goliath lost his head, the Hebrews made David their hero. People threw him a ticker-tape parade and sang, "Saul has slain his thousands, and David his ten thousands" (1 Samuel 18:7 NKJV).

Saul was very angry; this refrain displeased him greatly (v. 8).

Saul explodes with the pent-up fury of a volcano. The king is already a troubled soul, prone to angry eruptions, mad enough to eat bees. David's popularity splashes gasoline on Saul's temper. Saul tries to kill Bethlehem's golden boy six different times. First, he invites David to marry his daughter Michal. Seems like a kind gesture, until you read the crude dowry Saul

"The king wants no other price for the bride than a hundred Philistine foreskins" (v. 25).

required. One hundred Philistine foreskins. Surely one of the Philistines will kill David, Saul hopes. They don't. David doubles the demand and returns with the proof.

Saul doesn't give up. He orders his servants and Jonathan to kill David, but they refuse. He tries with the spear another time but misses. Saul sends messengers to David's house to kill him, but his wife, Michal, lowers him through a window. David stays one step ahead of Saul.

Saul's anger puzzles David. What has he done? He has brought musical healing to Saul's tortured spirit, hope to the enfeebled nation. He is the Abraham Lincoln of the Hebrew calamity, saving the republic and doing so modestly and honestly. Yet Mount Saul keeps erupting, rewarding David's deeds with flying spears and murder plots. We understand David's question to Jonathan: "What have I done? What is my iniquity, and what is my sin before your father, that he seeks my life?" (20:1 NKJV).

Saul told his son Jonathan and all the attendants to kill David (1 Samuel 19:1).

Michal let David down through a window (v. 12).

"How have I wronged your father, that he is trying to kill me?" (20:1).

1. Read 1 Samuel 18:1–9. What caused Saul to become jealous of David? What did those thoughts cause him to do?

   _____

   _____

   _____

2. Of all the people you've known, whose personality most closely resembles that of King Saul? What is life like with a person like that? Explain.

   _____

   _____

   _____

3. The writers of the Bible often cautioned about the dangers of envy and jealousy. Read the following passages and write down what God is saying to you about not falling prey to these negative feelings.

   Psalm 37:1–3: "Do not fret because of evildoers, nor be envious of the workers of iniquity. For they shall soon be cut down like the grass, and wither as the green herb. Trust in the LORD, and do good. Dwell in the land, and feed on His faithfulness" (NKJV).

   _____

   _____

   _____

   _____

   Proverbs 14:30: "A heart at peace gives life to the body, but envy rots the bones" (NIV).

   _____

   _____

   _____

   _____

1 Corinthians 13:4: "Love is patient, love is kind and is not jealous; love does not brag and is not arrogant" (NASB).

_____

_____

_____

Philippians 2:3: "When you do things, do not let selfishness or pride be your guide. Instead, be humble and give more honor to others than to yourselves" (NCV).

_____

_____

James 3:13–16: "Who is wise and understanding among you? Let them show it by their good life, by deeds done in the humility that comes from wisdom. But if you harbor bitter envy and selfish ambition in your hearts, do not boast about it or deny the truth. Such 'wisdom' does not come down from heaven but is earthly, unspiritual, demonic. For where you have envy and selfish ambition, there you find disorder and every evil practice" (NIV).

_____

_____

_____

_____

_____

4. Why did David keep returning to such a volatile situation? At what point did his responsibility to the king end and his responsibility to protect himself begin?

_____

_____

_____

_____

NOWHERE TO GO

Jonathan said to David, "Go in peace . . ." Then David left, and Jonathan went back to the town (1 Samuel 20:42).

After the sixth attempt on his life, David gets the point. *Saul doesn't like me.* With a price on his head and a posse on his trail, he kisses Michal and life in the court goodbye and runs. But where can he go? To Bethlehem and jeopardize the lives of his family? Into enemy territory and risk his own? That becomes an option later. For now, he chooses another hideout. He goes to church. "Now David came to Nob, to Ahimelech the priest" (1 Samuel 21:1 NKJV).

David stumbles in this story. Desperate souls always do. The city was holy; David was anything but. He lied each time he opened his mouth. And he gets worse before he gets better. He escapes to Gath, the hometown of Goliath. He tries to forge a friendship based on a mutual adversary. If your enemy is Saul and my enemy is Saul, we become friends, right?

David answered . . . "The king sent me on a mission" (1 Samuel 21:2).

In this case, wrong. The Gittites aren't hospitable. David panics. He's a lamb in a pack of wolves. Tall men, taller walls. Piercing glares, piercing spears. David doesn't see God; he sees trouble. So he takes matters into his own hands. He pretends to be insane, scratching on doors and drooling down his beard. Finally the king of Gath says to his men, "'Must you bring me a madman? We already have enough of them around here! Why should I let someone like this be my guest?' So David left Gath and escaped to the cave of Adullam" (21:14–22:1 NLT).

David fled from Saul and went to Achish king of Gath (v. 10).

[David] pretended to be insane (v. 13).

David has nowhere left to go. He can't go to the court of Saul or the house of Michal, the city of Samuel or the safety of Nob. So he goes to the only place he can—the place where no one goes, because nothing survives. He goes to the desert, the wilderness. To the honeycombed canyons that overlook the Dead Sea. He finds a cave, the cave called Adullam. In it he finds shade, silence, and safety. He stretches on the cool dirt and closes his eyes and begins his decade in the wilderness.

David left Gath and escaped to the cave of Adullam (22:1).

Can you relate to David's story? Has your Saul cut you off from the position you had and the people you love? In an effort to land on your feet, have you stretched the truth? Distorted the facts?

Are you seeking refuge in Gath? Under normal circumstances you would never go there. But these aren't normal circumstances, so you loiter in the breeding ground of giants. The hometown of trouble. Her arms or that bar. You walk shady streets and frequent questionable places. And, while there, you go crazy. So the crowd will accept you, so the stress won't kill you, you go wild. You wake up in a Dead Sea cave, in the grottoes of Adullam, at the lowest point of your life, feeling as dumb as a roomful of anvils. You stare out at an arid, harsh, unpeopled future and ask, "What do I do now?"

Blessed is the one who perseveres under trial (James 1:12).

I suggest you let David be your teacher. Sure, he goes wacko for a few verses. But in the cave of Adullam, he gathers himself. The faithful shepherd boy surfaces again. The giant-killer rediscovers courage. Yes, he has a price on his head. Yes, he has no place to lay his head, but somehow he keeps his head.

He returns his focus to God and finds refuge.

5. Goliath had wanted to kill David, yet David boldly faced him down on a field of battle. Why then, just a short time later, did David panic and flee when he realized Saul wanted to kill him?

_____

_____

_____

_____

_____

6. How do you explain the fact that David lied to protect himself instead of relying on the One who had kept him safe from a lion, a bear, and a murderous giant?

_____

_____

_____

_____

7. What's the most desperate thing you've ever done to escape a dicey situation? What were the results? With the benefit of hindsight, what would have been a better course of action? Explain.

_____

_____

_____

_____

8. How do you guard against the kind of spiritual shortsightedness that causes people to seek refuge where they shouldn't?

_____

_____

_____

_____

King Saul used every bit of his power to bring David down. It wasn't nearly enough. When Saul ended his own life on a battlefield, David was still alive and well—and positioned to assume Saul's throne. In the next study, we'll see how David embodied the notion that whatever doesn't kill you makes you stronger.

❧ POINTS TO REMEMBER ❧

❖ After a victory, our enemy will go on the attack and try to bring us to a low place where we doubt the love and provision of God.
❖ It is when we find ourselves cut off and in a lonely place that we will be tempted to seek refuge in things other than God.
❖ When we experience a setback and things are not going as planned, we need to regroup, rediscover our courage, and refocus ourselves on God.

❧ PRAYER FOR THE DAY ❧

Father, you are our refuge and source of security when situations turn ominous and spiral out of control. Give us the clarity of thought to seek you when we feel threatened. Protect us, as you did David, from those who would do us harm. In Jesus' name, amen.

Day Three: Strongholds

COLD IN THE VALLEY

You might hear the news from a policeman: "I'm sorry. He didn't survive the accident." You might return a friend's call, only to be told, "The surgeon brought bad news." Too many spouses have heard these words from grim-faced soldiers: "We regret to inform you . . ." In such moments, spring becomes winter, blue turns to gray, birds go silent, and the chill of sorrow settles in. It's cold in the valley of the shadow of death.

David's messenger isn't a policeman, friend, or soldier. He is a breathless Amalekite with torn clothing and hair full of dirt who stumbles into Camp Ziklag with the news: "The people have fled from the battle, many of the people are fallen and dead, and Saul and Jonathan his son are dead also" (2 Samuel 1:4 NKJV).

David knows the Hebrews are fighting the Philistines. He knows Saul and Jonathan are in for the battle of their lives. He's been awaiting the outcome. When the messenger presents David with Saul's crown and bracelet, David has undeniable proof—Saul and Jonathan are dead.

Jonathan. Closer than a brother. He had saved David's life and sworn to protect his children.

Saul. God's chosen. God's anointed. Yes, he had hounded David. He had badgered David. But he was still God's anointed.

God's chosen king—dead.

David's best friend—dead.

Leaving David to face yet another giant—the giant of grief.

David wept as creatively as he worshiped, and "sang this lament over Saul and his son Jonathan, and gave orders that everyone in Judah learn it by heart" (1:17–18 MSG). David called the nation to mourning. He rendered weeping a public policy. He refused to gloss over or soft-pedal death. He faced it, fought it, challenged it. But he didn't deny it. As his son Solomon explained, "There is . . . a time to mourn" (Ecclesiastes 3:1, 4 NIV).

1. Read 1 Samuel 20:1–42. How would you describe the relationship between David and Jonathan? What did Jonathan do to show his loyalty to David?

_____

_____

_____

_____

_____

The Philistines were in hot pursuit of Saul and his sons, and they killed his sons (1 Samuel 31:2).

Saul took his own sword and fell on it (v. 4).

A man arrived from Saul's camp with his clothes torn and dust on his head (2 Samuel 1:2).

"I took the crown that was on his head and the band on his arm" (v. 10).

David took up this lament concerning Saul and his son Jonathan (v. 17).

2. Read Psalm 103:13–22. What traces of mourning and grief do you find in David's words? How does David worship God in the midst of his grief?

_____

_____

_____

_____

_____

3. Who fills the role of Jonathan in your life? What would the loss of that person mean to you? If you've already lost that person, what impact has it had on your life? How would you describe your mourning process?

_____

_____

_____

_____

_____

4. In Luke 6:27–28, Jesus says, "But to you who are willing to listen, I say, love your enemies! Do good to those who hate you. Bless those who curse you. Pray for those who hurt you" (NLT). How did David show love to King Saul even though they had a complicated and contentious relationship?

_____

_____

_____

_____

_____

COILED RATTLESNAKE

They anointed David king over Israel (2 Samuel 5:3).

David cannot remain in mourning forever, for there is work to be done. As God's anointed, he must take the next step toward becoming king of Israel. That involves taking the stronghold of Jerusalem.

Strongholds: old, difficult, discouraging challenges. This is what David faced when he looked at Jerusalem. When you and I think of the city, we envision temples and prophets. We picture Jesus teaching, a New Testament church growing. We imagine a thriving, hub-of-history capital.

The king and his men marched to Jerusalem to attack the Jebusites, who lived there (v. 6).

When David sees Jerusalem in 1000 BC, he sees something else. He sees a millennium-old, cheerless fortress, squatting defiantly on the spine of a ridge of hills. A rugged outcropping elevates her. Tall walls protect her. Jebusites indwell her. No one bothers them. Philistines fight the Amalekites. Amalekites fight the Hebrews. But the Jebusites? They are a coiled rattlesnake in the desert. Everyone leaves them alone.

Everyone, that is, except David. The just-crowned king of Israel has his eye on Jerusalem. He's inherited a divided kingdom. The people need not just a strong leader but strong headquarters. David's present base of Hebron sits too far south to enlist the loyalties of the northern tribes. But if he moves north, he'll isolate the south. He seeks a neutral, centralized city.

He wants Jerusalem. We can only wonder how many times he's stared at her walls. He grew up in Bethlehem, only a day's walk to the south. He hid in the caves in the region of En Gedi, not far south. Surely he noticed Jerusalem. Somewhere he pegged the place as the perfect capital. The crown had scarcely been resized for his head when he set his eyes on his newest Goliath.

The Jebusites pour scorn on David like Satan dumps buckets of discouragement on you: "You'll never overcome your bad habits." "Born white trash; gonna die white trash." "Think you can overcome your addiction? Think again." If you've heard the mocking David heard, your story needs the word David's has. Did you see it?

The Jebusites said to David, "You will not get in here; even the blind and the lame can ward you off" (2 Samuel 5:6).

"*Nevertheless* David took the stronghold." Granted, the city was old. The walls were difficult. The voices were discouraging . . . *Nevertheless* David took the stronghold. Wouldn't you love God to write a nevertheless in your biography? Born to alcoholics, *nevertheless* led a sober life. Never went to college, *nevertheless* mastered a trade. Didn't read the Bible until retirement age, *nevertheless* came to a deep and abiding faith.

Nevertheless, David captured the fortress (v. 7).

We all need a nevertheless. And God has plenty to go around. Strongholds mean nothing to him.

5. Read Ecclesiastes 3:1–8. How do we know when a particular time—say, the time to mourn—is over? How do we, like David, know when it's time to move on to the next stage of life?

_____

_____

_____

_____

_____

_____

6. Moving on is exactly what David did. After he ascended to the throne of Israel, we see some of his most prominent character traits emerge. Read 2 Samuel 5:6–11. What can we conclude about him based on his plan to attack the seemingly impenetrable fortress of Jerusalem?

_____

_____

_____

_____

_____

_____

7. In 2 Samuel 5:12 we read, "Then David knew that the LORD had established him as king over Israel and had exalted his kingdom for the sake of his people Israel" (NIV). How does this explain David's early successes as king of Israel?

_____

_____

_____

_____

_____

8. David brought down a stronghold that few others had even attempted to confront. What strongholds are waiting to be brought down in your life? What principles from David's campaign for Jerusalem can you apply to your own struggles?

_____

_____

_____

_____

_____

David's popularity during the early years of his reign—with God and with the people of Israel—is perhaps unrivaled in the Old Testament. For a while, the man seemingly could do no wrong. Then something began to shift in him. David lost sight of who he was, where he had come from, and what his responsibilities were. As we'll see in the next study, when he fell, he fell hard.

⟿ POINTS TO REMEMBER ᖆ

❖ God calls us to respect those whom he has anointed, even if we disagree with them or don't get along with them.
❖ Like David, we must face our losses head-on—we can't gloss over or soft-pedal our grief.
❖ Strongholds mean nothing to God, and he can write a "nevertheless" into our biography.

⟿ PRAYER FOR THE DAY ᖆ

Father, remind us that no stronghold can withstand your power. Give us the courage and imagination to dream big where your work is concerned. Allow us to see impenetrable forces in our lives for what they really are: mere obstacles to overcome with your help. We give you all the honor and glory for our victories. In Jesus' name, amen.

*D*ay Four: Altitude Sickness

AN ALL-TIME HIGH

You can climb too high for your own good. It's possible to ascend too far, stand too tall, and elevate too much. Linger too long at high altitudes, and two of your senses suffer. Your hearing dulls. It's hard to hear people when you are higher than they. Voices grow distant. When you are up there, your eyesight dims. It's hard to focus on people when you are so far above them. They appear so small. Little figures with no faces. You can hardly distinguish one from the other. They all look alike.

You don't hear them. You don't see them. You are above them.

Which is exactly where David was. He had never been higher. The wave of his success crested at age fifty. Israel was expanding. In two decades on the throne, he distinguished himself as a warrior, musician, statesman, and king. His cabinet was strong, and his boundaries stretched for 60,000 square miles. No defeats on the battlefield. No blemishes on his administration. Loved by the people. Served by the soldiers. Followed by the crowds. David was at an all-time high.

Never higher, yet never weaker. David stands at the highest point of his life, in the highest position in the kingdom, at the highest place in the city—on the balcony overlooking Jerusalem. He should be with his men, at battle, astride his steed and against his foe. But he isn't. He is at home.

It's springtime in Israel. The nights are warm, and the air is sweet. David has time on his hands, love on his mind, and people at his disposal. His eyes fall upon a woman as she bathes. We'll always wonder if Bathsheba was bathing in a place where she shouldn't bathe, hoping David would look where he shouldn't look. We'll never know. But we know that he looks and likes what he sees. So he inquires about her.

The servant laces his information with a warning. He gives not only the woman's name but her marital status and the name of her husband. Why tell David she is married if not to caution him? And why give the husband's name unless David is familiar with it? Odds are, David knew Uriah. The servant hopes to deftly dissuade the king. But David misses the hint. The next verse describes his first step down a greasy slope. "So David sent messengers to bring Bathsheba to him. When she came to him, he had sexual relations with her" (2 Samuel 11:4 NCV).

David "sends" many times in this story. He sends Joab to battle (see verse 1). He sends the servant to inquire about Bathsheba (see verse 3). He sends for Bathsheba to have her come to him (see verse 4). When David learns of her pregnancy, he sends word to Joab (see verse 6) to send Uriah back to Jerusalem. David sends him to Bathsheba to rest, but Uriah is too noble.

Pride goes before destruction, a haughty spirit before a fall (Proverbs 16:18).

The LORD gave David victory wherever he went (2 Samuel 8:14).

In the spring, at the time when kings go off to war . . . David remained in Jerusalem (11:1).

From the roof he saw a woman bathing (v. 2).

The man said, "She is Bathsheba, the daughter of Eliam and the wife of Uriah the Hittite" (v. 3).

David sent messengers to get her (v. 4).

David was told, "Uriah did not go home" (v. 10).

Some of the men in David's army fell; moreover, Uriah the Hittite died (2 Samuel 11:17).

[Bathsheba] became his wife and bore him a son (v. 27).

David opts to send Uriah back to a place in the battle where he is sure to be killed. Thinking his cover-up is complete, David sends for Bathsheba and marries her (see verse 27).

We don't like this sending, demanding David. We prefer the pastoring David, caring for the flock; the dashing David, hiding from Saul; the worshiping David, penning psalms. We aren't prepared for the David who has lost his self-control, who sins as he sends.

1. "In the spring of the year, at the time when kings go out to battle . . . David remained at Jerusalem" (2 Samuel 11:1 NKJV). David's troubles began when he put himself in the wrong place at the wrong time. When was a time you made a similar mistake? What consequences did you have to face for your actions?

   _____

   _____

   _____

2. In Ephesians 4:27, Paul advises us to "not give the devil a foothold" (NIV). How did David give the devil a way to defeat him?

   _____

   _____

   _____

3. Temptation is problem for all of us. Read the following passages and write down what God is saying to you on how to avoid it.

   Matthew 26:41: "Watch and pray so that you will not fall into temptation. The spirit is willing, but the flesh is weak" (NIV).

   _____

   _____

   _____

   Ephesians 6:11: "Put on the full armor of God so that you can fight against the devil's evil tricks" (NCV).

   _____

   _____

   _____

   Hebrews 2:18: "For since [Jesus] Himself was tempted in that which He has suffered, He is able to come to the aid of those who are tempted" (NASB).

   _____

   _____

   _____

James 1:12: "When tempted, no one should say, 'God is tempting me.' For God cannot be tempted by evil, nor does he tempt anyone" (NIV).

_____

_____

_____

James 4:7: "Therefore submit to God. Resist the devil and he will flee from you" (NKJV).

_____

_____

_____

1 John 4:4: "My dear children, you belong to God and have defeated them; because God's Spirit, who is in you, is greater than the devil, who is in the world" (NCV).

_____

_____

_____

4. Obviously the servant's warnings carried little sway with David. What might a trusted advisor have said to the king to get his attention?

_____

_____

_____

AN ALL-TIME LOW

What has happened to David? Simple. Altitude sickness. He's been too high too long. The thin air has messed with his senses. He can't hear as he used to. He can't hear the warnings of the servant or the voice of his conscience. Nor can he hear his Lord. The pinnacle has dulled his ears and blinded his eyes.

Did David see Bathsheba? No. He saw Bathsheba bathing. He saw Bathsheba's body and Bathsheba's curves. He saw Bathsheba, the conquest. But did he see Bathsheba, the human being? The wife of Uriah? The daughter of Israel? The creation of God? No. David had lost his vision. Too long at the top will do that to you. Too many hours in the bright sun and thin air leaves you breathless and dizzy.

Of course, who among us could ever ascend as high as David? Who among us is a finger snap away from a rendezvous with anyone we choose? Presidents and kings might send people to do their bidding; we're lucky to send out for Chinese food. We don't have that kind of clout. We can understand David's other struggles. His fear of Saul. Long stretches hiding in the wilderness. We've been there. But David high and mighty? David's balcony is one place we've never been. Or have we?

Do you see a person wise in their own eyes? There is more hope for a fool than for them (Proverbs 26:12).

How is your hearing? Do you hear the servants whom God sends? Do you hear the conscience that God stirs? And your vision? Do you still see people? Or do you see only their functions? Do you see people who need you, or do you see people beneath you? The story of David and Bathsheba is less a story of lust and more a story of power. A story of a man who rose too high for his own good. A man who needed to hear these words: "Come down before you fall."

This must be why God hates arrogance. He hates to see his children fall. He hates to see his Davids seduce and his Bathshebas be victimized. God hates what pride does to his children. He doesn't dislike arrogance. He hates it. 'Tis far wiser to descend the mountain than fall from it.

Pursue humility. Humility doesn't mean you think less of yourself but that you think of yourself less. Embrace your poverty. We're all equally broke and blessed. Resist the place of celebrity. As Jesus said, "Go sit in a seat that is not important. When the host comes to you, he may say, 'Friend, move up here to a more important place.' Then all the other guests will respect you" (Luke 14:10 NCV).

Wouldn't you rather be invited up than put down?

God has a cure for the high and mighty: come down from the mountain. You'll be amazed what you hear and who you see. And you'll breathe a whole lot easier.

[God] mocks proud mockers but shows favor to the humble and oppressed (Proverbs 3:34).

Humble yourselves, therefore, under God's mighty hand, that he may lift you up in due time (1 Peter 5:6).

5. David had seen what happened to King Saul. How did he fail to recognize the danger signs of arrogance and pride in his own life?

_____

_____

_____

6. Proverbs 11:2 states, "Pride leads only to shame; it is wise to be humble" (NCV). How did power corrupt David's relationship with God? How does power, or even just the illusion of power, corrupt people today?

_____

_____

_____

7. Often, we ask God for just enough provisions, just enough wealth, just enough health, just enough wisdom, and just enough good fortune to live independently of him. Humility requires our admission that God is our sole source of strength and support in this life and that without him we have nothing. This pursuit of humility starts on our knees by thanking God for his blessings and acknowledging just how undeserving we are of them. With these observations in mind, what changes do you need to make to your prayer life?

_____

_____

_____

8. In Luke 14:11, Jesus said, "All those who exalt themselves will be humbled, and those who humble themselves will be exalted" (NIV). What steps can you take to pursue greater humility . . .

in your marriage or dating relationship?

_____

_____

_____

in your friendships?

_____

_____

_____

in your neighborhood?

_____

_____

_____

at your work or school?

_____

_____

_____

at your church?

_____

_____

_____

in your social media?

_____

_____

_____

in your interactions with strangers?

_____

_____

_____

David's plan to cover up his sin was nearly foolproof. He had devised a plausible explanation for anyone who got too curious about his relationship with Bathsheba and had eliminated the one person who could have blown the whistle on him. Sure, the servants in the palace likely knew, but he had been able to keep the people of Israel in the dark. Yet there was one loose thread—David failed to account for God. The Lord saw everything David had done and was not about to let him get away with it.

⁓ POINTS TO REMEMBER ⁓

❖ It is when we are at our highest that we tend to be at our weakest in respect to temptation and sin.

❖ God hates arrogance because he hates to see his children fall.

❖ Humility doesn't mean we think less of ourselves but that we think of ourselves less.

⁓ PRAYER FOR THE DAY ⁓

Father, where can we go from your presence? What can we do that escapes your notice? You see when we fall short of your standard. You see when we give in to our urges and temptations. You see the effect our transgressions have—not only on the people we wrong, but on ourselves, on our relationship with you, and on our self-image. In your holy mercy, you refuse to leave us in our sin. You expose our wrongdoing and compel us to make things right. Thank you for your tough love—and for the forgiveness you offer to all who repent. In Jesus' name, amen.

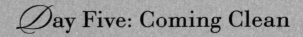

*D*ay Five: Coming Clean

A SIMPLE PARABLE

If a box of files existed documenting every second of your life, which would you burn? Do you have a season in which you indulged, imbibed, or inhaled? King David did. Could a collapse be more colossal than his? He seduces and impregnates Bathsheba, murders her husband, and deceives his general and soldiers. Then he marries her. She bears the child.

The thing David had done displeased the LORD (2 Samuel 11:27).

The cover-up appears complete. The casual observer detects no cause for concern. David has a new wife and a happy life. All seems well on the throne. But all is not well in David's heart. Guilt simmers. The guy is a walking wreck. Why? Because God keeps bringing it up.

God will be silent no more. David, the "sender," sits while God takes control. He sends Nathan to David. Nathan is a prophet, a preacher, a White House chaplain of sorts. The man deserves a medal for going to the king. He knows what happened to Uriah. David had killed an innocent soldier. What will he do with a confronting preacher?

The LORD sent Nathan to David (12:1).

Still, Nathan goes. Rather than declare the deed, he relates a story about a poor man with one sheep. David instantly connects. He shepherded flocks before he led people. He knows poverty. He's the youngest son of a family too poor to hire a shepherd. Nathan tells David how the poor shepherd loved this sheep—holding her in his own lap, feeding her from his own plate. She was all he had.

Enter, as the story goes, the rich jerk. A traveler stops by his mansion, so a feast is in order. Rather than slaughter a sheep from his own flock, the rich man sends his bodyguards to steal the poor man's animal. They come onto his property, snatch the lamb, and fire up the barbecue.

As David listens, hair rises on his neck. He grips the arms of the throne. He renders a verdict without a trial: fish bait by nightfall. "The man who has done this shall surely die!" (2 Samuel 12:5 NKJV).

Oh, David. You never saw it coming. You never saw Nathan erecting the gallows or throwing the rope over the beam. You never felt him tie your hands behind your back, lead you up the steps, and stand you squarely over the trap door. Only when he squeezed the noose around your neck did you gulp. Only when Nathan tightened the rope with four three-letter words: "You are the man!" (verse 7 NKJV).

[Nathan] said, "There were two men in a certain town, one rich and the other poor" (2 Samuel 12:1).

David burned with anger against the man (v. 5).

Then Nathan said to David, "You are the man!" (v. 7).

1. Read 1 Samuel 12:1–31. Remember that David had the power and authority to have Nathan killed. David had already shown he was capable of just about anything when it came to covering up his sins. How do you suppose Nathan felt about God's assignment? What can we learn from his example?

_____

_____

_____

2. Who do you know who could use the kind of wake-up call Nathan gave David? What steps would you need to take to deliver that wake-up call?

_____

_____

_____

3. Why do you think God directed Nathan to tell the story of the rich man taking the poor man's lamb? How was this more effective in getting David to recognize his sin that just confronting him outright? What does this tell us about how God convicts us of our sin?

_____

_____

_____

4. How could David have failed to recognize himself in Nathan's story? How did his pride play a part in blinding him?

_____

_____

WAVING THE WHITE FLAG

David's face pales; his Adam's apple bounces. A bead of sweat forms on his forehead. He slinks back in his chair. He makes no defense. He utters no response. He has nothing to say. God, however, is just clearing his throat. Through Nathan he proclaims:

> I made you king over Israel. I freed you from the fist of Saul. I gave you your master's daughter and other wives to have and to hold. I gave you both Israel and Judah. And if that hadn't been enough, I'd have gladly thrown in much more. So why have you treated the word of GOD with brazen contempt, doing this great evil? You murdered Uriah the Hittite, then took his wife as your wife. Worse, you killed him with an Ammonite sword! (2 Samuel 12:7–9 MSG).

God's words reflect hurt, not hate; bewilderment, not belittlement. Your flock fills the hills. Why rob? Beauty populates your palace. Why take from someone else? Why would the wealthy steal? David has no excuse.

So God levies a sentence.

> Now, therefore, the sword will never depart from your house, because you despised me and took the wife of Uriah the Hittite to be your own. This is what the LORD says: "Out of your own household I am going to bring calamity upon you. Before your very eyes I will take your wives and give them to one who is close to you, and he will sleep with your wives in broad daylight. You did it in secret, but I will do this thing in broad daylight before all Israel" (verses 10–12 NIV).

From this day forward, turmoil and tragedy mark David's family. Even the child of this adultery will die. He must. Surrounding nations now question the holiness of David's God. David had soiled God's reputation, blemished God's honor. And God, who jealously guards his glory, punishes David's public sin in a public fashion. The infant perishes. The king of Israel discovers the harsh truth of Numbers 32:23: "You can be sure that your sin will track you down" (MSG).

Have you found this to be true in your life? Colossal collapses won't leave us alone. Unconfessed sins sit on our hearts like festering boils, poisoning, expanding. And God, with gracious thumbs, applies the pressure.

God takes your sleep, your peace. He takes your rest. Why? Because he wants to take away your sin. Can a mom do nothing as toxins invade her child? Can God sit idly as sin poisons his? He will not rest until we do what David did: confess our fault. "Then David said to Nathan, 'I have sinned against the LORD.' Nathan replied, 'The LORD has taken away your sin. You are not going to die'" (2 Samuel 12:13 NIV).

"Why did you despise the word of the LORD by doing what is evil in his eyes?" (2 Samuel 12:9).

"You did it in secret, but I will do this thing in broad daylight before all Israel" (v. 12).

On the seventh day the child died (v. 18).

David said to Nathan, "I have sinned against the LORD" (v. 13).

Nathan replied, "The LORD has taken away your sin" (v. 13).

Interesting. David sentenced the imaginary sheep stealer to death. God is more merciful. He put away David's sin. Rather than cover it up, he lifted it up and put it away. "As far as the east is from the west, so far has he removed our transgressions from us. As a father has compassion on his children, so the LORD has compassion on those who fear him" (Psalm 103:12–13 NIV).

David denied his wrongdoing for at least nine months until the child was born. It took a prophet to bring the truth to the surface, but when he did, David finally waved the white flag. No more combat with God. No more arguing with heaven. He came clean with God. What was the result of such honesty? "I confessed all my sins to you and stopped trying to hide my guilt. I said to myself, 'I will confess my rebellion to the LORD.' And you forgave me! All my guilt is gone" (Psalm 32:5 NLT).

Want to get rid of your guilt? Then come clean with God.

If we confess our sins, [God] is faithful and just and will forgive us (1 John 1:9).

5. What did the giants of lust and pride do to David that Goliath could not? What were the long-term consequences for David? For his family? For the people of Israel and the surrounding nations?

_____
_____
_____
_____
_____

6. In Psalm 139:23–24, David wrote, "Search me, O God, and know my heart! Try me and know my thoughts! And see if there be any grievous way in me, and lead me in the way everlasting!" (ESV). Why was it important for David—someone whom who had fallen—to make himself accountable to God?

_____
_____
_____
_____

7. Read Galatians 6:1–10. What warnings does Paul give to those who think too highly of themselves? What does he advise us to do when a fellow believer has fallen into sin? How are we to be like Nathans to confront and restore others? Who would be the ideal candidate to fill that role in your life?

_____
_____
_____
_____
_____

8. If you invited God to search you and know your heart—to try you and know your thoughts—what would he find there right now?

_____

_____

_____

_____

"God testified concerning him: 'I have found David son of Jesse, a man after my own heart; he will do everything I want him to do'" (Acts 13:22).

The Bible tells us that God called David "a man after my own heart" (Acts 13:22 NIV). He gave the appellation to no one else. Not Abraham or Moses or Joseph. He called Paul an apostle, John his beloved, but neither was tagged a man after God's own heart.

One might read David's story and wonder what God saw in him. The fellow fell as often as he stood, stumbled as often as he conquered. He stared down Goliath, yet ogled at Bathsheba; defied God-mockers in the valley, yet joined them in the wilderness. An Eagle Scout one day. Chumming with the Mafia the next. He could lead armies but couldn't manage a family. Raging David. Weeping David. Bloodthirsty. God-hungry. Eight wives. One God.

A man after God's own heart? That God saw him as such gives hope to us all. David's life has little to offer the unstained saint. Straight-*A* souls find David's story disappointing. The rest of us find it reassuring. We ride the same roller coaster. We alternate between swan dives and belly flops, soufflés and burnt toast.

In David's good moments, no one was better. In his bad moments, could one be worse? The heart God loved was a checkered one.

We need David's story. Giants lurk in our neighborhoods. Rejection. Failure. Revenge. Remorse. Giants. We must face them, yet we need not face them alone. Focus first, and most, on God. The times David did, giants fell. The days he didn't, David did.

In David's battle against Goliath, his God-thoughts outnumber Goliath-thoughts nine to two. How does this ratio compare with yours? Do you ponder God's grace four times as much as you ponder your guilt? Is your list of blessings four times as long as your list of complaints? Is your mental file of hope four times as thick as your mental file of dread? Are you four times as likely to describe the strength of God as you are the demands of your day?

No? Then David is your man.

Some note the absence of miracles in his story. No Red Sea openings, chariots flaming, or dead Lazaruses walking. No miracles.

But there is one. David is one. A rough-edged walking wonder of God who neon-lights this truth:

Focus on giants—you stumble. Focus on God—your giants tumble.

Are you afraid of a giant? Then recall the lion and the bear. Remember the times God has come through for you in the past. Don't look forward in fear; look backward in appreciation. God's proof is God's past. Forgetfulness sires fearfulness, but a good memory makes for a good heart.

So lift your eyes, giant-slayer. The God who made a miracle out of David stands ready to make one out of you.

Be careful that you do not forget the LORD, who brought you out of Egypt, out of the land of slavery (Deuteronomy 6:12).

❧ POINTS TO REMEMBER ☙

- ❖ We may think we have covered up our sins, but God promises we always reap what we sow.
- ❖ God forgives our sins, but we will still have to face the consequences of our actions.
- ❖ David's life proves we don't have to be "perfect saints" in order to be people after God's own heart.

❧ PRAYER FOR THE DAY ☙

Lord, thank for you the stories of men like David in the Bible. Thank you for showing us that even at our worst we are never outside your love. Help us to focus on our blessings instead of our complaints, our hopes instead of our fears, and on your goodness instead of our own shortcomings and weaknesses. In Jesus' name, amen.

❧ WEEKLY MEMORY VERSE ☙

Therefore confess your sins to each other and pray for each other so that you may be healed. The prayer of a righteous person is powerful and effective.
JAMES 5:16 (NIV)

For Further Reading

Selections throughout this lesson were taken from *Facing Your Giants* (Nashville: Thomas Nelson, 2006); *The Applause of Heaven* (Nashville: Thomas Nelson, 1990); and *Come Thirsty* (Nashville: Thomas Nelson, 2004).

LESSON 6

JOSEPH

GIANT PROBLEMS AND COLOSSAL COLLAPSES

GABRIEL MUST HAVE SCRATCHED HIS HEAD at this one. He wasn't one to question his God-given missions. Sending fire and dividing seas were all in an eternity's work for this angel. When God sent, Gabriel went.

And when word got out that God was to become man, Gabriel was enthused. He could envision the moment: The Messiah in a blazing chariot. The King descending on a fiery cloud. An explosion of light from which the Messiah would emerge.

That's what he expected. What he never expected, however, was what he got: a slip of paper with a Nazarene address. "God will become a baby," it read. "Tell the mother to name the child Jesus. And tell her not to be afraid."

Gabriel was never one to question, but this time he had to wonder.

God will become a baby? Gabriel had seen babies before. He had been platoon leader on the bulrush operation. He remembered what little Moses looked like.

That's okay for humans, he thought to himself. *But God?*

The heavens can't contain him; how could a body? Besides, have you seen what comes out of those babies? Hardly befitting for the Creator of the universe. Babies must be carried and fed, bounced and bathed. To imagine some mother burping God on her shoulder—why, that was beyond what even an angel could imagine.

And what of this name—what was it—*Jesus*? Such a common name. There's a Jesus in every cul-de-sac. Come on, even *Gabriel* has more punch to it than Jesus. Call the baby *Eminence* or *Majesty* or *Heaven-sent*. Anything but *Jesus*.

So Gabriel scratched his head. What happened to the good ol' days? The Sodom and Gomorrah stuff. Flooding the globe. Flaming swords. That's the action he liked.

But Gabriel had his orders. Take the message to Mary. *Must be a special girl*, he assumed as he traveled. But Gabriel was in for another shock.

You his angels, you mighty ones who do his bidding, who obey his word (Psalm 103:20).

Therefore the Lord himself will give you a sign: The virgin will conceive and give birth to a son, and will call him Immanuel (Isaiah 7:14).

Will God really dwell on earth with humans? The heavens, even the highest heavens, cannot contain you (2 Chronicles 6:18).

God sent . . . Gabriel to Nazareth,
a town in Galilee, to a virgin
pledged to be married to a man
named Joseph (Luke 1:26–27).

One peek told him Mary was no queen. The mother-to-be of God was not regal. She was a Jewish peasant who'd barely outgrown her acne and had a crush on a guy named Joe.

And speaking of Joe—what does this fellow know? Might as well be a weaver in Spain or a cobbler in Greece. He's a carpenter. Look at him over there, sawdust in his beard and nail apron around his waist. You're telling me God is going to have dinner every night with him? You're telling me the source of wisdom is going to call this guy "Dad"? You're telling me a common laborer is going to be charged with giving food to God?

What if he gets laid off?

What if he gets cranky?

What if he decides to run off with a pretty young girl from down the street? Then where will we be? It was all Gabriel could do to keep from turning back.

"This is a peculiar idea you have, God," he must have muttered to himself.

Are God's guardians given to such musings? Are we?

The angel said to her . . .
"You will conceive and give birth to
a son, and you are to call him Jesus"
(vv. 30–31).

Only heaven knows how long Gabriel fluttered unseen above Mary before he took a breath and broke the news. But he did. He told her the name. He told her the plan. He told her not to be afraid. And when he announced, "With God nothing is impossible!" he said it as much for himself as for her.

For even though he couldn't answer the questions, he knew who could, and that was enough. And even though we can't answer them all, taking time to ask a few would be a good start.

"No word from God will
ever fail" (v. 37).

1. What do you suppose God saw in Joseph, beyond the sawdust and nail apron, that made him say, "There, *that's* the man whom I will entrust to raise my Son on earth"?

   _____

   _____

   _____

   _____

2. What does God see beyond *your* exterior that causes him to say, "Oh, yes, I can do big things with this one"?

   _____

   _____

   _____

   _____

Joseph's calling was extraordinary and utterly unique. No man before or since has been asked to raise the Messiah—God himself—as his own son. Yet Joseph's calling was also fairly typical in that God didn't require him to radically alter his personality or suddenly acquire a new skill set. Unbeknownst to Joseph, God had equipped him for the task that awaited him. Now he would call on Joseph to draw from what he had been given and see his plan through to completion.

That's what God's call involves: using the gifts he has given us for a specific purpose, for his glory. As for where his call may lead us, though, all bets are off. As we'll see in this first study, God's call took Joseph to places he had never imagined and exposed him to situations he never could have predicted.

❧ PRAYER FOR THE WEEK ❧

Father, thank you for the inspiring example of Joseph, a regular person who found himself in extraordinary circumstances. Thank you for giving us the opportunity to be a part of something much bigger than ourselves. Help us to use our talents and abilities in ways that will make a difference in your kingdom. In Jesus' name, amen.

Day One: The Branch-Sitter

LIFE IN A STABLE PLACE

When it comes to questions, nothing stirs up so many as the birth of Christ. Characters appear and disappear before we can ask them anything. The innkeeper too busy to welcome God—did he ever learn who he turned away? The shepherds—did they ever hum the song the angels sang? The wise men who followed the star—what was it like to worship a toddler? And Joseph. Especially Joseph. I've got questions for Joseph.

Did you and Jesus arm wrestle? Did he ever let you win?

Did you ever look up from your prayers and see Jesus listening?

How do you say "Jesus" in Egyptian?

What ever happened to the wise men? What ever happened to *you*?

We don't know what happened to Joseph. His role in Act I is so crucial that we expect to see him in the rest of the drama—but with the exception of a short scene with twelve-year-old Jesus in Jerusalem, he never reappears. The rest of his life is left to speculation, and we are left with our questions.

We do know Joseph was at a stable place in life when God called him to go out on a limb. He was perched firmly on his branch in the tree. It was thick, reliable, and perfect for sitting. It was so strong he didn't tremble when the storms came, nor did he shake when the winds blew. No, this branch was predictable and solid, and Joseph had no intention of leaving it.

Now, as he sat securely on his branch, he looked up at the one God wanted him to climb. He'd never seen one so thin! *That's no place for a man to*

Suddenly a great company of the heavenly host appeared with the angel, praising God (Luke 2:13).

"Where is the one who has been born king of the Jews? We saw his star when it rose and have come to worship him" (Matthew 2:2).

Joseph her husband was faithful to the law (1:19).

No one knows the thoughts of God except the Spirit of God (1 Corinthians 2:11).

go! he said to himself. *There's no place to sit. There's no protection from the weather. And how could you sleep dangling from that quivering twig?*

I can see him inching back a bit, leaning against the trunk, and pondering the situation. Common sense told him not to go out on the limb. *Conceived by the Holy Spirit? Come on!* Self-defense told him not to do it. *Who will believe me? What will our families think?* Convenience told him not to do it. *Just when I was hoping to settle down and raise a family.* Pride told him not to do it. *If she expects me to buy a tale like that . . .*

But God had told him to do it. And that's what bothered him. It bothered him because he was happy where he was. Life next to the trunk was good. His branch was big enough to allow him to sit in comfort. He was near scores of other branch-sitters and had made some valid contributions to the tree community. Surely God wouldn't want him to leave. He had . . . well, you could say that he had *roots* here.

Besides, he knew the kind of fellow who goes out on a limb. Radical. Extremist. Liberal. Always going overboard. Always stirring the leaves. Guys with their heads full of strange ideas in search of foreign fruit. Why, the stable ones are the ones who know how to stay close to home and leave well enough alone.

I have a feeling some of you can relate to Joseph. You know how he feels because you've been there. You know the imbalance that comes from having one foot in your will and one foot in God's. You, too, have sunk your fingernails into the bark of your secure limb to get a better grip. You know too well the butterflies that swarm in the pit of your stomach when you realize changes are in the air.

Do not conform to the pattern of this world, but be transformed by the renewing of your mind (Romans 12:2).

1. Joseph was in the prime of his life and seemed to be in a good place. He had a fiancée. He had a career. He had a good standing in the community. How do you think he envisioned his future?

   _____

   _____

   _____

2. Read Matthew 1:18–24. Joseph was no doubt filled with awe while he was in the presence of God's messenger. But when the angel departed and Joseph was alone once again, what do you suppose was his first thought? Explain.

   _____

   _____

   _____

3. The word *angel* in English comes from the Greek word *angelos*, which means "messenger of God." In the Bible we find many instances of angels encountering people and delivering God's words to them. Look up the following verses. What was the angel's message? How did the recipient respond?

Hagar in the desert: Genesis 16:7–13

_____

_____

_____

Lot at Sodom: Genesis 19:12–25

_____

_____

_____

Gideon in the winepress: Judges 6:11–18

_____

_____

_____

Elijah in the wilderness: 1 Kings 19:3–9

_____

_____

_____

Zachariah in the temple: Luke 1:8–22

_____

_____

_____

Philip on the desert road: Acts 8:26–31

_____

_____

_____

4. What questions did the angel's visit raise for Joseph during his encounter? How was he able to come to grips with God's extraordinary plan for his life?

_____

_____

_____

OUT ON A LIMB

Maybe right now you're in the midst of a decision. It's disrupting, isn't it? You like your branch. You've grown accustomed to it, and it to you. And, like Joseph, you're a pretty good branch-sitter. And then you hear the call.

"I need you to go out on a limb and take a stand. Some of the local churches are organizing an anti-pornography campaign. They need some volunteers."

Live a life worthy of the calling you have received (Ephesians 4:1).

"I need you to go out on a limb and forgive that person. It doesn't matter who hurt who first. What matters is that you go and build the bridge."

"I need you to go out on a limb and evangelize. That new family down the block? They don't know anyone in town. Go meet them."

"I need you to go out on a limb and sacrifice. The orphanage has a mortgage payment they can't meet. Remember the bonus you received last week?"

Regardless of the nature of the call, the consequences are the same: civil war. Though your heart may say yes, your feet say no. Excuses blow as numerously as golden leaves in an autumn wind. "That's not my talent." "It's time for someone else to take charge." "Not now. I'll get to it tomorrow." But eventually you're left staring at a bare tree and a hard choice: God's will or yours?

Joseph made his choice. After all, it was really the only option. He knew that the only thing worse than a venture into the unknown was the thought of denying his Master. So, resolute, he grasped the smaller limb. With tight lips and a determined glint in his eye, he placed one hand in front of the other until he dangled in the air with only his faith in God as a safety net.

As things turned out, Joseph's fears were justified. Life wasn't as comfortable as it had been. The limb he grasped was, indeed, a slender one: the Messiah was to be born to Mary and to be raised in his home. He took cold showers for nine months so the baby could be born of a virgin. He had to push away the sheep and clear out the cow patties so his wife would have a place to give birth. He became a fugitive of the law. He spent two years trying to understand Egyptian.

At times that limb must have bounced furiously in the wind. But Joseph just shut his eyes and held on. But you can be sure of one thing. He never regretted it. Sweet was the reward for his courage. One look in the face of that heavenly toddler and he knew he would do it again in a heartbeat.

Have you been called to go out on a limb for God? You can bet it won't be easy. Limb-climbing has never been easy. Ask Joseph. Or, better yet, ask Jesus. He knows better than anyone the cost of hanging on a tree.

5. Joseph's comfort zone was in his place and position in society. What is your comfort zone—the people, situations, circumstances, and surroundings in which you feel most at ease?

_____

_____

_____

_____

_____

_____

_____

_____

_____

_____

_____

"Yet not my will, but yours be done" (Luke 22:42).

[Joseph] did what the . . . Lord had commanded him and took Mary home as his wife (Matthew 1:24).

He did not consummate their marriage (v. 25).

[Joseph] took the child and his mother during the night and left for Egypt (2:14).

6. What's the furthest from your comfort zone that you've ever found yourself? What were the circumstances that took you to that place?

_____

_____

_____

_____

7. Why do God's plans frequently take us outside of our comfort zone?

_____

_____

_____

8. What are the payoffs for leaving your comfort zone? How do they compare to the risks and discomfort?

_____

_____

_____

Joseph's plans for the future—his hopes for a traditional, comfortable life with Mary—weren't the only things that took a hit when the angel showed up. As we'll see in the next study, Joseph's reputation—his standing in the community, which he had likely worked hard to build—was suddenly threatened by Mary's pregnancy. Joseph discovered that when you commit to God's plan, people look at you differently. And sometimes they talk about you as well.

❧ POINTS TO REMEMBER ❧

❖ It is when we are in a secure and stable place that God will often nudge us to help us grow in our faith.
❖ Eventually, when faced with a hard choice, we have to decide whether we will follow God's will or our own.
❖ Following God's call to go out on a limb is nerve-wracking, but it is something we will never regret doing.

❧ PRAYER FOR THE DAY ❧

Father, thank you for pulling us out of our comfort zone—
for taking us places we would never go on our own and letting us experience
things we wouldn't experience without you. Thank you for broadening our
perspective as to what we're capable of. Strengthen our hearts, O Lord.
Give us the courage and confidence to pursue your will, regardless of
where it takes us. In Jesus' name, amen.

*D*ay Two: Tanking Your Reputation

CAUGHT IN THE MIDDLE

We cannot, at once, promote two reputations. We can either promote God's and forget our own, or promote ours and forget God's. We must choose. Joseph did.

Matthew describes Jesus' earthly father as a craftsman. "Isn't this the carpenter's son? Isn't his mother's name Mary, and aren't his brothers James, Joseph, Simon and Judas?" (Matthew 13:55 NIV). He lives in Nazareth, a single-camel map dot on the edge of boredom. And he never speaks in the New Testament. Instead, he *does* much. He sees an angel, marries a pregnant girl, and leads his family to Bethlehem and Egypt. He does much, but says nothing.

"Isn't this the carpenter's son?" (Matthew 13:55).

"Nazareth! Can anything good come from there?" Nathanael asked (John 1:46).

A small-town carpenter who never said a Scripture-worthy word. Doesn't God have better options? An eloquent priest from Jerusalem or a scholar from the Pharisees? Why Joseph? A major part of the answer lies in his reputation: he gives it up for Jesus. "Then Joseph [Mary's] husband, being a just man, and not wanting to make her a public example, was minded to put her away secretly" (Matthew 1:19 NKJV).

[Joseph] did not want to expose her to public disgrace, [so] he had in mind to divorce her quietly (Matthew 1:19).

With the phrase "a just man," Matthew recognizes the status of Joseph. He was a *tsadiq* (tsa-deek), a serious student of the Torah. Nazareth viewed Joseph as we might view an elder, deacon, or Bible class teacher. *Tsadiqs* studied God's law. They recited and lived the Shema daily. They supported the synagogue, observed holy days, and followed the food restrictions. For a common carpenter to be known as a *tsadiq* was no small thing. Joseph likely took pride in his standing, but Mary's announcement jeopardized it. *I'm pregnant.*

Mary was pledged to be married to Joseph (v. 18).

Mary's parents, by this point, have signed a contract and sealed it with a dowry. Mary belongs to Joseph; Joseph belongs to Mary. Legally and matrimonially bound.

Now what? What's a *tsadiq* to do? His fiancée is pregnant, blemished, tainted . . . he is righteous, godly. On one hand, he has the law. On the other, he has his love. The law says, stone her. Love says, forgive her. Joseph is caught in the middle. But Joseph is a kind man. "Not wanting to disgrace her, [he] planned to send her away secretly" (verse 19 NASB).

A quiet divorce. How long would it stay quiet? Likely not long. But for a time, this was the solution.

1. Read Deuteronomy 22:13–21. What was Joseph, a *tsadiq*, required to do to uphold this law? Why do you think he chose an alternate course of action?

   _____

   _____

   _____

2. What did Joseph stand to lose if he continued his relationship with Mary? What do you stand to lose if you follow God's call as Joseph did—whether that involves sharing your faith with people or confronting a friend or loved one about a destructive habit?

_____
_____
_____

3. In James 1:17 we read, "Every good and perfect gift is from above, coming down from the Father of the heavenly lights, who does not change like shifting shadows" (NIV). How would this verse change the perspective of those who are worried about what they will lose if they follow God's calling?

_____
_____
_____
_____

4. What "good and perfect gifts" have you received when you submitted to God's will for your life as Joseph did?

_____
_____

SURRENDERING THE COMMON LIFE

So Joseph put together a plan to save his reputation as a *tsadiq*. But then comes the angel. "While he thought about these things, behold, an angel of the Lord appeared to him in a dream, saying, 'Joseph, son of David, do not be afraid to take to you Mary your wife, for that which is conceived in her is of the Holy Spirit'" (Matthew 1:20 NKJV).

Mary's growing belly gives no cause for concern, but reason to rejoice. "She carries the Son of God in her womb," the angel announces. But who would believe it? Who would buy this tale? Envision Joseph being questioned by the city leaders.

"Joseph," they say. "We understand that Mary is with child."

He nods.

"Is the child yours?"

He shakes his head.

"Do you know how she became pregnant?"

Gulp. A bead of sweat forms beneath Joseph's beard. He faces a dilemma. Make up a lie and preserve his place in the community or tell the truth and kiss his *tsadiq* goodbye. He makes his decision. "Joseph . . . did as the angel of the Lord commanded him and took to him his wife, and did not know

"Joseph son of David, do not be afraid to take Mary home as your wife, because what is conceived in her is from the Holy Spirit" (Matthew 1:20).

He did what the angel of the Lord had commanded (v. 24).

125

her till she had brought forth her firstborn Son. And he called His name Jesus" (verses 24–25 NKJV).

Joseph tanked his reputation. He swapped his *tsadiq* diploma for a pregnant fiancée and an illegitimate son and made the big decision of discipleship. He placed God's plan ahead of his own.

Would you be willing to do the same? God grants us an uncommon life to the degree we surrender our common one. "If you try to keep your life for yourself, you will lose it. But if you give up your life for me, you will find true life" (Matthew 16:25 NLT). Would you forfeit your reputation to see Jesus born into your world?

"Whoever wants to save their life will lose it, but whoever loses their life for me will find it" (Matthew 16:25).

5. Read Matthew 13:53–56, Mark 6:1–3, Luke 4:16–22, and John 6:41–42. According to these accounts, how did the people of Jesus' hometown regard him? What does this tell you about the way in which he was raised by Joseph and Mary?

   _____

   _____

   _____

   _____

6. The Gospel story makes no mention of Joseph delivering a speech to the people of Nazareth to defend himself or to explain the extraordinary positions in which he and Mary found themselves. Instead, Joseph seems to have gone about the business of being a loving and supportive partner to Mary and father to Jesus. What can we conclude about Joseph based on his deeds?

   _____

   _____

   _____

   _____

7. It took humility for Joseph to follow God and tank his reputation, and it takes humility for us to do the same. Read Philippians 2:5–11. What does this passage say about Jesus, our model of humility? How did God set the example by sending Jesus into this world to pay the price for our sins?

   _____

   _____

   _____

   _____

8. When was a time your reputation took a hit because of your relationship with Jesus? How did you respond?

   _____

   _____

   _____

Joseph might have assumed he knew where God's plan would take him, but he would soon discover he didn't have a clue. How could he have envisioned sitting in a stable in Bethlehem, watching the birth of the Son of God with assorted barnyard animals? How could he have predicted Herod's order of infanticide and his family's desperate flight to Egypt? As we'll see in the next study, Joseph didn't simply commit to a one-time role in God's plan. He said to God, in effect, "My life is yours. Do with it as you will." And God did.

⟋ POINTS TO REMEMBER ⟍

❖ We can choose to promote God's reputation or choose to promote our own, but we can't choose both.
❖ Following God requires us to step out in faith and see things from an eternal perspective rather than an earthly one.
❖ God grants us an uncommon life to the degree we are willing to give up our common one.

⟋ PRAYER FOR THE DAY ⟍

Father, we praise you for the wisdom and intricacy of your plan, for the way you bring order from chaos and good from bad. Give us the courage of Joseph in committing ourselves to your will for life. Grant us the peace of mind to embrace the fact that though we may not know what the future holds, we know who holds the future. In Jesus' name, amen.

⟋ay Three: A Lowly Place

GOD ENTERS THE WORLD

The noise and the bustle began earlier than usual in the village. As night gave way to dawn, people were already on the streets. Vendors were positioning themselves on the corners of the most heavily traveled avenues. Store owners were unlocking the doors to their shops. Children were awakened by the excited barking of the street dogs and the complaints of donkeys pulling carts.

The owner of the inn had awakened earlier than most in the town. After all, the inn was full, all the beds taken. Every available mat or blanket had been put to use. Soon all the customers would be stirring and there would be a lot of work to do.

Joseph also went up from the town of Nazareth in Galilee to Judea, to Bethlehem the town of David, because he belonged to the house and line of David. He went there to register with Mary, who was pledged to be married to him (Luke 2:4–5).

While they were there, the time come for the baby to be born, and [Mary] gave birth to her firstborn, a son (Luke 2:6–7).

One's imagination is kindled thinking about the conversation of the innkeeper and his family at the breakfast table. Did anyone mention the arrival of the young couple the night before? Did anyone ask about their welfare? Did anyone comment on the pregnancy of the girl on the donkey? Perhaps. Perhaps someone raised the subject. But, at best, it was raised, not discussed. There was nothing that novel about them. They were, possibly, one of several families turned away that night.

Besides, who had time to talk about them when there was so much excitement in the air? Augustus did the economy of Bethlehem a favor when he decreed that a census should be taken. Who could remember when such commerce had hit the village?

In those days Caesar Augustus issued a decree that a census should be taken of the entire Roman world (v. 1).

No, it is doubtful that anyone mentioned the couple's arrival or wondered about the condition of the girl. They were too busy. The day was upon them. The day's bread had to be made. The morning's chores had to be done. There was too much to do to imagine that the impossible had occurred.

God had entered the world as a baby. Yet, were someone to chance upon the sheep stable on the outskirts of Bethlehem that morning, what a peculiar scene they would behold. The stable stinks like all stables do. The stench of urine, dung, and sheep reeks pungently in the air. The ground is hard, the hay scarce. Cobwebs cling to the ceiling and a mouse scurries across the dirt floor.

[Mary] wrapped [Jesus] in cloths and placed him in a manger, because there was no guest room available for them (v. 7).

A more lowly place of birth could not exist.

1. Seven hundred years before Jesus was born, the prophet Micah wrote, "But you, Bethlehem Ephrathah, though you are little among the thousands of Judah, yet out of you shall come forth to Me the One to be Ruler in Israel, whose goings forth are from of old, from everlasting" (Micah 5:2 NKJV). Read Luke 2:1–7. What events occurred to fulfill this prophecy?

   _____

   _____

   _____

   _____

2. The prophet Isaiah wrote, "Hear now, you house of David! Is it not enough to try the patience of humans? Will you try the patience of my God also? Therefore the Lord himself will give you a sign: The virgin will conceive and give birth to a son, and will call him Immanuel" (7:14 NIV). The people of Israel knew these prophecies of the coming Messiah. Why, then, do you think so many of the Israelites missed the significance of Jesus' birth when it happened?

   _____

   _____

   _____

   _____

3. Read Matthew 25:1–13. What does this parable say about the importance of being vigilant for what God is doing? Why is this important for us today as we wait for Jesus to return to this earth?

_____

_____

_____

_____

4. How do we stay vigilant and watchful in spiritual matters?

_____

_____

_____

_____

MAJESTY IN THE MUNDANE

Near the young mother sits Joseph, the weary father. If anyone is dozing, he is. He can't remember the last time he sat down. And now that the excitement has subsided a bit, now that Mary and the baby are comfortable, he leans against the wall of the stable and feels his eyes grow heavy. He still hasn't figured it all out. The mystery of the event puzzles him. But he hasn't the energy to wrestle with the questions.

What's important is that the baby is fine and that Mary is safe. As sleep comes, he remembers the name the angel told him to use . . . Jesus. "We will call him Jesus."

Wide awake is Mary. Her head rests on the soft leather of Joseph's saddle. The pain has been eclipsed by wonder. She looks into the face of the baby. Her son. Her Lord. His Majesty. At this point in history, the human being who best understands who God is and what he is doing is a teenage girl in a smelly stable. She can't take her eyes off him. Somehow Mary knows she is holding God. So this is he. She remembers the words of the angel. "His kingdom will never end" (Luke 1:33 NIV).

He looks like anything but a king. His face is prunish and red. His cry, though strong and healthy, is still the helpless and piercing cry of a baby. And he is absolutely dependent on Mary and Joseph for his well-being.

Majesty in the midst of the mundane. Holiness in the filth of sheep manure and sweat. Divinity entering the world on the floor of a stable, through the womb of a teenager and in the presence of a carpenter.

She touches the face of the infant-God. How long was your journey!

This baby had overlooked the universe. These rags keeping him warm were the robes of eternity. His golden throne room had been abandoned in

"You will conceive and give birth to a son, and you are to call him Jesus" (Luke 1:31).

"He will reign over Jacob's descendants forever; his kingdom will never end" (v. 33).

For to us a child is born, to us a son is given, and the government will be on his shoulders. And he will be called Wonderful Counselor, Mighty God, Everlasting Father, Prince of Peace (Isaiah 9:6).

*But God chose the foolish things
of the world to shame the wise;
God chose the weak things of the
world to shame the strong*
(1 Corinthians 1:27).

favor of a dirty sheep pen. And worshiping angels had been replaced with kind but bewildered shepherds.

Meanwhile, the city hums. The merchants are unaware God has visited their planet. The innkeeper would never believe he had just sent God into the cold. And the people would scoff at anyone who told them the Messiah lay in the arms of a teenager on the outskirts of their village. They were all too busy to consider the possibility.

Those who missed His Majesty's arrival that night missed it not because of evil acts or malice; no, they missed it because they simply weren't looking. Little has changed in the last two thousand years, has it?

5. Seeing Mary so close to giving birth after carrying the baby to term must have driven home to Joseph that he was a supporting player in God's plan. He'd had nothing to do with the conception and would have little to do with the birth. If, say, the innkeeper had stumbled onto the scene and asked him, "What is your purpose here?" what do you think Joseph would have said?

_____

_____

_____

_____

_____

_____

_____

6. What kind of personality excels in a supporting role? Why are people in supporting roles so vital to God's plan?

_____

_____

_____

_____

_____

_____

_____

7. The shepherds would come soon, the wise men a little later. But at the moment of Jesus' birth, Joseph and Mary were alone, save for a menagerie of barnyard animals. That moment was a crucible for Joseph. Prophecy had become reality. The Messiah had arrived. And Joseph was responsible for raising, protecting, and caring for him. What thoughts do you suppose were racing through his mind at that moment?

_____

_____

_____

_____

8. What responsibilities would Joseph have felt?

_____
_____
_____
_____
_____

9. The story of Jesus' birth is the story of God working through ordinary people, places, and events. In what ways has he worked through the everyday experiences in your life? How have you seen the miraculous in the mundane?

_____
_____
_____
_____
_____
_____
_____
_____
_____
_____

In that stable in Bethlehem, Joseph watched the final hours of the Old Testament era tick away. He was no doubt feeling confused, scared, uncertain, overwhelmed—and perhaps a little excited. After all, the Jewish people had been looking for the Messiah for centuries, and Joseph was about to meet him face-to-face. And call him son.

"Bethlehem Ephrathah, though you are small among the clans of Judah, out of you will come for me one who will be ruler over Israel, whose origins are from of old, from ancient times" (Micah 5:2).

⤳ POINTS TO REMEMBER ↶

❖ God chose to enter the world not in splendor but in the most mundane of environments possible.
❖ God chooses to use that which the world deems foolish in order to humble those who think they are wise.
❖ If we are not watching, we can miss the miraculous things God is doing around us every day.

⤳ PRAYER FOR THE DAY ↶

Father, we praise you for giving roles to everyone in your plans—from Type As and Type Bs to those who defy categorization. Keep us ever mindful of the fact that while some roles are more prominent and public than others, all are equally important and pleasing to you. In Jesus' name, amen.

Day Four: To Obey or Not Obey

SO MANY QUESTIONS

[Herod] asked them where the Messiah was to be born. "In Bethlehem in Judea," [the Magi] replied (Matthew 2:4–5).

Of all the questions I have about the birth of Christ, I'd like to know about that night in the stable. I can picture Joseph there. Moonlit pastures. Stars twinkle above. Bethlehem sparkles in the distance. There he is, pacing outside the stable.

What was he thinking while Jesus was being born? What was on his mind while Mary was giving birth? He'd done all he could do—heated the water, prepared a place for Mary to lie. He'd made Mary as comfortable as she could be in a barn and then he stepped out. She'd asked to be alone, and Joseph had never felt more so.

In that eternity between his wife's dismissal and Jesus' arrival, what was he thinking? He walked into the night and looked into the stars. Did he pray?

For some reason, I don't see him silent; I see Joseph animated, pacing. Head shaking one minute, fist shaking the next. This isn't what he had in mind. I wonder what he said . . .

This isn't the way I planned it, God. Not at all. My child being born in a stable? This isn't the way I thought it would be. A cave with sheep and donkeys, hay and straw? My wife giving birth with only the stars to hear her pain?

This isn't at all what I imagined. No, Lord, I imagined family. I imagined grandmothers. I imagined neighbors clustered outside the door and friends standing at my side. I imagined the house erupting with the first cry of the infant. Slaps on the back. Loud laughter. Jubilation.

That's how I thought it would be.

The midwife would hand me my child and all the people would applaud. Mary would rest and we would celebrate. All of Nazareth would celebrate.

But now. Now look. Nazareth is five days' journey away. And here we are in a . . . in a sheep pasture. Who will celebrate with us? The sheep? The shepherds? The stars?

This doesn't seem right. What kind of husband am I? I provide no midwife to aid my wife. No bed to rest her back. Her pillow is a blanket from my donkey. My house for her is a shed of hay and straw.

The smell is bad; the animals are loud. Why, I even smell like a shepherd myself.

Did I miss something? Did I, God?

When you sent the angel and spoke of the son being born—this isn't what I pictured. I envisioned Jerusalem, the temple, the priests, and the people gathered to watch. A pageant perhaps. A parade. A banquet at least. I mean, this is the Messiah!

Or, if not born in Jerusalem, how about Nazareth? Wouldn't Nazareth have been better? At least there I have my house and my business. Out here, what do I have? A weary mule, a stack of firewood, and a pot of warm water. This is not the way I wanted it to be! This is not the way I wanted my son.

There were shepherds living out in the fields nearby, keeping watch over their flocks at night. An angel of the Lord appeared to them, and the glory of the Lord shone around them, and they were terrified. But the angel said to them, "Do not be afraid. I bring you good news that will cause great joy for all the people. Today in the town of David a Savior has been born to you; he is the Messiah, the Lord. This will be a sign to you: You will find a baby wrapped in cloths and lying in a manger" (Luke 2:8–12).

Oh my, I did it again. I did it again, didn't I, Father? I don't mean to do that; it's just that I forget. He's not my son . . . he's yours. The child is yours. The plan is yours. The idea is yours. And forgive me for asking, but . . . is this how God enters the world? The coming of the angel, I've accepted. The questions people asked about the pregnancy, I can tolerate. The trip to Bethlehem, fine. But why a birth in a stable, God?

I'm unaccustomed to such strangeness, God. I'm a carpenter. I make things fit. I square off the edges. I follow the plumb line. I measure twice before I cut once. Surprises are not the friend of a builder. I like to know the plan. I like to see the plan before I begin.

But this time I'm not the builder, am I? This time I'm a tool. A hammer in your grip. A nail between your fingers. A chisel in your hands. This project is yours, not mine. I guess it's foolish of me to question you. Forgive my struggling. Trust doesn't come easy to me, God. But you never said it would be easy, did you?

You, LORD, are our Father. We are the clay, you are the potter; we are all the work of your hand (Isaiah 64:8).

1. Joseph was still a relative newcomer to God's plan, but he'd had some time to think about it. Which of the following words best describes how Joseph might have felt when he witnessed Jesus' *actual* arrival? Why?

   ❏ Disappointed
   ❏ Stunned
   ❏ Powerless
   ❏ Guilty (for failing to provide a better birthplace)
   ❏ Scared
   ❏ Disoriented
   ❏ Overwhelmed

   _____
   _____
   _____
   _____

2. Think of a time when your expectations as to how God would answer a prayer proved to be way off. What was your reaction to his actual answer?

   _____
   _____
   _____
   _____

3. Is understanding God's plan always a prerequisite for obeying? Why or why not? Explain.

   _____
   _____
   _____
   _____
   _____
   _____

4. In spite of Joseph's questions, he recognized he was "a chisel in God's hands" and was obedient to God's plans. What do the following verses say to you personally about the importance of being obedient to God?

Matthew 6:24: "No one can serve two masters. Either you will hate the one and love the other, or you will be devoted to the one and despise the other" (NIV).

_____

_____

_____

Luke 6:47–49: "Whoever comes to Me, and hears My sayings and does them, I will show you whom he is like: He is like a man building a house, who dug deep and laid the foundation on the rock. And when the flood arose, the stream beat vehemently against that house, and could not shake it, for it was founded on the rock. But he who heard and did nothing is like a man who built a house on the earth without a foundation, against which the stream beat vehemently; and immediately it fell. And the ruin of that house was great" (NKJV).

_____

_____

_____

_____

John 14:21: "Those who know my commands and obey them are the ones who love me, and my Father will love those who love me. I will love them and will show myself to them" (NCV).

_____

_____

_____

_____

James 1:22–25: "Do not merely listen to the word, and so deceive yourselves. Do what it says. Anyone who listens to the word but does not do what it says is like someone who looks at his face in a mirror and, after looking at himself, goes away and immediately forgets what he looks like. But whoever looks intently into the perfect law that gives freedom, and continues in it—not forgetting what they have heard, but doing it—they will be blessed in what they do" (NIV).

_____

_____

_____

_____

A SKY BLACKENED WITH DOUBT

I wonder. Did Joseph ever pray such a prayer? Perhaps he did. Perhaps he didn't. But you probably have. You've stood where Joseph stood. Caught between what God says and what makes sense. You've done what he told you to do only to wonder if it was him speaking in the first place. You've stared into a sky blackened with doubt. And you've asked what Joseph asked.

You've asked if you're still on the right road. You've asked if you were supposed to turn left when you turned right. And you've asked if there is a plan behind this scheme. Things haven't turned out like you thought they would.

Each of us knows what it's like to search the night for light. Not outside a stable, but perhaps outside an emergency room. On the gravel of a roadside. On the manicured grass of a cemetery. We've asked our questions. We questioned God's plan. And we've wondered why God does what he does.

The Bethlehem sky is not the first to hear the pleadings of a confused pilgrim.

If you are asking what Joseph asked, let me urge you to do what Joseph did. Obey. That's what he did. He obeyed. He obeyed when the angel called. He obeyed when Mary explained. He obeyed when God sent.

He was obedient to God.

He was obedient when the sky was bright. He was obedient when the sky was dark.

He didn't let his confusion disrupt his obedience. He didn't know everything. But he did what he knew. He shut down his business, packed up his family, and went to another country. Why? Because that's what God said to do.

What about you? Just like Joseph, you can't see the whole picture. Just like Joseph, your task is to see that Jesus is brought into your part of the world. And just like Joseph, you have a choice: to obey or disobey. Because Joseph obeyed, God used him to change the world.

Can he do the same with you?

Trust in the LORD with all your heart (Proverbs 3:5).

"I am the light of the world. Whoever follows me will never walk in darkness, but will have the light of life" (John 8:12).

5. If you could get God to answer one question, what would it be? What impact would it have on your life if you got your answer? What impact would it have if you never got an answer in this lifetime?

_____

_____

_____

6. In 1 Corinthians 13:12, Paul wrote, "For now we see only a reflection as in a mirror; then we shall see face to face. Now I know in part; then I shall know fully, even as I am fully known" (NIV). What comfort can you take from Paul's words when the situation is unclear to you?

_____

_____

_____

_____

7. What are some reasons God might withhold certain information from us?

_____

_____

_____

_____

_____

_____

_____

8. If you could ask Joseph for advice on how to stay faithful when you can't see God's whole plan, what do you think he would say?

_____

_____

_____

_____

_____

_____

_____

Joseph and Mary would soon discover they weren't the only ones anticipating Jesus' arrival. As we'll see in the next study, an encounter with a devout man named Simeon made them realize that others had a vested interest in their son. They had to come to grips with the fact that the son of Joseph and Mary was first and foremost the Son of God and Son of Man.

❧ POINTS TO REMEMBER ☙

❖ Most of the time, the way *we* envision our life turning out and the way *God* envisions it will not be the same.

❖ At times we all have doubts—questions about God's plan and why he does what he does.

❖ When we can't see the whole picture, we have to make the choice to obey God and trust him for the results.

❧ PRAYER FOR THE DAY ☙

*Father, we praise you for defying our expectations at every turn.
People anticipated the Messiah's arrival for centuries, yet no one expected it
to come as it did. Help us remember that the next time we struggle with an
unanswered prayer or a situation that doesn't go as we expect.
In Jesus' name, amen.*

Day Five: Final Scenes

SIMEON'S WAIT

Funny how Scripture remembers different people. Abraham is remembered trusting. Envision Moses, and you envision a person leading. Paul's place in Scripture was carved by his writing, and John is known for his loving. But Simeon is remembered, interestingly enough, not for leading nor preaching nor loving, but rather for looking.

"Now in Jerusalem there was a man named Simeon. He was an upright and devout man; he *looked forward* to Israel's comforting and the Holy Spirit rested on him" (Luke 2:25 TJB, emphasis mine).

Our brief encounter with Simeon occurs eight days after the birth of Jesus. Joseph and Mary have brought their son to the temple. It's the day of a sacrifice, the day of circumcision, the day of dedication. But for Simeon, it's the day of celebration.

Let's imagine a white-headed, wizened fellow working his way down the streets of Jerusalem. People in the market call his name and he waves but doesn't stop. Neighbors greet him and he returns the greeting but doesn't pause. Friends chat on the corner and he smiles but doesn't stop. He has a place to be and he hasn't time to lose.

Luke 2:27 contains this curious statement: "Prompted by the Spirit he came to the Temple" (TJB). Simeon apparently had no plans to go to the temple. God, however, thought otherwise. We don't know how the prompting came—a call from a neighbor, an invitation from his wife, a nudging within the heart—we don't know. But somehow Simeon knew to clear his calendar and put away his golf clubs.

"I think I'll go to church," he announced.

On this side of the event, we understand the prompting. Whether Simeon understood or not, we don't know. We do know, however, that this wasn't the first time God tapped him on the shoulder. At least one other time in his life, he had received a message from God. "The Holy Spirit had revealed to him that he would not die until he had seen him—God's anointed King" (verse 26 TLB).

Simeon reminds us to "wait forwardly." Patiently vigilant. But not so patient that we lose our vigilance. Nor so vigilant that we lose our patience.

In the end, the prayer of Simeon was answered. "Simeon took the baby in his arms and thanked God: 'Now, Lord, you can let me, your servant, die in peace, as you said'" (Luke 2:28–29 NCV).

One look into the face of Jesus, and Simeon knew that it was finally time to go home. And one look into the face of our Savior, and we will know the same.

When the time came for the purification rites required by the Law of Moses, Joseph and Mary took him to Jerusalem to present him to the Lord (Luke 2:22).

Now there was a man in Jerusalem called Simeon (v. 25).

Moved by the Spirit, he went into the temple courts (v. 27).

It had been revealed to him by the Holy Spirit that he would not die before he had seen the Lord's Messiah (v. 26).

Simeon took him in his arms and praised God (v. 28).

1. Read Luke 2:25–35. As we discussed previously, there were few people in Israel who recognized the Messiah when he was born. Simeon, however, was one of them. How had he been vigilant in watching for the promised birth? How did he react when he saw Jesus?

_____

_____

_____

2. We don't know how long Simeon had been waiting for the Messiah. It might have been a week. A month. A year. Maybe even twenty years. Regardless, he was vigilant and acted when God called him. What are the benefits of waiting for an answer to prayer—even though it is difficult to do?

_____

_____

_____

3. The prophet Isaiah wrote, "Though youths grow weary and tired, and vigorous young men stumble badly, yet those who wait for the LORD will gain new strength; they will mount up with wings like eagles, they will run and not get tired, they will walk and not become weary" (Isaiah 40:30–31 NASB). What is the key to maintaining patient vigilance? What promise does this verse provide for those who wait and place their hope in the Lord?

_____

_____

_____

4. Think about Simeon's words in Luke 2:34–35: "Behold, this Child is destined for the fall and rising of many in Israel, and for a sign which will be spoken against (yes, a sword will pierce through your own soul also)" (NKJV). How would you have reacted to this prophecy if you were Mary and Joseph?

_____

_____

_____

SPENDING TIME IN THE TEMPLE

Then Simeon blessed them and said to Mary . . . "This child is destined to cause the falling and rising of many in Israel" (Luke 2:34).

Luke tells us that Mary and Joseph were "amazed at what Simeon had said" about Jesus (Luke 2:33 NCV). Luke goes on to recount one last story with the family at the temple in Jerusalem before Joseph forever exits the Gospels. It occurs twelve years later during the Passover Feast. "When he was twelve years old, they went to the feast as they always did. After the feast days were over, they started home. The boy Jesus stayed behind in Jerusalem, but his parents did not know it" (Luke 2:42–43 NCV).

For three days Joseph and Mary were separated from Jesus. "After three days they found Jesus sitting in the Temple with the teachers, listening to them and asking them questions. All who heard him were amazed at his understanding and answers" (verses 46–47). The temple was the last place they thought to search. But it was the first place Jesus went.

Jesus didn't go to a cousin's house or a buddy's playground. The son of Joseph the carpenter didn't go among the carpenters but among teachers of faith and interpreters of the Torah. He sought the place of godly thinking. Though he was beardless and unadorned, this boy's thoughts were profound. Just ask the theologians with whom he conversed and confounded. This boy did not think like a boy.

Why? What made Jesus different? The Bible is silent about his IQ. When it comes to the RAM size of his mental computer, we are told nothing. But when it comes to his purity of mind, we are given this astounding claim: Christ "knew no sin" (2 Corinthians 5:21 NKJV). Peter says Jesus "did no sin, neither was guile found in his mouth" (1 Peter 2:22 KJV). John lived next to him for three years and concluded, "In Him there is no sin" (1 John 3:5 NKJV).

The word *sinless* has never survived cohabitation with another person. Those who knew Christ best, however, spoke of his purity in unison and with conviction. And because he was sinless, his mind was stainless. No wonder people were "amazed at his teaching" (Mark 1:22 NCV). His mind was virus-free.

The twelve-year-old boy in the temple—the one with sterling thoughts and pure mind? Guess what—he represents God's goal for you! You are made to be like Christ! God's priority is that you be "transformed by the renewing of your mind" (Romans 12:2 NIV). You may have been born virus-prone, but you don't have to live that way. There is hope for your head!

Are you a worrywart? Don't have to be one forever. Guilt plagued and shame stained? Prone to anger? Jealousy? God can take care of that. God can change your mind. Heaven is the land of sinless minds. Virus-free thinking. Absolute trust. No fear or anger. Shame and second-guessing are practices of a prior life. Heaven will be wonderful, not because the streets are gold, but because our thoughts will be pure.

So what are you waiting on? Apply God's antivirus. "Set your mind on things above, not on things on the earth" (Colossians 3:2 NKJV). Give him your best thoughts, and see if he doesn't change your mind.

5. Read Luke 2:41–52. How did Joseph and Mary lose track of Jesus for three days? What does this tell you about the family system at the time?

_____

_____

_____

_____

When [Jesus] was twelve years old, [Mary and Joseph] went up to the festival (Luke 2:42).

After three days they found him in the temple courts (v. 46).

"Why were you searching for me?" [Jesus] asked. "Didn't you know I had to be in my Father's house?" (v. 49).

We do not have a high priest who is unable to empathize with our weaknesses, but we have one who has been tempted in every way, just as we are—yet he did not sin (Hebrews 4:15).

We all, who with unveiled faces contemplate the Lord's glory, are being transformed into his image with ever-increasing glory, which comes from the Lord, who is the Spirit (2 Corinthians 3:18).

Set your minds on things above (Colossians 3:2).

6. Luke tells us that "Jesus kept increasing in wisdom and stature, and in favor with God and men" (verse 52 NASB). This statement is practically the sum total of the Bible's information about Jesus from the time his parents found him in the temple in Jerusalem to the time he started his public ministry at age thirty. It summarizes more than two decades of Jesus' life! Think about these "missing years." What role might Joseph have played in helping Jesus grow in wisdom? In stature? In favor with God? In favor with men? Explain.

_____

_____

_____

_____

7. The temple was the last place Joseph and Mary thought to search, but it was the first place Jesus went. What did Jesus mean when he said, "I had to be in My Father's house" (verse 49 NIV)? What does this say about his priorities? What does it say about what our priorities should be?

_____

_____

_____

_____

_____

8. How is God making you more like Christ in your thoughts? How is he transforming you through the renewal of your mind?

_____

_____

_____

_____

"And surely I am with you always, to the very end of the age" (Matthew 28:20).

God still looks for Josephs today. Men and women who believe that he is not through with this world. Common people who serve an uncommon God.

Will you be that kind of person? Will you serve . . . even when you don't understand? Will you choose to "trust in the LORD with all your heart and lean not on your own understanding" (Proverbs 3:5 NIV)?

The Bethlehem sky is not the first to hear the pleadings of an honest heart, nor the last. Perhaps God didn't answer every question that Joseph asked. But he answered the most important one: "Are you still with me, God?"

And through the first cries of the God-child the answer came: "Yes. Yes, Joseph. I'm with you."

There are many questions about the Bible that we won't be able to answer until we get home. Many times we will muse, "I wonder . . ."

But in our wonderings, there are some questions we never need to ask. Does God care? Do we matter to God? Does he still love his children?

Through the small face of the stable-born baby, he says yes.

Yes, your sins are forgiven.

Yes, your name is written in heaven. Yes, death has been defeated. And yes, God has entered your world. Immanuel. God is with us.

The Word became flesh and made his dwelling among us (John 1:14).

POINTS TO REMEMBER

❖ Simeon's story reminds us to "wait forwardly" on God and be patiently vigilant in the work he is doing in our midst.
❖ God's priority is for us to be like the twelve-year-old Jesus in the temple, with sterling thoughts and a virus-free mind.
❖ God still looks for men and women who believe he is not through with this world and are obedient to follow his call.

PRAYER FOR THE DAY

God, help us to wait patiently but vigilantly on you. Renew our minds and give us your thoughts. Help us to be Josephs for you and obediently answer the call you put on our lives. Thank you that you never give up on us but renew our strength each day. In Jesus' name, amen.

WEEKLY MEMORY VERSE

Cast all your anxiety on him because he cares for you.
1 PETER 5:7 (NIV)

For Further Reading

Selections throughout this lesson were taken from *When God Whispers Your Name* (Nashville: Thomas Nelson, 1999); *He Still Moves Stones* (Nashville: Thomas Nelson, 1993); *God Came Near* (Nashville: Thomas Nelson, 1986); *When Christ Comes* (Nashville: Thomas Nelson, 1998); *Next Door Savior* (Nashville: Thomas Nelson, 2003); *Cure for the Common Life* (Nashville: Thomas Nelson, 2006).

LESSON 7

REDEFINING GOD'S FAMILY

AS JESUS WAS GOING DOWN THE ROAD, he saw Matthew sitting at his tax-collection booth. "'Follow me and be my disciple,' Jesus said to him. So Matthew got up and followed him" (Matthew 9:9 NLT).

The surprise in this invitation is the one invited—a tax collector. Combine the greed of an embezzling executive with the presumption of a hokey television evangelist. Throw in the audacity of an ambulance-chasing lawyer and the cowardice of a drive-by sniper. Stir in a pinch of a pimp's morality, and finish it off with the drug peddler's code of ethics—and what do you have?

A first-century tax collector.

According to the Jews, these guys ranked barely above plankton on the food chain. Caesar permitted these Jewish citizens to tax almost anything—your boat, the fish you caught, your house, your crops. As long as Caesar got his due, they could keep the rest.

Matthew was a *public* tax collector. Private tax collectors hired other people to do the dirty work. Public publicans, like Matthew, just pulled their stretch limos into the poor side of town and set up shop. As crooked as corkscrews.

His given name was Levi, a priestly name. Did his parents aspire for him to enter the priesthood? If so, he was a flop in the family circle.

You can bet he was shunned. The neighborhood cookouts? Never invited. High-school reunions? Somehow his name was left off the list. The guy was avoided like the flu. They all kept their distance from Matthew.

Everyone except Jesus. "'Come, be my disciple,' Jesus said to him. So Matthew got up and followed him" (Matthew 9:9 NLT).

Matthew must have been ripe. Jesus hardly had to tug. Within a punctuation mark, Matthew's shady friends and Jesus' green followers are swapping email addresses. "Then Levi gave a big dinner for Jesus at his house. Many tax collectors and other people were eating there, too" (Luke 5:29 NCV).

As Jesus went on from there, he saw a man named Matthew sitting at the tax collector's booth. "Follow me," he told him (Matthew 9:9).

Now the tax collectors and sinners were all gathering around to hear Jesus (Luke 15:1).

[Jesus] saw Levi son of Alphaeus sitting at the tax collector's booth (Mark 2:14).

Then Levi held a great banquet for Jesus at his house (Luke 5:29).

1. What did Jesus see in Matthew? What did Matthew see in Jesus?

_____

_____

_____

2. Why do you think Matthew was so willing to drop everything and follow Jesus? What might have caused him to want to make a drastic change?

_____

_____

_____

Matthew's story sheds light on our own discipleship. After all, if we're better than Matthew, it's only by increments. If people could know our hearts and the thoughts we sometimes entertain, they would see we're far from disciple material. But Jesus sees—and still he calls us to follow him. He sees value in us. He wants a relationship with us. For that reason, we can look to Matthew's story for clues as to how to maximize the potential of that relationship.

⌁ PRAYER FOR THE WEEK ⌁

Father, thank you for looking past our reputation, our weaknesses, and our failings. Thank you for seeing the potential in us as you did with Matthew. Bless our efforts to understand you better. Deepen our relationship with you. In Jesus' name, amen.

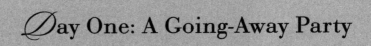

$\mathcal{D}$ay One: A Going-Away Party

A FRIEND IS A FRIEND

While Jesus was having dinner at Levi's house, many tax collectors and sinners were eating with him and his disciples (Mark 2:15).

What do you suppose led up to that party? Let's try to imagine. I can see Matthew going back to his office and packing up. He removes the Roman Collaborator of the Year Award from the wall and boxes up the Shady Business School certificate. His coworkers start asking questions.

"What's up, Matt? Headed on a cruise?"

"Hey, Matthew, the Missus kick you out?"

Matthew doesn't know what to say. He mumbles something about a job change. But as he reaches the door, he pauses. Holding his box full of office supplies, he looks back. They're giving him hangdog looks—kind of sad, puzzled.

He feels a lump in his throat. Oh, these guys aren't much. Parents warn their kids about this sort. Salty language. Mardi Gras morals. They keep the number of the bookie on their phones. The bouncer at the Gentlemen's Club sends them birthday cards. But a friend is a friend.

Yet what can he do? Invite them to meet Jesus? Yeah, right. They like preachers the way sheep like butchers. So, not knowing what else to do, he shrugs his shoulders and gives them a nod. "These stupid allergies," he says, rubbing the mist from one eye.

Later that day the same thing happens. He goes to the bar to settle up his account. The décor is blue-collar chic: a seedy, smoky place with a Budweiser chandelier over the pool table and a jukebox in the corner. Not the country club, but for Matthew, it's his home on the way home.

And when he tells the owner he's moving on, the bartender responds, "Whoa, Matt. What's comin' down?"

Matthew mumbles an excuse about a transfer but leaves with an empty feeling in his gut.

A friend loves at all times, and a brother is born for a time of adversity (Proverbs 17:17).

1. In 2 Corinthians 3:18, Paul wrote, "We all, with unveiled face, beholding as in a mirror the glory of the Lord, are being transformed into the same image from glory to glory, just as by the Spirit of the Lord" (NKJV). Think about this process of being transformed into the image of Christ. Is this something that happens immediately, or does it take place more gradually? Explain.

   _____

   _____

   _____

   _____

2. In 2 Corinthians 5:17, Paul added, "Therefore, if anyone is in Christ, he is a new creation; old things have passed away; behold, all things have become new" (NKJV). How did Matthew become a "new creation" after meeting Jesus? What parts of us "pass away" and get left behind with the old life?

   _____

   _____

   _____

3. How do you suppose Matthew explained his decision to follow Jesus to his family, friends, and acquaintances?

   _____

   _____

   _____

4. Have your family members, friends, and acquaintances recognized that a new life has begun in you? If so, what reactions or comments have you received from them? If not, how do you explain that?

_____

_____

_____

INVITE 'EM OVER

Later on, Matthew meets up with Jesus at a diner and shares his problem. "It's my buddies—you know, the guys at the office. And the fellows at the bar."

"What about them?" Jesus asks.

"Well, we kinda run together, you know. I'm gonna miss 'em. Take Josh for instance—as slick as a can of motor oil, but he visits orphans on Sunday. And Bruno at the gym? Can crunch you like a roach, but I've never had a better friend. He's posted bail for me three times."

Jesus motions for him to go on. "What's the problem?"

"Well, I'm gonna miss those guys. I mean, I've got nothing against Peter and James and John, Jesus . . . but they're Sunday morning, and I'm Saturday night. I've got my own circle, ya know?"

Jesus starts to smile and shake his head. "Matthew, Matthew, you think I came to quarantine you? Following me doesn't mean forgetting your friends. Just the opposite. I want to meet them."

"Are you serious?"

"Is the high priest a Jew?"

"But, Jesus, these guys . . . half of them are on parole. Josh hasn't worn socks since his bar mitzvah . . ."

"I'm not talking about a religious service, Matthew. Let me ask you—what do you like to do? Bowl? Play Monopoly? How's your golf game?"

Matthew's eyes brighten. "You ought to see me cook. I get on steaks like a whale on Jonah."

"Perfect." Jesus smiles. "Then throw a little going-away party. A hang-up-the-clipboard bash. Get the gang together."

Matthew's all over it. Calling the caterer, his housekeeper, his secretary. "Get the word out, Thelma. Drinks and dinner at my house tonight. Tell the guys to come and bring a date."

5. When Matthew invited Jesus to his home, the party included many of his fellow tax collectors and "sinners." Read 2 Corinthians 6:14–18. In this passage, Paul told believers not to be unequally yoked with unbelievers. Does this mean we are not to associate with any non-Christians? How do you reconcile this passage with Jesus' decision to be around Matthew's friends?

_____

_____

_____

Two are better than one, because they have a good return for their labor: If either of them falls down, one can help the other up (Ecclesiastes 4:9–10).

Above all, love each other deeply, because love covers over a multitude of sins (1 Peter 4:8).

6. The problem Paul was addressing in Corinth was the believers' tendency to engage in the sinful practices of their former lives—practices they found difficult to abandon. When people make a decision to follow Christ as Matthew did, why is it important for them to remove themselves from certain situations? What does this often require in terms of their relationship with the people of their "old life"—people who *don't* follow Christ?

_____

_____

_____

_____

7. In John 10:10 Jesus stated, "The thief comes only to steal and kill and destroy; I have come that they may have life, and have it to the full" (NIV). How does Jesus reach us where we are to offer us this life? What does that compel us to do after we receive it?

_____

_____

_____

_____

8. How do you pitch the abundance that Jesus offers to someone who seems to be enjoying the "good life" of partying and acquiring wealth and possessions?

_____

_____

_____

_____

Jesus was interested in Matthew's friends not because he shared their taste for debauchery but because he could envision their potential. He saw their passion, their energy, their longings. He also saw their pain, their guilt, their damaged self-image. Jesus knew he could offer them something none of their vices could. He could offer true joy and fulfillment. He could offer freedom. He could offer a fresh start. As we'll see in the next study, Jesus was more than willing to engage Matthew's friends where they lived—and partied.

❧ POINTS TO REMEMBER ❧

❖ Jesus reaches out to those who are shunned by society and invites them to come and be his disciples.
❖ When Jesus calls, we must leave everything behind and follow him.
❖ Following Jesus doesn't mean forgetting our friends—he wants to reach them as well.

─◦ PRAYER FOR THE DAY ◦─

Father, thank you for the new life you offer. May we never lose sight of the sacrifice, forgiveness, and grace that was necessary for you make our new beginnings possible. Guide our attitudes and actions so we may be effective spokespeople for the abundant life you give. Work in us and through us to make a difference in the lives of people who haven't yet experienced your abundance. In Jesus' name, amen.

𝒟ay Two: Being Normal

AN ICY BREEZE

While Jesus was having dinner at Matthew's house, many tax collectors and sinners came and ate with him and his disciples (Matthew 9:10).

And so Jesus ends up at Matthew's house, a classy split-level with a view of the Sea of Galilee. Parked out front is everything from BMWs to Harleys to limos. And the crowd inside tells you this is anything but a clergy conference.

Earrings on the guys and tattoos on the girls. Moussified hair. Music that rumbles teeth roots. And buzzing around in the middle of the group is Matthew, making more connections than an electrician.

He hooks up Peter with the tax collector bass club and Martha with the kitchen staff. Simon the Zealot meets a high school debate partner. And Jesus? Beaming. What could be better? Sinners and saints in the same room, and no one's trying to determine who is which.

When the teachers of the law who were Pharisees saw him eating with the sinners and tax collectors, they asked his disciples: "Why does he eat with tax collectors and sinners?" (Mark 2:16).

But an hour or so into the evening the door opens, and an icy breeze blows in. "The Pharisees and the men who taught the law for the Pharisees began to complain to Jesus' followers, 'Why do you eat and drink with tax collectors and sinners?'" (Luke 5:30 NCV). Enter the religious police and their thin-lipped piety. Big black books under arms. Cheerful as Siberian prison guards. Clerical collars so tight that veins bulge. They like to grill too. But not steaks.

Matthew is the first to feel the heat. "Some religious fellow you are," one says, practically pulling an eyebrow muscle. "Look at the people you hang out with."

On hearing this, Jesus said, "It is not the healthy who need a doctor, but the sick" (Matthew 9:12).

Matthew doesn't know whether to get mad or get out. Before he has time to choose, Jesus intervenes, explaining that Matthew is right where he needs to be. "Healthy people don't need a doctor—sick people do. I have come to call not those who think they are righteous, but those who know they are sinners and need to repent" (verses 31–32 NLT).

1. Read Luke 5:27–32. The Pharisees no doubt considered themselves the heroes in this story. They were, after all, Israel's most learned religious

leaders, and they were trying to keep people from violating God's law. So why does Jesus respond to them the way he does? What did the Pharisees get wrong?

_____

_____

_____

_____

2. Many of the Pharisees were experts in the letter of God's law but not in the spirit of God's grace and mercy behind those laws. How does Jesus attempt to correct some of these attitudes in the following verses?

Matthew 15:3, 6–9: "Jesus replied, 'And why do you break the command of God for the sake of your tradition? . . . You nullify the word of God for the sake of your tradition. You hypocrites! Isaiah was right when he prophesied about you: "These people honor me with their lips, but their hearts are far from me. They worship me in vain; their teachings are merely human rules"'" (NIV).

_____

_____

_____

_____

Matthew 23:13–14: "How terrible for you, teachers of the law and Pharisees! You are hypocrites! You close the door for people to enter the kingdom of heaven. You yourselves don't enter, and you stop others who are trying to enter. How terrible for you, teachers of the law and Pharisees. You are hypocrites. You take away widows' houses, and you say long prayers so that people will notice you. So you will have a worse punishment" (NCV).

_____

_____

_____

_____

Luke 14:1–4, 7: "The Pharisees and the teachers of the law muttered, 'This man welcomes sinners and eats with them.' Then Jesus told them this parable: 'Suppose one of you has a hundred sheep and loses one of them. Doesn't he leave the ninety-nine in the open country and go after the lost sheep until he finds it? . . . I tell you that in the same way there will be more rejoicing in heaven over one sinner who repents than over ninety-nine righteous persons who do not need to repent'" (NIV).

_____

_____

_____

_____

Luke 18:10–14: "Two men went up to the temple to pray, one a Pharisee and the other a tax collector. The Pharisee stood and was praying this to himself: 'God, I thank You that I am not like other people: swindlers, unjust, adulterers, or even like this tax collector. I fast twice a week; I pay tithes of all that I get.' But the tax collector, standing some distance away, was even unwilling to lift up his eyes to heaven, but was beating his breast, saying, 'God, be merciful to me, the sinner!' I tell you, this man went to his house justified rather than the other; for everyone who exalts himself will be humbled, but he who humbles himself will be exalted" (NASB).

_____
_____
_____
_____
_____

3. D.T. Niles described Christianity as "one beggar telling another beggar where he found bread." What does that mean to you?

_____
_____
_____
_____

4. How does (or should) that beggar image affect the way we talk to others about Jesus and our relationship with him?

_____
_____
_____
_____

WHICH SIDE OF THE TABLE

Quite a story. Matthew goes from double-dealer to disciple. He throws a party that makes the religious right uptight, but Christ proud. The good guys look good, and the bad guys hit the road. Some story indeed.

What do we do with it?

That depends on which side of the tax collector's table you find yourself. You and I are Matthew. Don't look at me that way. There's enough hustler in the best of us to qualify for Matthew's table. Maybe you've never taken taxes, but you've taken liberty with the truth, taken credit that wasn't yours, taken advantage of the weak. You and me? Matthew.

If you're still at the table, you receive an invitation. "Follow me." So what if you've got a questionable reputation? So did Matthew. You may end up writing your own gospel.

For all have sinned and fall short of the glory of God (Romans 3:23).

"My sheep listen to my voice; I know them, and they follow me" (John 10:27).

If you've left the table, you receive a clarification. You don't have to be weird to follow Jesus. You don't have to stop liking your friends to follow him. Just the opposite. A few introductions would be nice. Do you know how to grill a steak?

Some time ago I was asked to play a game of golf. The foursome included two preachers, a church leader, and a "Matthew-before-Christ." The thought of four hours with three Christians, two of whom were pulpiteers, did not appeal to him. His best friend, a Christ follower and his boss, insisted, so he agreed.

I'm happy to report that he proclaimed the experience painless. On the ninth hole he turned to one of us and said, smiling, "I'm so glad you guys are normal." I think he meant this: "I'm glad you didn't get in my face or club me with a King James driver. Thanks for laughing at my jokes and telling a few yourself. Thanks for being normal." We didn't lower standards. But neither did we saddle a high horse. We were nice. Normal and nice.

Discipleship is sometimes defined by being normal.

A woman in a small Arkansas community was a single mom with a frail baby. Her neighbor would stop by every few days and keep the child so she could shop. After some weeks her neighbor shared more than time; she shared her faith, and the woman did what Matthew did. She followed Christ.

The friends of the young mother objected. "Do you know what those people teach?" they contested.

"Here is what I know," she told them. "They held my baby." I think Jesus likes that kind of answer, don't you?

I have become all things to all people so that by all possible means I might save some. I do all this for the sake of the gospel (1 Corinthians 9:22–23).

Let us consider how we may spur one another on toward love and good deeds, not giving up meeting together (Hebrews 10:24–25).

5. Jesus told his disciples, "You are the light that gives light to the world. A city that is built on a hill cannot be hidden. And people don't hide a light under a bowl. They put it on a lampstand so the light shines for all the people in the house" (Matthew 5:14–15 NCV). What does it mean to let your light shine to the world? How might your good deeds cause someone else to glorify God?

_____

_____

_____

_____

_____

_____

6. In what situations or circumstances might you be most tempted to hide your light?

_____

_____

_____

_____

7. Being a witness for Christ does not mean lowering your standards, but neither does it mean saddling your high horse. In what ways can you be an example for Christ by just doing life with others? In what ways do actions often speak louder than words when showing others what being a Christian is about?

_____

_____

_____

8. Jesus once said this prayer for his disciples: "My prayer is not that you take them out of the world but that you protect them from the evil one. They are not of the world, even as I am not of it" (John 17:15–16 NIV). How does the work God wants us to do involve meeting people where they are? What does it mean to be in this world but not of it?

_____

_____

_____

_____

_____

_____

Jesus' interest in Matthew was more than reciprocated. Matthew was eager to get to know Christ and learn everything he could about this extraordinary teacher. He wasn't alone in his curiosity. As Jesus' fame spread, many people sought him out. And the passion and zeal with which they did revealed something about them.

─◦ POINTS TO REMEMBER ◦─

❖ When it comes down to it, none of us are really saints—we are all sinners in need of God's grace.
❖ Jesus came to help the sick (which is all of us), call us to repentance, and heal us.
❖ Discipleship is sometimes defined by just being normal and doing everyday life with those around us.

─◦ PRAYER FOR THE DAY ◦─

_Father, thank you for the light you ignite in us. Help us recognize the importance of shining that light at all times and in all circumstances—especially our normal everyday interactions. When people see you in us,
grant us the wisdom and humility to give all the glory and honor
for it to you. In Jesus' name, amen._

Day Three: Seeking Christ

HUNGER IN HIS HEART

What's fascinating about Matthew's story is that he wasn't content to just *meet* with Jesus. He wanted to *know* Jesus. As you remember, Matthew was converted at work. He was sitting at his tax booth when the Master said, "Follow me." In the very next verse, we find Jesus sitting at Matthew's dining room table. "Jesus was having dinner at Matthew's house" (Matthew 9:10 NCV).

A curbside conversion couldn't satisfy his heart, so Matthew took Jesus home. Something happens over a dinner table that doesn't happen over an office desk. Take off the tie, heat up the grill, break out the sodas, and spend the evening with the suspender of the stars. "You know, Jesus, forgive me for asking but I've always wanted to know . . ." Matthew wanted to know Jesus, and because God "rewards those who truly want to find him" (Hebrews 11:6 NCV), Matthew was rewarded with the presence of Christ in his home.

Of course, it only made sense that Jesus would spend time with Matthew. After all, Matthew was a top draft pick, shoulder-tapped to write the first book of the New Testament. Jesus hangs out only with the big guys like Matthew and Andrew and John. Right?

May I counter that opinion with an example? Zacchaeus was far from a big guy. He was small, so small he couldn't see over the crowd that lined the street the day Jesus came to Jericho. Of course, the crowd might have let him elbow up to the front, except that he, like Matthew, was a tax collector. But he, like Matthew, had a hunger in his heart to see Jesus.

It wasn't enough to stand at the back of the crowd. It wasn't enough to peer through a cardboard telescope. It wasn't enough to listen to someone else describe the parade of the Messiah. Zacchaeus wanted to see Jesus with his own eyes.

So he went out on a limb. Clad in a name-brand suit and brand-new Italian loafers, he shimmied up a tree in hopes of seeing Christ.

I wonder if you would be willing to do the same. Would you go out on a limb to see Jesus? Not everyone would.

1. Read Luke 19:1–10. Matthew followed Jesus because the Lord told him to do so. However, in this situation, Zacchaeus was the one who sought out Jesus. What motivated him to go to such considerable lengths to investigate Jesus? What was Zacchaeus looking for in Christ?

   _____

   _____

   _____

   _____

Levi got up and followed him (Mark 2:14).

[God] rewards those who earnestly seek him (Hebrews 11:6).

Jesus entered Jericho and was passing through. A man was there by the name of Zacchaeus; he was a chief tax collector and was wealthy (Luke 19:1–1).

He wanted to see who Jesus was, but because he was short he could not see over the crowd. So he ran ahead and climbed a sycamore-fig tree (vv. 3–4).

When Jesus reached the spot, he looked up and said, "Zacchaeus, come down . . . I must stay at your house today" (v. 5).

2. When Jesus saw Zacchaeus up in the tree, he said, "Zacchaeus, come down immediately. I must stay at your house today" (verse 5 NIV). What does Jesus' response to Zacchaeus tell us about the Lord?

_____

_____

_____

3. How did the crowds respond when they heard Jesus' invitation? How did Zacchaeus respond?

_____

_____

_____

4. What do you suppose Zacchaeus and Matthew discovered about Jesus in this one-on-one setting that forever changed the course of their lives?

_____

_____

_____

NOT SATISFIED

A certain ruler asked him, "Good teacher, what must I do to inherit eternal life?" (Luke 18:1).

In the same Bible where we read about Zacchaeus crawling across the limb, we read about a young ruler. Unlike the crowd's reaction to Zacchaeus, it parted to make room for him. He was the . . . ahem . . . *rich* young ruler. Upon learning that Jesus was in the area, he called for the limo, cruised across town, and approached the carpenter.

Note the question the rich young ruler had for Jesus: "Teacher, what good thing must I do to have life forever?" (Matthew 19:16 NCV). Bottom-line sort of fellow, this ruler. No time for formalities or conversations. "Let's get right to the issue. Your schedule is busy; so is mine. Tell me how I can get saved, and I'll leave you alone."

There was nothing wrong with his question, but there was a problem with his heart. Contrast his desire with that of Zacchaeus, "Can I make it up that tree?"

Or John and Andrew, "Where are you staying?"

Or Matthew, "Can you spend the evening?"

Or Simeon, "Can I stay alive until I see him?"

Or the Magi, "Saddle up the camels. We aren't stopping until we find him."

Or the shepherds, "Let's go . . . Let's see."

Jesus answered them, "It is not the healthy who need a doctor, but the sick" (Luke 5:31).

See the difference? The rich young ruler wanted medicine. The others wanted the Physician. The ruler wanted an answer to the quiz. They wanted the Teacher. He was in a hurry. They had all the time in the world. He settled for a cup of coffee at the drive-through window. They wouldn't settle for anything less than a full-course meal at the banquet table. They wanted more than salvation. They wanted the Savior. They wanted to see Jesus.

They were earnest in their search. One translation renders Hebrews 11:6: "God . . . rewards those who *earnestly* seek him" (NIV, emphasis mine). And another: "God . . . rewards those who *sincerely* look for him" (TLB, emphasis mine). I like the King James translation: "He is a rewarder of them that *diligently* seek him" (emphasis mine).

Diligently—what a great word. Be diligent in your search. Be hungry in your quest, relentless in your pilgrimage. Step away from the puny pursuits of possessions and positions, and seek your King.

Don't be satisfied with angels. Don't be content with stars in the sky. Seek him out as the shepherds did. Long for him as Simeon did. Worship him as the wise men did. Do as John and Andrew did: Ask for his address. Do as Matthew did: Invite Jesus into your house. Imitate Zacchaeus. Risk whatever it takes to see Christ.

Press on toward the goal to win the prize (Philippians 3:14).

Peter answered him, "We have left everything to follow you!" (Matthew 19:27).

5. Read Matthew 19:16–30. Keep in mind that in first-century Israel, wealth was considered a sign of blessing from God. Not only did the young man have plenty of wealth, but also he was quick to point out he had obeyed *all* of the commandments. What affirmation was he looking to receive from Jesus?

   _____

   _____

   _____

   _____

6. Why did Jesus tell the man to sell his possessions and give them to the poor? How did his response reveal the condition of his heart and his actual priorities?

   _____

   _____

   _____

7. After the rich young ruler had departed, Peter said, "We have left everything to follow you! What then will there be for us?" (verse 27 NIV). What had the disciples given up to follow Jesus? What reward did Jesus say was in store for those who had left everything to follow him?

   _____

   _____

   _____

8. As you look at these stories, do you find that you tend to desire "medicine" like the rich young ruler, or the "Physician" like Matthew and Zacchaeus? How are you being diligent in search for more of Jesus?

   _____

   _____

   _____

Matthew and the disciples were not content to be bystanders when it came to being with Jesus—they left their former lives behind to follow him. Yet for all the time they spent learning about Jesus, and for all the miracles and healings they witnessed, they never quite grasped the sheer magnitude of his power and authority. As we'll see in the next study, nowhere is that more evident than in Matthew's account of a harrowing boat trip across the Sea of Galilee.

—☙ POINTS TO REMEMBER ❧—

❖ There is a big difference between being content to simply *meet* Jesus and actually desiring to *know* him.
❖ Often we settle for the medicine when God is welcoming us to come and get to know the Physician.
❖ To be a follower of Christ means being diligent in our search, hungry in our quest, and relentless in our pilgrimage.

—☙ PRAYER FOR THE DAY ❧—

Father, thank you for the opportunity to follow you, to share in your work, and to strive toward your goals. Thank you for giving us a deeper purpose—and ultimately a deeper satisfaction—than anything else life has to offer. Focus our thoughts and guide our perspective. May we never lose sight of the fact that the "sacrifices" we make for you will be rewarded beyond anything we can imagine. In Jesus' name, amen.

$\mathcal{D}$ay Four: *Seismos* Storms

ERUPTION AT SEA

Jesus said to his disciples, "Let us go over to the other side of the lake." So they got into a boat and set out (Luke 8:22).

Matthew, as it turns out, would end up writing one of the four accounts we have of Jesus' life on earth. His is the first in our Bibles, the Gospel that bears his name. As one of Jesus' disciples, he was an eyewitness to everything he writes about, including a memorable scene that took place one day on the Sea of Galilee. "Jesus got into a boat," he wrote, "and his followers went with him. A great storm arose on the lake so that waves covered the boat" (Matthew 8:23–24 NCV).

Matthew remembered well the pouncing tempest and bouncing boat and was careful in his terminology. Not just any noun would do. He pulled his Greek thesaurus off the shelf and hunted for a descriptor that exploded like the waves across the bow. He bypassed common terms for spring shower, squall, cloudburst, or downpour. He recalled more than winds and white-caps. His finger followed the column of synonyms down, down until he landed on a word that worked. "Ah, there it is." *Seismos*—a quake, a trembling eruption of sea and sky. "A great *seismos* arose on the lake."

The term still occupies a spot in our vernacular. A *seis*mologist studies earthquakes, a *seis*mograph measures them, and Matthew, along with a crew of recent recruits, felt a *seismos* that shook them to the core. He used the word on only two other occasions: once at Jesus' death when Calvary shook (see Matthew 27:51–54) and again at Jesus' resurrection when the graveyard tremored (see 28:2). Apparently, the stilled storm shares equal billing in the trilogy of Jesus' great shake-ups: defeating sin on the cross, death at the tomb, and here silencing fear on the sea.

Peter and John, seasoned sailors, struggle to keep down the sail. Matthew, confirmed landlubber, struggles to keep down his breakfast. The storm is not what the tax collector bargained for. Meanwhile, "Jesus was sleeping" (Matthew 8:24 NCV).

Now there's a scene. The disciples scream; Jesus dreams. Thunder roars; Jesus snores. He doesn't doze, catnap, or rest. He slumbers. Could you sleep at a time like this? Could you snooze during a roller coaster loop-the-loop? In a wind tunnel? At a rock concert? Jesus sleeps through all three at once!

Suddenly a furious storm came up on the lake, so that the waves swept over the boat (Matthew 8:24).

The earth shook, the rocks split (27:51).

There was a violent earthquake (28:2).

Jesus was in the stern, sleeping on a cushion (Mark 4:38).

1. In the New Testament, the Greek word *seismos* is almost always used to refer to an earthquake (see, for example, Acts 16:26 and Revelation 6:12). What does the fact Matthew uses this word to describe the storm at sea tell us about its fury? What does it tell us about his feelings after having witnessed the event?

   _____

   _____

   _____

   _____

2. Given the strength of the storm, why is Jesus' response so surprising?

   _____

   _____

   _____

3. When was a time in your life when you faced a "storm" and Jesus seemed to be sleeping? How did you react?

   _____

   _____

   _____

   _____

4. As you look back at that situation, how do you see that Jesus was in control all the time?

_____

_____

_____

_____

_____

SPIRITUAL AMNESIA

The disciples woke him and said to him, "Teacher, don't you care if we drown?" (Mark 4:38).

Jesus' snooze troubles the disciples. "Lord, save us! We will drown!" they say (Matthew 8:25 NCV). They do not ask about Jesus' strength: "Can you still the storm?" His knowledge: "Are you aware of the storm?" Or his know-how: "Do you have any experience with storms?"

Matthew and the other disciples had reason to trust Jesus. By now they'd seen him "healing all kinds of sickness and all kinds of disease among the people" (Matthew 4:23 NKJV). They had just witnessed him heal a leper with a touch and a servant with a command (see 8:3, 13). Peter saw his sick mother-in-law recover (see verses 14–15), and they all saw demons scatter like bats out of a cave. "He cast out the spirits with a word, and healed all who were sick" (verse 16 NKJV).

I will remember the deeds of the LORD; yes, I will remember your miracles of long ago (Psalm 77:11).

Shouldn't someone mention Jesus' track record or review his résumé? Do they remember the accomplishments of Christ? They may not. Fear creates a form of spiritual amnesia. It dulls our miracle memory. It makes us forget what Jesus has done and how good God is.

"You of little faith, why are you so afraid?" (Matthew 8:26)

Jesus' response that Matthew records is a good one. Jesus lifts his head from the pillow, steps out from the stern into the storm, and asks, "Why are you fearful, O you of little faith?" (verse 8:26 NKJV). Might it be that God views all our *seismos* storms this same way? "Jesus got up and gave a command to the wind and the waves, and it became completely calm" (verse 26 NCV).

He got up and rebuked the wind and the raging waters; the storm subsided (Luke 8:24).

Jesus handles the great quaking with a great calming. The sea becomes as still as a frozen lake, and the disciples are left wondering, "What kind of man is this? Even the winds and the waves obey him!" (verse 27 NCV).

What kind of man, indeed.

They asked one another, "Who is this?" (v. 25).

5. At first glance the disciples' reaction seems reasonable, considering the circumstances. Why did Jesus call them people "of little faith"? What would someone of great faith have done differently?

_____

_____

_____

_____

_____

6. Fear creates a form of spiritual amnesia within us. What do the following passages command us to do in regard to our fears?

Deuteronomy 7:21: "Do not be terrified . . . for the LORD your God, who is among you, is a great and awesome God" (NIV).

_____

_____

_____

Joshua 1:9: "Remember that I commanded you to be strong and brave. Don't be afraid, because the LORD your God will be with you everywhere you go" (NCV).

_____

_____

_____

Psalm 56:3–4: "When I am afraid, I will put my trust in you. I praise God for what he has promised. I trust in God, so why should I be afraid? What can mere mortals do to me?" (NLT).

_____

_____

_____

Proverbs 29:25: "Fear of man will prove to be a snare, but whoever trusts in the LORD is kept safe" (NIV).

_____

_____

2 Timothy 1:7: "God has not given us a spirit of fear, but of power and of love and of a sound mind" (NKJV).

_____

_____

1 John 4:18: "Where God's love is, there is no fear, because God's perfect love drives out fear. It is punishment that makes a person fear, so love is not made perfect in the person who fears" (NCV).

_____

_____

_____

7. Why is it so easy to fall into a what-have-you-done-for-me-lately approach to our Christian faith? What is the problem with having this kind of attitude?

_____

_____

_____

_____

_____

8. At the end of this story, the disciples said, "What kind of man is this? Even the winds and the waves obey him!" (Matthew 8:27 NIV). How did this response capture their understanding of Jesus' power? How does it shape your understanding of what Jesus can do in your *seismos* situation?

_____

_____

_____

_____

Jesus' ability to calm a raging storm certainly made an impression on those who witnessed it. However, less than two years later, Matthew and the other disciples would face an even greater crisis when the Roman and Jewish leaders took Jesus into custody and led him to the cross. Suddenly, the one they called "Master" was gone from their midst. How would they respond? Would they remember Jesus was the one who calmed the wind and the waves and stand bravely by his side? Or would they allow their old fears and doubts to again cause them to suffer from spiritual amnesia?

⤳ POINTS TO REMEMBER ↫

❖ When the storms of life are raging around us, we tend to forget Jesus' strength, his knowledge, and his know-how to get us through them.
❖ It may seem to us at times that God is sleeping or doesn't hear our prayers, but he is always watching over us.
❖ Regardless of what we face, we must have faith and remember that God is *always* in control.

⤳ PRAYER FOR THE DAY ↫

Father, we, like Matthew and the disciples, occasionally need reminders that no storm is beyond your ability to calm. Forgive us for those times when we forget—when our faith slips and our old fears come rushing back. Lead us on the adventure you have laid out for us. Strengthen our resolve and bolster our faith so we may make the most of it. In Jesus' name, amen.

*D*ay Five: Betrayed by All

ALONE IN THE GARDEN

"Get up, we must go. Look, here comes the man who has turned against me" (Matthew 26:46 NCV). These words Matthew records were spoken to Judas, but they could have been spoken to anyone. They could have been spoken to John, to Peter, to Matthew himself. They could have been spoken to the Roman soldiers, to the Jewish leaders. They could have been spoken to Pilate, to Herod, to Caiaphas. They could have been spoken to every person who praised him last Sunday but abandoned him tonight.

Everyone turned against Jesus that night. *Everyone.*

Judas did. Matthew tells us, "Judas had planned to give them a signal, saying, 'The man I kiss is Jesus. Arrest him.' At once Judas went to Jesus and said, 'Greetings, Teacher!' and kissed him" (verses 48–49 NCV). What was your motive, Judas? Why did you do it? Were you trying to call his hand? Did you want the money? Were you seeking some attention? And why, dear Judas, why did it have to be a kiss? You could have pointed. You could have just called his name. But you put your lips to his cheek and kissed. A snake kills with his mouth.

The people did. "Then the people came and grabbed Jesus and arrested him" (verse 50 NCV). We wonder who was in the crowd. Who were the bystanders? Matthew just says they were *people.* Regular folks like you and me with bills to pay and kids to raise and jobs to do. Individually they never would have turned on Jesus, but collectively they wanted to kill him. Even the instantaneous healing of an amputated ear didn't sway them (see verse 51). They suffered from mob blindness. They blocked each other's vision of Jesus.

The disciples did. "All of Jesus' followers left him and ran away" (verse 56 NCV). Matthew must have written those words slowly. He was in that group. *All* the disciples were. Jesus told them they would scamper. They vowed they wouldn't, but they did. When the choice came between their skin and their friend, they chose to run. Oh, they stood for a while. But their courage was as fleeting as their feet. When they saw Jesus was going down, they got out.

Everyone turned against Jesus. Though the kiss was planted by Judas, the betrayal was committed by all. Every person took a step, but no one took a stand. As Jesus left the garden, he walked alone. The world had turned against him. He was betrayed.

"The Son of Man is delivered into the hands of sinners. Rise! Let us go! Here comes my betrayer!" (Matthew 26:45–46).

The betrayer had arranged a signal with them (v. 48).

The men stepped forward, seized Jesus and arrested him (v. 50).

One of Jesus' companions reached for his sword (v. 51).

All the disciples deserted him and fled (v. 56).

My close friend, someone I trusted, one who shared my bread, has turned against me (Psalm 41:9).

1. Read Matthew 26:31–56. Remember that Matthew himself is relating the events of that night. How do you think he felt as he wrote these words?

What regrets were going through his mind as he relived the memory of this night?

_____

_____

_____

2. After everything the disciples had seen and experienced to this point, why do you suppose they abandoned Jesus that night?

_____

_____

_____

3. Not all abandonments are quite so dramatic as the ones we read about in this story. People abandon the Lord in many other ways—such as when they choose their way over his, or allow a habit to control them, or trade what they know is right for that which feels good. In what ways have you been guilty of this type of abandonment in the past?

_____

_____

_____

4. What did that do to your relationship with Christ? How did he convict you of that betrayal and seek to restore you?

_____

_____

_____

EVERYTHING CHANGES

They came to a place called Golgotha . . . [and] crucified him (Matthew 27:33,35).

Chicken-hearted disciples. A two-timing Judas. A pierced side. Spineless Pharisees. A hard-hearted high priest. A trial before Pilate. The crucifixion, death, and burial. Matthew records these final moments in Jesus' life. Christ rarely speaks on that Friday. He doesn't have to—his accusers provide accurate play-by-play.

At dawn on the first day of the week, Mary Magdalene and the other Mary went to look at the tomb (28:1).

But that's not the end of Matthew's Gospel. Three days after Christ dies on the cross, two women named Mary go to look at the tomb and are met with an earthquake. An angel comes down from heaven, rolls away the stone, and announces, "He is not here. He has risen from the dead as he said he would" (Matthew 28:6 NCV).

How conditions have changed since Friday. The crucifixion was marked by sudden darkness, silent angels, and mocking soldiers. At the empty tomb the soldiers are silent, an angel speaks, and light erupts. The one who was dead is said to be alive, and the soldiers, who are alive, look as if they are dead. The women can tell something is up. What they don't know is Someone is up. So the angel informs them: "Don't be afraid! . . . I know

There was a violent earthquake . . . an angel of the Lord came down from heaven and . . . rolled back the stone and sat on it (v. 2).

you are looking for Jesus, who was crucified. He isn't here! He has been raised from the dead, just as he said would happen. Come, see where his body was lying" (verses 5–6 NLT).

Take a look at the vacated tomb Matthew describes. Did you know the opponents of Christ never challenged its vacancy? No Pharisee or Roman soldier ever led a contingent back to the burial site and declared, "The angel was wrong. The body is here. It was all a rumor." The best the religious leaders could do was pay the soldiers who guarded the tomb and say, "Tell the people that Jesus' followers came during the night and stole the body" (verse 13 NLT).

It wasn't enough. Within weeks Matthew and the other disciples are occupying every Jerusalem street corner, announcing a risen Christ. What quicker way for the enemies of the church to shut them up than to produce a cold and lifeless body? Display the cadaver, and Christianity is stillborn. But they had no cadaver to display.

Helps explain the later Jerusalem revival. When the apostles argued for the empty tomb, the people looked to the Pharisees for a rebuttal. But they had none to give. Fast-forward forty days after the resurrection, and the same men who had gone into hiding at the crucifixion were now a force of life-changing fury. Peter is preaching in the precinct where Christ was arrested. Followers of Christ defy the enemies of Christ. Whip them and they'll worship. Lock them up and they'll launch a jailhouse ministry. As bold after the resurrection as they were cowardly before it. Explanation:

Greed? They made no money.

Power? They gave all the credit to Christ.

Popularity? Most were killed for their beliefs.

Only one explanation remains—a resurrected Christ and his Holy Spirit. The courage of these men and women was forged in the fire of the empty tomb. The disciples did not dream up a resurrection. The resurrection fired up the disciples. It prompted Matthew to write his Gospel and end with this amazing promise from Christ: "I will be with you always, even until the end of this age" (verse 20 NCV).

5. Read 1 Corinthians 15:1–28. Why does the apostle Paul recount all of the people to whom Christ appeared after he came back to life? Why does Paul put such emphasis on the resurrection?

_____

_____

_____

6. For two days—the day of Jesus' arrest, trial, and crucifixion, and the following (Sabbath) day in which his corpse lay in the tomb—Matthew and the other disciples embodied Paul's description of "people most to be pitied" (verse 18 NIV). Why was this the case?

_____

_____

_____

The angel said to the women . . . "He is not here; he has risen" (Matthew 28:5–6).

When the chief priests had met with the elders and devised a plan, they gave the soldiers a large sum of money, telling them, "You are to say, 'His disciples came during the night and stole him away while we were asleep'" (vv. 12–13).

Every day they continued to meet together in the temple courts. They broke bread in their homes and ate together with glad and sincere hearts, praising God and enjoying the favor of all the people. And the Lord added to their number daily those who were being saved (Acts 2:46–47).

"Don't be alarmed," [the angel] said. "You are looking for Jesus the Nazarene, who was crucified. He has risen! He is not here. See the place where they laid him" (Mark 16:6).

7. Something changed inside Matthew and the other disciples the moment they heard three words from the women who had visited Jesus' tomb: "He has risen" (Matthew 28:6 NCV). Church history tells us Matthew became a fervent Christian evangelist, helping to spread the news of Jesus throughout Judea and other countries. Eventually his faith made him a target of the Roman government, and he was put to death for boldly proclaiming Christ's message. Think back to Matthew's beginnings as a tax collector for the Romans. How do you explain such a sudden, profound, and lasting change in his life?

_____

_____

_____

_____

8. What do Jesus' resurrection and his promise to be with you "until the end of this age" (verse 20 NCV) mean to you? How do they affect the way you approach your daily life?

_____

_____

_____

_____

_____

Had you and I been present during the time of Matthew, we would have looked at the "family" of Jesus and seen little to impress us. None of his followers was of noble birth. No deep pockets or prestige. Peter had his swagger. John had his temper. Matthew, of course, had his checkered past and colorful friends.

The Spirit you received brought about your adoption to sonship. And by him we cry, "Abba, Father" (Romans 8:15).

Like Jacob's sons in the Egyptian court, they seemed outclassed and out of place. Yet Jesus was not embarrassed to call them his family. He laid claim to them in public. He lays claim to us as well. "Jesus, who makes people holy, and those who are made holy are from the same family. So he is not ashamed to call them his brothers and sisters" (Hebrews 2:11 NCV). Jesus redefined his family to include all who come near him.

❧ POINTS TO REMEMBER ❧

❖ Although the kiss was planted by Judas, the truth is that each of us has betrayed Jesus at one time or another in our lives.
❖ The only explanation to account for the disciples' actions after Jesus' death is that Christ was truly resurrected from the dead.
❖ Jesus redefined family to include all those who come near to him and, like Matthew and the disciples, choose to follow him.

⎯◞ PRAYER FOR THE DAY ◟⎯

Jesus, it is difficult to comprehend the amazing love you have for us—a love that compelled you to take on our sins alone and suffer on the cross for our sakes. Thank you for your sacrifice and for the gift of life you have given to us through your resurrection. Thank you for choosing us to be part of your family. Forgive us for our betrayals and cover us with your grace when we fall short of your standard. In Jesus' name, amen.

⎯◞ WEEKLY MEMORY VERSE ◟⎯

So in Christ Jesus you are all children of God through faith.
GALATIANS 3:26 (NIV)

For Further Reading

Selections throughout this lesson were taken from *Next Door Savior* (Nashville: Thomas Nelson, 2003); *And the Angels Were Silent* (Nashville: Thomas Nelson, 1987); *Just Like Jesus* (Nashville: Thomas Nelson, 1998); *Fearless* (Nashville: Thomas Nelson, 2009); and *You'll Get Through This* (Nashville: Thomas Nelson, 2013).

LESSON 8

*L*AZARUS

IMAGINE YOU ARE IN A COURTROOM, a nearly empty courtroom. Present are four people: a judge, a lawyer, an orphan, and a would-be guardian. The judge is God, Jesus is the one who seeks to be the guardian, and you are the orphan. You have no name, no inheritance, no home. The lawyer is proposing that you be placed in Jesus' care.

Who is the lawyer? A Galilean fisherman by the name of John.

Six testimonies have been given. Six miracles have been verified. John gestures toward the table where sit the articles of evidence. The jugs of water that Jesus had turned into wine. The signed affidavit of the doctor who'd treated the sick son Jesus had healed. The cot of the crippled man who for thirty-eight years had not walked. The basket of the boy with the lunch Jesus had used to feed the five thousand. A broken oar to show the strength of a storm at sea. A cup and cane left by a blind man who didn't need to beg anymore.

"And now," John says, turning to the judge, "we have one final witness to call and one more piece of evidence to submit."

John goes to his table and returns with a white linen sheet. "This is a burial shroud," he explains. Placing the clothing on the table he requests, "Your honor permitting, I call our final witness to the chair, Lazarus of Bethany."

Heavy courtroom doors open, and a tall man enters. He strides down the aisle and pauses before Jesus long enough to place a hand on his shoulder and say, "Thank you." You can hear the tenderness in his voice. Lazarus turns and takes his seat in the witness chair.

"State your name for the court."

"Lazarus."

"Have you heard of a man called Jesus of Nazareth?"

"Who hasn't?"

"How do you know him?"

We have an advocate with the Father—Jesus Christ (1 John 2:1).

James . . . and his brother John . . . were in a boat with their father (Matthew 4:21).

Jesus went throughout Galilee . . . healing every disease and sickness among the people (v. 23).

Lazarus . . . was from Bethany, the village of Mary and her sister Martha (John 11:1).

If anyone acknowledges that Jesus is the Son of God, God lives in them (1 John 4:15).

"He is my friend. We—my sisters and I—have a house in Bethany. When he comes to Jerusalem, he often stays with us. My sisters, Mary and Martha, have become believers in him as well."

"Believers?"

"Believers that he is the Messiah. The Son of God."

"Why do you believe that?"

Lazarus smiles. "Well, let me tell you my story."

1. Put yourself in this courtroom scenario. Imagine someone approaches you and asks, "How do you know Jesus?" What would your answer be?

_____

_____

_____

_____

_____

_____

_____

2. What story would you tell? How would that story demonstrate the relationship you have with Christ?

_____

_____

_____

_____

_____

_____

_____

_____

We all have a story to tell, but Lazarus's testimony was extraordinary. Most stories will touch *someone*, but few will touch *everyone*. As we'll see in the first study, Jesus' raising of Lazarus wasn't just a defining moment in his earthly ministry but also a sneak preview of his ultimate conquering of death.

─◌ PRAYER FOR THE WEEK ◌─

Father, thank you for giving us a story to tell. Thank you for the happily-ever-after ending you've written for us. Give us the wisdom, courage, and humility to share our story—along with Lazarus's and dozens of others from the pages of your Word—in ways that make a difference in the lives of others. In Jesus' name, amen.

*D*ay One: An Extraordinary Story

ONE SANDAL IN THE GRAVE

"I've always been sickly," Lazarus continues. "That's why I've stayed with my sisters, you know. They care for me. My heart never has been the strongest, so I have to be careful. Martha, the oldest sister, she's . . . well, she's like a mother to me. It was Martha who called Jesus when my heart failed."

"Go on," says John.

"Well, I lingered for a few days, but I knew I was near the edge. The doctors would just come in and shake their heads and walk out. I had one sandal in the grave."

"Is that when Jesus came?"

"No. We kept hoping he would. Martha would sit by the bed at night, and she would whisper over and over and over, 'Be strong, Lazarus. Jesus will be here any minute.' We just knew he would come. I mean, he had healed all those strangers; surely he would heal me. I was his friend."

"What delayed him?"

"For the longest time we didn't know. I thought he might be in prison or something. I kept waiting and waiting. Every day I got weaker. My vision faded, and I couldn't see. I drifted in and out. Every time someone entered my room, I thought it might be him. But it never was. He never came."

"Were you angry?"

"More confused than angry. I just didn't understand."

"Then what happened?"

"Well, I woke up one night. My chest was so tight I could hardly breathe. I must have sat up because Martha and Mary came to my bed. They took my hand. I heard them calling my name, but then I began to fall. It was like a dream. I was falling, spinning wildly in midair. Their voices grew fainter and fainter and then nothing. The spinning stopped, the falling stopped. And the hurting stopped. I was at peace."

1. Read John 11:1–16. What did Jesus say when he heard Lazarus was sick? What did he mean by this? What actions did he take in response to the news?

   _____

   _____

2. When was a time you endured a vigil for a sick or injured loved one, perhaps similar to the one Mary and Martha endured at Lazarus's bedside? How did you approach God during that time?

   _____

   _____

Lazarus now lay sick (John 11:2).

When [Jesus] heard that Lazarus was sick, he stayed where he was two more days (v. 6).

"Our friend Lazarus has fallen asleep; but I am going there to wake him up." His disciples replied, "Lord, if he sleeps, he will get better." Jesus had been speaking of his death, but his disciples thought he meant natural sleep (vv. 12–13).

3. What was your emotional state? Were you afraid for the person's life? Were you angry at God for allowing your loved one to suffer? Were you confused, not knowing quite what to do? Were you wrestling with regret over things you'd said—or hadn't said—to your loved one? Were you feeling sorry for yourself? Explain.

_____

_____

_____

4. How did the situation turn out? What impact did the experience have on your relationship with Jesus? Explain.

_____

_____

_____

THE VOICE OF JESUS

John pauses, letting the silence of the courtroom speak. The judge listens. The guardian listens. And you, the orphan, say nothing.

He will wipe every tear from their eyes. There will be no more death or mourning or crying or pain (Revelation 21:4).

"At *peace?*" John says, breaking the silence.

"Like I was asleep. Resting. Tranquil. I was dead."

"Then what happened?"

"Well, Martha can tell you the details. The funeral was planned. The family came. Friends traveled from Jerusalem. They buried me."

"Did Jesus come to the funeral?"

"No."

"He still wasn't there?"

"No, when he heard I was buried, he waited an extra four days."

"Why?"

Lazarus stopped and looked at Jesus. "To make his point."

John smiles knowingly. "What happened next?"

"I heard his voice."

"Whose voice?"

"The voice of Jesus."

"But I thought you were dead."

"I was."

"I, uh, thought you were in a grave."

"I was."

"How does a dead man in a grave hear the voice of a man?"

"He doesn't. The dead hear only the voice of God. I heard the voice of God."

"What did he say?"

"He didn't say it; he shouted it."

"What did he shout?"

"Lazarus is dead, and for your sake I am glad I was not there, so that you may believe" (John 11:14–15).

"'Lazarus, come out!'"

"And you heard him?"

"As if he were in the tomb with me. My eyes opened; my fingers moved. I lifted my head. I was alive again. I heard the stone being rolled away. The light poured in. It took a minute for my eyes to adjust."

"What did you see?"

"A circle of faces looking in at me."

"Then what did you do?"

"I stood up. Jesus gave me his hand and pulled me out. He told the people to get me some real clothes, and they did."

"So you died, were in the tomb four days, then Jesus called you back to life? Were there any witnesses to this?"

Lazarus chuckles. "Only a hundred or so."

"That's all, Lazarus, thank you. You may step down."

Jesus called in a loud voice, "Lazarus, come out!" (John 11:43).

Jesus said . . . "Take off the grave clothes and let him go" (v. 44).

5. "On his arrival, Jesus found that Lazarus had already been in the tomb for four days" (John 11:17 NIV). Why did Jesus wait so long to travel to Bethany?

_____

_____

_____

6. Lazarus heard the voice of Christ, even though he was in the grave. What does this tell us about God's presence with us even in death?

_____

_____

_____

7. How do you suppose the people in the crowd reacted when they saw Lazarus walk out of his tomb? What might skeptics in the crowd have said?

_____

_____

_____

8. Two thousand years later, what is your reaction to Lazarus's resurrection? What do modern skeptics say about it?

_____

_____

_____

Jesus came to be at Lazarus's burial site thanks to the efforts of a friend who cared enough to deliver the news and urgent longings of Lazarus's family to the Lord. As we'll see in the next study, the selfless act of that unnamed friend has tremendous implications for anyone who enjoys a personal relationship with Jesus.

☙ POINTS TO REMEMBER ❧

❖ We don't always know why God delays in answering our request, but we can trust in his timing.
❖ Everything changes when we hear the voice of Jesus.
❖ Our stories of what God has done for us serve as powerful testimonies to others of God's goodness and grace.

☙ PRAYER FOR THE DAY ❧

Father, thank you for the testimony of Lazarus. Keep the details of his story fresh in our minds when we come face-to-face with mortality . . . when your timetable doesn't make sense to us . . . or when the boldness of our faith starts to wane. Help us understand that you cause all things to work together for good. In Jesus' name, amen.

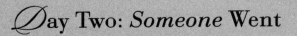

$\mathcal{D}$ay Two: *Someone* Went

A DILIGENT AMBASSADOR

If Scripture boasted a list of the famous dead, Lazarus would be near the top. But I'd like you to think about someone else in this story. His name is not important. His looks are immaterial. His gender is of no concern. His title is irrelevant. He is important not because of who he is but because of what he did.

So the sisters sent word to Jesus (John 11:3).

He is someone who went to Jesus on behalf of a friend. Lazarus was sick, and Jesus could help, and someone needed to go to Jesus, so someone went. Others cared for the sick man in other ways. Some brought food; others provided treatment; still others comforted the family. Each role was crucial. Each person was helpful, but none was more vital than the one who went to Jesus.

He went because he was asked to go. An earnest appeal came from the family of the afflicted. "We need someone who will tell Jesus that my brother is sick. We need someone to ask him to come. Will you go?"

The question came from Mary and Martha. They would have gone themselves, but they couldn't leave their brother's bedside. They needed someone else to go for them. Not just anyone, mind you, for not just anyone could. Some were too busy; others didn't know the way. Some fatigued too quickly; others were inexperienced on the path. Not everyone could go.

And not everyone would go. This was no small request the sisters were making. They needed a diligent ambassador, someone who knew how to find Jesus. Someone who wouldn't quit mid-journey. Someone who would make sure the message was delivered. Someone who was as convinced as they were that Jesus must know what had happened.

They knew of a trustworthy person, and to that person they went. They entrusted their needs to someone, and that someone took those needs to Christ. "So Mary and Martha sent *someone* to tell Jesus, 'Lord, the one you love is sick'" (John 11:3 NCV, emphasis mine).

Someone carried the request. *Someone* walked the trail. *Someone* went to Jesus on behalf of Lazarus. And because *someone* went, Jesus responded.

1. If you had to entrust someone with the responsibility Martha gave her unnamed friend, to whom would you turn? Why would you trust that person?

_____

_____

_____

_____

2. What are the characteristics of an ideal ambassador? Do you know anyone who might choose you as their ambassador to Christ? Explain.

_____

_____

_____

_____

3. The unnamed friend of Mary and Martha served as an ambassador to deliver the news of Lazarus's impending death to Christ. In the same way, God calls us to serve as ambassadors to him—though he calls us to proclaim the message of Jesus' eternal life that he offers to all! What do the following passages say about how you should serve as an ambassador for God?

Mark 16:15–16: "Go everywhere in the world, and tell the Good News to everyone. Anyone who believes and is baptized will be saved, but anyone who does not believe will be punished" (NCV).

_____

_____

_____

Luke 10:2: "The harvest is plentiful, but the workers are few. Ask the Lord of the harvest, therefore, to send out workers into his harvest field" (NIV).

_____

_____

_____

I heard the voice of the Lord saying, "Whom shall I send? And who will go for us?" And I said, "Here am I. Send me!" (Isaiah 6:8).

Romans 10:14–15: "How then will they call on Him in whom they have not believed? How will they believe in Him whom they have not heard? And how will they hear without a preacher?" (NASB).

_____

_____

_____

2 Corinthians 5:20: "Now then, we are ambassadors for Christ, as though God were pleading through us: we implore you on Christ's behalf, be reconciled to God" (NKJV)

_____

_____

_____

2 Timothy 4:5: "But you should control yourself at all times, accept troubles, do the work of telling the Good News, and complete all the duties of a servant of God" (NCV).

_____

_____

_____

4. What steps can you take to become a more faithful ambassador to Jesus for your loved ones, your friends, and your acquaintances?

_____

_____

_____

THE ONE YOU LOVE

"Lord, the one you love is sick"
(John 11:3).

The phrase the friend of Lazarus uses is worth noting. When he tells Jesus of the illness, he says, "Lord, the one you love is sick" (John 11:3 NCV). He doesn't base his appeal on the imperfect love of the one in need but on the perfect love of the Savior. He doesn't say, "The one *who loves you* is sick." He says, "The one *you love* is sick."

When he heard this, Jesus said, "This sickness will not end in death" (v. 4).

The power of the prayer, in other words, does not depend on the one who makes the prayer but on the One who hears the prayer. "When Jesus *heard* this, he said, 'This sickness will not end in death'" (verse 4 NCV, emphasis mine). The Master heard the request. Jesus stopped whatever he was doing and took note of the man's words. This anonymous courier was heard by God. His voice matters in heaven.

Now you are the body of Christ, and each one of you is a part of it (1 Corinthians 12:27).

How important was this friend in the healing of Lazarus? How essential was his role? Some might regard it as secondary. After all, didn't Jesus know everything? Certainly he knew Lazarus was sick. Granted, but he didn't respond to the need until someone came to him with the message.

When was Lazarus healed? After *someone* made the request. Oh, I know the healing wouldn't unfold for several days, but the timer was set when the appeal was made. All that was needed was the passage of time.

Would Jesus have responded if the messenger had not spoken? Perhaps, but we have no guarantee. We do, however, have an example: The power of God was triggered by prayer. Jesus looked down the very throat of death's cavern and called Lazarus back to life . . . all because someone prayed.

In the economy of heaven, the prayers of saints are a valued commodity.

"Ask and it will be given to you; seek and you will find; knock and the door will be opened to you" (Matthew 7:7).

5. A matter of life and death, like Lazarus's, obviously must be taken to the Lord. But what about the smaller things? Are there any matters too trivial or too mundane to take to the Lord? Explain.

_____

_____

_____

6. In John 14:13–14, Jesus said to his disciples, "I will do whatever you ask in my name, so that the Father may be glorified in the Son. You may ask me for anything in my name, and I will do it" (NIV). What promise are we given in this passage? How does this bring God glory?

_____

_____

_____

7. In 1 John 5:14–15, we read, "Now this is the confidence that we have in Him, that if we ask anything according to His will, He hears us. And if we know that He hears us, whatever we ask, we know that we have the petitions that we have asked of Him" (NKJV). What does it mean to pray according to God's will? How does this provide us with confidence in prayer?

_____

_____

_____

_____

8. Paul said we should "rejoice always, pray continually, give thanks in all circumstances" (1 Thessalonians 5:16–18 NIV). What steps can you take to do this more effectively in your life?

_____

_____

_____

When Jesus finally arrived in Bethany, Lazarus had already been in the tomb for four days. Martha was in despair, confused, and perhaps even angry with Jesus for delaying so long. Why had he waited? The reason, as we'll see in the next study, would soon become perfectly clear to her. Jesus was about to make a resounding and final statement on who had the ultimate authority over life and death.

⤙⤚ POINTS TO REMEMBER ⤙⤚

❖ Jesus responded to Mary and Martha's request because *someone* went to him on their behalf.
❖ There are no secondary roles in God's kingdom, for each of us has an important part to play.
❖ In the economy of heaven, our prayers are a valued commodity.

⤙⤚ PRAYER FOR THE DAY ⤙⤚

Father, thank you for the privilege of speaking to you—for the opportunity to lay our fears, concerns, and desperate needs at your feet. Thank you for involving yourself in the things that matter to us. Thank you for the ambassadors, known and unknown, who carry our concerns and needs to you. Bless our efforts to become ambassadors for others. In Jesus' name, amen.

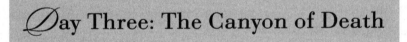

$\mathscr{D}$ay Three: The Canyon of Death

A FAMILIAR PLACE

Though I walk through the darkest valley, I will fear no evil, for you are with me (Psalm 23:4).

The canyon of death. It is a desolate canyon. The dry ground is cracked and lifeless. A blistering sun heats the wind that moans eerily and stings mercilessly. Tears burn and words come slowly as visitors to the canyon are forced to stare into the ravine. The bottom of the crevice is invisible, the other side unreachable. You can't help but wonder what is hidden in the darkness. And you can't help but long to leave.

Have you been there? Have you been called to stand at the thin line that separates the living from the dead? Have you lain awake at night listening to machines pumping air in and out of your lungs? Have you watched sickness corrode and atrophy the body of a friend? Have you lingered behind at the cemetery long after the others have left, gazing in disbelief at the metal casket that contains the body that contained the soul of the one you can't believe is gone?

Jesus answered . . . "Anyone who walks in the daytime will not stumble, for they see by this world's light. It is when a person walks at night that they stumble, for they have no light" (John 11:9–10).

If so, then this canyon is familiar to you. You've heard the lonesome whistle of the winds. You've heard the painful questions—*why?* and *what* for?—ricochet answerless off the canyon walls. And you've kicked loose rocks off the edge and listened for the sound of their crashing, which never comes.

Martha found herself in that canyon when her brother died. Her words to Jesus are full of despair. "Lord, if you had been here . . ." (John 11:21 NCV). She stares into the Master's face with confused eyes. She'd been strong long enough; now it hurt too badly. Lazarus was dead. Her brother was gone. And the one man who could have made a difference didn't. He hadn't even made it for the burial.

Something about death makes us accuse God of betrayal. "If God were here, there would be no death!" we claim. After all, if God is God anywhere, he has to be God in the face of death. Pop psychology can deal with depression. Pep talks can deal with pessimism. Prosperity can handle hunger. But only God can deal with our ultimate dilemma—death. And only the God of the Bible has dared to stand on the canyon's edge and offer an answer.

On his arrival, Jesus found that Lazarus had already been in the tomb for four days (John 11:17).

"Lord," Martha said to Jesus, "if you had been here, my brother would not have died" (v. 21).

1. Read John 11:18–21. Why did Martha feel free to question—and even challenge—Jesus' inaction when her brother was on his deathbed?

_____

_____

_____

2. How do you think she felt about Jesus at that time?

_____

_____

_____

I am the Living One . . . I hold the keys of death (Revelation 1:18).

3. Many of us can relate to Martha standing in the canyon of death. The loss of our loved one is so painful, and like Martha we say to God, "If only you had been here." Why does death tend to make us accuse God of betrayal?

_____

_____

_____

_____

4. What's the best comfort or advice you can offer someone who is standing on a canyon's edge?

_____

_____

_____

A HINGE POINT IN HISTORY

Jesus wasn't angry with Martha. Perhaps it was his patience that caused her to change her tone from frustration to earnestness. "I know that even now," she said, "God will give you whatever you ask."

"Lord," Martha said . . . "I know that even now God will give you whatever you ask" (John 11:22).

Jesus said . . . "Your brother will rise again" (John 11:23).

Martha answered, "I know he will rise again" (v. 24).

Jesus said to her, "I am the resurrection and the life. The one who believes in me will live, even though they die" (v. 25).

Death has been swallowed up in victory (1 Corinthians 15:54).

"Do you believe this?" (John 11:26).

"Yes, Lord," she replied, "I believe that you are the Messiah, the Son of God, who is to come into the world" (v. 27).

Jesus then made one of those claims that place him either on the throne or in the asylum: "Your brother will rise and live again."

Martha misunderstood. (Who wouldn't have?) "I know that he will rise again in the resurrection on the last day" (John 11:21–24 NCV).

That wasn't what Jesus meant. Don't miss the context of the next words. Imagine the setting: Jesus has intruded on the enemy's turf; he's standing in Satan's territory, Death Canyon. His stomach turns as he smells the sulfuric stench of the ex-angel, and he winces as he hears the oppressed wails of those trapped in the prison. Satan has been here. He has violated one of God's creations.

With his foot planted on the serpent's head, Jesus speaks loudly enough that his words echo off the canyon walls. "I am the resurrection and the life. The one who believes in me will live, even though they die; and whoever lives by believing in me will never die" (verses 25–26 NIV).

It is a hinge point in history. A chink has been found in death's armor. The keys to the halls of hell have been claimed. The buzzards scatter and the scorpions scurry as Life confronts death—and wins! But Jesus isn't through with Martha. With eyes locked on hers he asks the greatest question found in Scripture, a question meant as much for you and me as for Martha.

"Do you believe this?"

Wham! There it is. The bottom line. The dimension that separates Jesus from a thousand gurus and prophets who have come down the pike. The question that drives any responsible listener to absolute obedience to or total rejection of the Christian faith.

Jesus didn't pose this query as a topic for discussion in Sunday schools. It was never intended to be dealt with while basking in the stained glass sunlight or while seated on padded pews.

No. This is a canyon question. A question which makes sense only during an all-night vigil or in the stillness of hospital waiting rooms. A question that makes sense when all of our props, crutches, and costumes are taken away. For then we must face ourselves as we really are: rudderless humans tail-spinning toward disaster. And we are forced to see him for what he claims to be: our only hope.

As much out of desperation as inspiration, Martha said yes. As she studied the tan face of that Galilean carpenter, something told her she'd probably never get closer to the truth than she was right now. So she gave him her hand and let him lead her away from the canyon wall.

5. Read John 11:22–27. How did this event represent a "hinge point" in history? How was Jesus invading the devil's turf in this passage?

_____

_____

_____

_____

_____

6. Think of a canyon time you've experienced. If Jesus had been *physically* present during that experience, as he was here with Martha, what would you have said, asked, or requested from him?

_____

_____

_____

_____

_____

7. How might Jesus' words to Martha apply to your situation?

_____

_____

_____

_____

_____

8. Canyons are precarious places. Not everyone emerges from them with their faith strengthened, as Martha did. What might cause a person to emerge from a canyon with their faith weakened—or perhaps even broken?

_____

_____

_____

_____

_____

Jesus allowed Martha and Mary to wrestle with the question of why this had happened to them, but he didn't let them stay in that place of uncertainty for long. With a single command to the four-days-deceased Lazarus, Jesus would fulfill his plan. However, as we will see in the next study, before that miracle took place he would stop and do something very human and yet very unexpected: he would *weep* for the sisters' loss.

❧ POINTS TO REMEMBER ☙

❖ Something about death makes us accuse God of betrayal—after all, if he is anywhere, he has to be God in the canyon of death.

❖ Jesus is the resurrection and the life, and those who believe in him will never face spiritual death.

❖ It is when we see Jesus as our only hope and receive his life that he leads us away from the canyon of death.

⟿ PRAYER FOR THE DAY ⟿

Father, we ask you today to guide us through our canyon experiences.
Work in our hearts and minds through the power of the Holy Spirit to keep us
close to you when life-or-death circumstances threaten to drive us away.
Help us recognize only you can lead us through the valley of the shadow
of death and into eternal life. In Jesus' name, amen.

Day Four: Come Out!

JESUS WEEPS

Martha sat in a damp world, cloudy, tearful. And Jesus sat in it with her. "I am the resurrection and the life. Those who believe in me, even though they die, will live" (John 11:25 NRSV). Hear those words in a Superman tone, if you like. Clark Kent descending from nowhere, ripping shirt and popping buttons to reveal the *S* beneath. "I am THE RESURRECTION AND THE LIFE!" Do you see a Savior bypassing the tears of Martha and Mary and, in doing so, telling them and all grievers to buck up and trust?

When Jesus saw [Mary] weeping, and the Jews who had come along with her also weeping, he was deeply moved in spirit and troubled (John 11:33).

I don't. I don't because of what Jesus does next. He weeps. He sits on the pew between Mary and Martha, puts an arm around each, and sobs. Among the three, a tsunami of sorrow is stirred; a monsoon of tears is released. Tears that reduce to streaks the watercolor conceptions of a cavalier Christ. Jesus weeps.

He weeps with them.

He weeps for them.

He weeps with us.

He weeps for us.

Jesus wept (v. 35).

He weeps so we will know: Mourning is not disbelieving. Flooded eyes don't represent a faithless heart. A person can enter a cemetery certain of life after death and still have a crater in the heart. Christ did. He wept. And his tears give us permission to shed our own. Grief does not mean we don't trust; it simply means we can't stand the thought of another day without the Lazaruses of our lives.

Jesus wept not for the dead but for the living. He wept not for the one in the cave of death but for those in the cave of fear. He wept for those who, though alive, were dead. He wept for those who, though free, were prisoners, held captive by their fear of death. He touches Martha's cheek, gives Mary a hug, stands, and turns to face the corpse. The casket lid is closed.

Then the Jews said, "See how he loved him!" (v. 36).

"Move the stone." The command was soft but firm.

"But, Jesus, it will . . . it will stink."
"Move the stone so you will see God." Stones have never stood in God's way. Mary pauses. Turning to the funeral home director, she says, "Open it."

1. Read John 11:28–37. Jesus knew what he was getting ready to do. He had been planning it since he received word of Lazarus's illness. Why, then, did he cry when he saw Mary and the others mourning?

_____

_____

_____

2. The author of Hebrews wrote, "Since, then, we have a great high priest who has passed through the heavens, Jesus, the Son of God, let us hold fast to our confession. For we do not have a high priest who is unable to sympathize with our weaknesses, but we have one who in every respect has been tested as we are, yet without sin" (4:14–15 NRSV). Jesus felt the pain—physical and emotional—that we feel, and he is able to empathize with us. Why was that necessary?

_____

_____

_____

_____

_____

3. What does the fact that Jesus can relate to us mean to someone who is struggling with the illness or loss of a loved one?

_____

_____

_____

_____

4. Paul wrote that Jesus "made himself nothing by taking the very nature of a servant, being made in human likeness" (Philippians 2:7 NIV). How does knowing that Jesus became like us, with all our human emotions, affect the way we feel about him? How does it affect the way we talk to and relate to him?

_____

_____

_____

_____

> *"Take away the stone," he said. "But, Lord," said Martha . . . "by this time there is a bad odor. . . ." Jesus said, "Did I not tell you that if you believe, you will see the glory of God?" (John 11:39–40).*

FOR THE LIVING

Some years ago, a visitor to our house showed my daughters some tricks. Magic acts. Simple sleight-of-hand stuff. I stood to the side and watched the girls' responses. They were amazed. When the coin disappeared, they gasped. When it reappeared, they were stunned. At first I was humored by their bewilderment.

But with time, my bewilderment became concern. Part of me didn't like what was happening. My kids were being duped. He was tricking them. They, the innocent, were being buffaloed by him, the sneak. I didn't like that. I didn't like seeing my children fooled.

So I whispered to my daughters. "It's in his sleeve." Sure enough it was. "It's behind his ear." And what do you know, I was right! Maybe I was rude to interfere with the show, but I don't enjoy watching a trickster pull one over on my children.

Neither does God.

Jesus couldn't bear to sit and watch the bereaved be fooled. Please understand, he didn't raise the dead for the sake of the dead. He raised the dead for the sake of the living.

Jesus, once more deeply moved, came to the tomb (John 11:38).

"Lazarus, come out!" (v. 43).

"Lazarus, come out!" (John 11:43 NCV).

Martha was silent as Jesus commanded. The mourners were quiet. No one stirred as Jesus stood face-to-face with the rock-hewn tomb and demanded that it release his friend.

No one stirred, that is, except for Lazarus. Deep within the tomb, he moved. His stilled heart began to beat again. Wrapped eyes popped open. Wooden fingers lifted. And a mummied man in a tomb sat up. And want to know what happened next?

The dead man came out, his hands and feet wrapped with strips of linen, and a cloth around his face (v. 44).

Let John tell you. "The dead man came out, his hands and feet wrapped with pieces of cloth, and a cloth around his face" (verse 44 NCV).

Question: What's wrong with this picture?

Answer: Dead men don't walk out of tombs.

Question: What kind of God is this?

Answer: The God who holds the keys to life and death. The kind of God who rolls back the sleeve of the trickster and reveals death for the parlor trick it is. The kind of God you want present at your funeral.

He'll do it again, you know. He's promised he would. And he's shown that he can. "The Lord himself will come down from heaven with a loud command. . . . And those who have died believing in Christ will rise" (1 Thessalonians 4:16 NCV).

The dead in Christ will rise (1 Thessalonians 4:16).

The same voice that awakened the corpse of Lazarus will speak again. The earth and the sea will give up their dead. There will be no more death.

Jesus made sure of that.

5. Read John 11:38–44. Martha surely knew who Jesus was. She had seen what he was capable of doing. So why was she reluctant to follow his instructions to roll away the stone in front of Lazarus's tomb?

_____

_____

_____

_____

6. What Martha seemed to be asking was, "Lord, are you sure you know what you're doing?" Before you judge her too harshly, ask yourself the same question when it comes to following some of Jesus' commands that run counter to our human nature. Read the following passages and write down why it is easier or more difficult for you to follow that specific command.

"But I tell you, don't stand up against an evil person. If someone slaps you on the right cheek, turn to him the other cheek also" (Matthew 5:39 NCV).

_____

_____

_____

_____

_____

"If anyone wants to sue you and take your shirt, let him have your coat also. . . . Give to him who asks of you, and do not turn away from him who wants to borrow from you" (Matthew 5:40, 42 NASB).

_____

_____

_____

_____

_____

"Judge not, that you be not judged. For with the judgment you pronounce you will be judged, and with the measure you use it will be measured to you" (Matthew 7:1–2 ESV).

_____

_____

_____

_____

_____

"But to you who are listening I say: Love your enemies, do good to those who hate you, bless those who curse you, pray for those who mistreat you" (Luke 6:27–28 NIV).

_____

_____

_____

_____

_____

"When you give a dinner or a supper, do not ask your friends, your brothers, your relatives, nor rich neighbors, lest they also invite you back, and you be repaid. But when you give a feast, invite the poor, the maimed, the lame, the blind" (Luke 14:12–13 NKJV).

_____

_____

_____

_____

7. The Bible is clear that God holds the keys to life and death. Why, then, does death have the ability to fool us into believing it is the end of everything?

_____

_____

_____

_____

8. What comfort does the story of Jesus raising Lazarus from the dead offer today, some two thousand years after it happened?

_____

_____

_____

_____

Therefore many of the Jews . . . believed in him (John 11:45).

The story of Jesus raising Lazarus from the dead ends with this note: "Therefore many of the Jews who had come to visit Mary, and had seen what Jesus did, believed in him" (John 11:45 NIV). Lazarus's life would serve as a testimony to the power of Christ. That was his part to play in God's story, but as we will see in the next study, his sisters had their parts to play as well.

☙ POINTS TO REMEMBER ☙

❖ Grief over death does not mean we fail to trust in Christ but that we can't stand the thought of losing our loves ones.
❖ Jesus' tears at his friend's death give us permission to shed our own.
❖ The same voice who awaked the corpse of Lazarus will speak again and raise us to eternal life.

☙ PRAYER FOR THE DAY ☙

Father, thank you for robbing death of its power. May we be ever mindful that your final victory over death required you first to suffer and die. Grant us the wisdom and boldness to share the hope of resurrection and eternal life with those who are struggling with a fear of death. In Jesus' name, amen.

*D*ay Five: Play Your Part

EVERY CHURCH NEEDS ONE

After Jesus performed this miracle, the family of Lazarus, Mary, and Martha decided to honor Jesus by having a party on his behalf. "Martha served the food, and Lazarus was one of the people eating with Jesus" (John 12:2 NCV). In a prior visit, Martha had become angry because Mary—horror of horrors—had been sitting at the feet of Jesus. How impractical! How irrelevant! How unnecessary!

"Lord," she had complained, "don't you care that my sister has left me alone to do all the work? Tell her to help me" (Luke 10:40 NCV). My, my! Aren't we testy? All of a sudden Martha went from serving Jesus to making demands of him. The room fell silent. The disciples ducked their eyes. Mary flushed red. And Jesus spoke.

"Martha, Martha, you are worried and upset about many things. Only one thing is important. Mary has chosen the better thing, and it will never be taken away from her" (verses 41–42 NCV). Apparently Martha got the point, for here at this dinner party we find her serving again.

Every church needs a Martha. Change that. Every church needs a hundred Marthas. Sleeves rolled and ready, they keep the pace for the church. Because of Marthas, the church budget gets balanced, the church babies get bounced, and the church building gets built. Marthas are ones who just keep going and going and going. They store strength like a camel stores water. Since they don't seek the spotlight, they don't live off the applause. That's not to say they don't need it. They just aren't addicted to it.

What is Mary doing? Is she in the kitchen? No, she is worshiping, for that is what she loves to do. Mary brings a pint of very expensive perfume and pours it on Jesus' feet, and then wipes his feet with her hair. The smell of the perfume fills the house, just like the sound of praise can fill a church.

Every church desperately needs some Marys. We need them to put passion in our worship. We need them to write songs of praise and sing songs of glory. We need them to kneel and weep and lift their hands and pray. We need them because we tend to forget how much God loves worship. Marys don't forget. They know that God wants to be known as a father. They know that a father likes nothing more than to have his children sit as his feet and spend time with him.

1. Anyone who wonders why Lazarus and his family held such a special place in Jesus' heart need only look at the story in Luke 10. Although Martha and Mary differed in their methods, they both focused their time

Six days before the Passover, Jesus came to Bethany, where Lazarus lived, whom Jesus had raised from the dead (John 12:1).

Martha was distracted by all the preparations that had to be made (Luke 10:40).

"Mary has chosen what is better" (v. 41).

God has placed in the church . . . gifts of healing, of helping, of guidance (1 Corinthians 12:28).

Mary took about a pint of pure nard, an expensive perfume; she poured it on Jesus' feet and wiped his feet with her hair. And the house was filled with the fragrance of the perfume (John 12:3).

Worship the LORD with gladness; come before him with joyful songs (Psalm 100:2).

and energy on the Lord as guided by their personalities and spiritual gifts. Do you see yourself as being more like Martha or Mary? Explain.

_____

_____

_____

_____

2. Who do you know who fills the opposite role—the Martha to your Mary, or vice versa? What qualities do you see in that person?

_____

_____

_____

3. Why is a balance of those two roles necessary—not just in the church but also in your circle of loved ones, friends, and acquaintances?

_____

_____

_____

4. What specific things can you do this week to encourage the "Martha" or "Mary" in your life?

_____

_____

_____

A PLACE AT THE TABLE

A dinner was given in Jesus' honor. Martha served, while Lazarus was among those reclining at the table with him (John 12:2).

What about Lazarus? As far as we know, he did nothing at this dinner. He saved his actions for outside the house. "A large crowd of people heard that Jesus was in Bethany. So they went there to see not only Jesus but Lazarus, whom Jesus raised from the dead . . . Because of Lazarus many Jews were leaving [the priests] and believing in Jesus" (John 12:9, 11 NCV).

On account of [Lazarus] many of the Jews were going over to Jesus and believing in him (v. 11).

Wow! Because of Lazarus many Jews were "believing in Jesus." Lazarus had been given a trumpet. He had a testimony to give—and what a testimony he had!

"I was always a good fellow," he would say. "I paid my bills. I loved my sisters. I even enjoyed being around Jesus. But I wasn't one of the followers. I didn't get as close as Peter and James and those guys. I kept my distance. Nothing personal. I just didn't want to get carried away.

"But then I got sick. And then I died. I mean, I died *dead*.

"Nothing left. Stone cold. No life. No breath. Nothing. And then Jesus called me from the grave. When he spoke, my heart beat and my soul stirred, and I was alive again. And I want you to know he can do the same for you."

In the orchestra of life, God had given Martha a bass drum of service. He had given Mary a flute for praise. And he had given Lazarus a trumpet. And Lazarus stood on center stage and played it.

God still gives trumpets. God still calls people from the pits. God still gives pinch-me-I'm-dreaming, too-good-to-be-true testimonies. But not everyone has a dramatic testimony. Who wants a band full of trumpets?

Some convert the lost. Some encourage the saved. And some keep the movement in step. All are needed.

So, if God has called you to be a Martha, then serve! Remind the rest of us that there is evangelism in feeding the poor and there is worship in nursing the sick.

If God has called you to be a Mary, then worship! Remind the rest of us that we don't have to be busy to be holy. Urge us with your example to put down our clipboards and megaphones and be quiet in worship.

If God has called you to be a Lazarus, then testify. Remind the rest of us that we, too, have a story to tell. We, too, have neighbors who are lost. We, too, have died and been resurrected.

Each of us has our place at the table.

Declare his glory among the nations, his marvelous deeds among all peoples (Psalm 96:3).

We have different gifts, according to the grace given to each of us. If your gift is prophesying, then prophesy in accordance with your faith; if it is serving, then serve; if it is teaching, then teach; if it is to encourage, then give encouragement; if it is giving, then give generously; if it is to lead, do it diligently; if it is to show mercy, do it cheerfully (Romans 12:6–8).

5. None of us have a testimony as dramatic as Lazarus's, but all we have a story to tell of what God has done in our lives. What is one thing God has done in your life that would give hope and encouragement to another person?

_____

_____

_____

_____

6. In Luke 8:39, Jesus told a man whom he had delivered from demons to "return home and tell how much God has done for you" (NIV). How would your story draw others to Christ and help them realize how much God has done for them?

_____

_____

_____

7. Read 1 Corinthians 12:12–31. What does Paul say about the value each person's specific gift adds to the body of Christ? Why are all the gifts important?

_____

_____

_____

8. In what ways have you been tempted to discount the gifts God has given to you? How can you see yourself using those gifts for his glory?

_____

_____

_____

_____

_____

_____

_____

Back in the courtroom, Lazarus has offered his testimony and is back in his seat.

John turns to the judge to present his closing arguments.

"You have heard the testimonies," he begins. "We started this case with the wedding in Cana." He paces as he speaks, measuring each word. "They had no wine, none at all. But when Jesus spoke, water became wine. The best wine. Delicious wine. You heard the testimony of the wedding attendants. They saw it happen.

The master of the banquet tasted the water that had been turned into wine (John 2:9).

"Then we heard the words of the foreign official. His son was nearly dead." You nod, remembering the man's testimony. Through his thickened accent the dignitary had explained, "I had no other choice. I went to him out of desperation. Look! Look what the teacher did for my son." The boy had stood, and you had stared. It was hard to believe such a healthy youngster had ever been near death.

"Go," Jesus replied, "your son will live" (4:50).

"And, your honor," John continues, "don't forget the crippled man near the pool. For thirty-eight years he had not walked. But then Jesus came and, well, the court saw him. Remember? We saw him walk into this room. We heard his story.

Jesus said to him, "Get up! Pick up your mat and walk" (5:8).

"And, as if that was not enough, we also heard the testimony of the boy with the lunch. He was part of a crowd of thousands who had followed Jesus in order to hear him teach and to see him heal. Just when the little boy was about to open his lunch basket to eat, he was asked to bring it to Jesus. One minute it held a lunch; the next it held a feast.

Jesus then took the loaves, gave thanks, and distributed to those who were seated as much as they wanted (6:11).

"Then there was the storm. Peter described it to us. The boat bouncing on the waves. Thunder. Lightning. Storms like that can kill. I know. I used to make a living on a boat! Peter's testimony about what happened was true. I was there. The Master walked on the water. And the moment he stepped into the boat, we were safe."

They saw Jesus approaching the boat, walking on the water (v. 19).

John pauses again. Sunlight squared by a window makes a box on the floor. John steps into the box. "Then, yesterday, you met a man who had never seen light. His world was dark. Black. He was blind. Blind from birth."

The man went and washed, and came home seeing (9:7).

John pauses. "Just now, you have heard testimony from Lazarus. Four days after the funeral, Jesus came calling. Literally calling, 'Lazarus, come out!' Try to picture Lazarus as he hears those words. Heaven-sent Lazarus.

Heaven-happy Lazarus. Four days into his measureless days. Now, with a wave and within a wink, he's reunited with his body and waking up on a cold slab in a wall-hewn grave. The rock to the entrance has been moved. Mummy-wrapped, he stiffly sits up and walks out."

John has concluded his closing arguments. He turns to face the judge one last time. "Your honor, I leave the decision in your hands." With that he returns to the table and takes his seat.

The guardian stands. He doesn't identify himself. He doesn't need to. All recognize him. He is Jesus Christ.

Jesus' voice fills the courtroom. "I represent an orphan who is the sum of all you have seen. Like the party that had no wine, this one has no cause for celebration. Like the dignitary's son, this child is spiritually ill. Like the cripple and the beggar, he can't walk and is blind. He is starving, but earth has no food to fill him. He faces storms, but earth has no compass to guide him. And, most of all, he is dead. Just like Lazarus. Dead. Spiritually dead. I will do for him what I did for them. I'll give him joy, strength, healing, sight, safety, nourishment, new life. All are his. If you will permit."

Jesus answered him, "Truly I tell you, today you will be with me in paradise" (Luke 23:43).

The judge speaks his answer. "You are my Son, whom I love, and I am very pleased with you" (Luke 3:22 NCV). God looks at you. "I will permit it," he says, "on one condition. That the orphan request it."

John has presented the witnesses. The witnesses have told their stories.

The Master has offered to do for you what he did for them. He will bring wine to your table, sight to your eyes, strength for your step and, most of all, power over your grave. He will do for you what he did for them.

The Judge has given his blessing. The rest is up to you. Now the choice is yours.

Believe in the Lord Jesus, and you will be saved (Acts 16:31).

❦ POINTS TO REMEMBER ❦

- ❖ If God has called you to be a Martha, serve others and remind the rest of us there is evangelism in feeding the poor and nursing the sick.
- ❖ If God has called you to be a Mary, worship the Lord and remind the rest of us we don't have to be busy to be holy.
- ❖ If God has called you to be a Lazarus, testify for Christ and remind the rest of us that we also have a story to tell.

❦ PRAYER FOR THE DAY ❦

Father, we were spiritually dead before you sent your Son into the world to give us life. Help our lives to be a testimony to others of the saving work of grace you have done within us. Help us to point others to Jesus through our words, our deeds, our gifts, and our very lives. In all things, we seek to bring you glory. In Jesus' name, amen.

⚬ WEEKLY MEMORY VERSES ⚬

For I am convinced that neither death nor life, neither angels nor demons, neither the present nor the future, nor any powers, neither height nor depth, nor anything else in all creation, will be able to separate us from the love of God that is in Christ Jesus our Lord.

ROMANS 8:38–39 (NIV)

For Further Reading

Selections throughout this lesson were taken from *God Came Near* (Nashville: Thomas Nelson, 1986); *He Still Moves Stones* (Nashville: Thomas Nelson, 1993); *A Gentle Thunder* (Nashville: Thomas Nelson, 1995); *Great House of God* (Nashville: Thomas Nelson, 1997); and *Next Door Savior* (Nashville: Thomas Nelson, 2003).

LESSON 9

PETER

GOSPEL OF THE SECOND CHANCE

IT WAS LIKE SPOTTING A LITTLE PEARL in a box of buttons or stumbling across a ten-dollar bill in a drawer full of envelopes.

It was small enough to overlook. Only two words. I know I'd read that passage a hundred times. But I'd never seen it. Maybe I'd passed over it in the excitement of the resurrection. Or, since Mark's account of the resurrection is by far the briefest of the four, maybe I'd just not paid too much attention. Or, maybe since it's in the last chapter of the Gospel, my weary eyes had always read too quickly to note this little phrase.

But I won't miss it again. It's highlighted in yellow and underlined in red. You might want to do the same.

Look in Mark, chapter 16. Read the first five verses about the women's surprise when they find the stone moved to the side. Then feast on that beautiful phrase spoken by the angel, "He is not here, he is risen," but don't pause for too long. Go a bit further. Get your pencil ready and enjoy this jewel in the seventh verse (here it comes). The verse reads like this: "But go, tell his disciples and Peter that he is going before you to Galilee."

Did you see it? Read it again. (This time I italicized the words.)

"But go, tell his disciples *and Peter* that he is going before you to Galilee."

Now tell me if that's not a hidden treasure.

If I might paraphrase the words, "Don't stay here, go tell the disciples," a pause, then a smile, "and especially tell Peter, that he is going before you to Galilee." What a line. It's as if all of heaven had watched Peter fall—and it's as if all of heaven wanted to help him back up again. "Be sure and tell Peter that he's not left out. Tell him that one failure doesn't make a flop."

Whew! No wonder they call it the gospel of the second chance.

Not many second chances exist in the world today. Just ask the kid who didn't make the Little League team or the fellow who got the pink slip or the mother of three who got dumped for a "pretty little thing."

"See the place where they laid him.
But go, tell his disciples and Peter,
'He is going ahead of you into Galilee'"
(Mark 16:6–7).

Let us then approach God's throne of grace with confidence, so that we may receive mercy and find grace to help us in our time of need (Hebrews 4:16).

Not many second chances. Nowadays it's more like, "It's now or never." "Around here we don't tolerate incompetence." "Gotta get tough to get along." "Not much room at the top." "Three strikes and you're out." "It's a dog-eat-dog world!"

Jesus has a simple answer to our masochistic mania. "It's a dog-eat-dog world?" he would say. "Then don't live with the dogs." That makes sense, doesn't it? Why let a bunch of other failures tell you how much of a failure you are?

Sure you can have a second chance. Just ask Peter.

1. Life can seem like a minefield. One wrong move, one bad decision, one momentary lapse of judgment can explode in our faces and change everything. What was one such incident that left you feeling like a failure?

_____

_____

_____

_____

_____

2. Have you received a second chance—a shot at redemption and an opportunity to learn from your failure? How did it come about?

_____

_____

_____

_____

_____

The apostle Peter had no way of knowing how meaningful his story would become to generations of believers. His story serves both as a cautionary tale and as an inspiration to all of us who have our less-than-perfect moments. Peter demonstrated just how far someone could fall—and still get back up again.

─❧ PRAYER FOR THE WEEK ❧─

Father, thank you for refusing to allow us to be defined by our failures. Thank you for the wisdom, experience, and perseverance found only at our lowest points. Open our eyes to the second chances you offer. Give us the courage and humility to pick ourselves up and start again after we fall. In Jesus' name, amen.

*D*ay One: What God Can Do

LET'S FISH!

Luke's Gospel tells us that one day when Jesus was standing on the shore of the Sea of Galilee, a crowd of people was pressing in to hear him teach. Jesus saw two boats on the shore, one of which belonged to a man named Simon. Jesus would later call him "Rocky," but we know him as Peter. And while we don't know all the thoughts going through this fisherman's head at that moment, I imagine they might have been something like this.

As Jesus was standing by the Lake of Gennesaret, the people were crowding around him and listening to the word of God. He saw at the water's edge two boats, left there by the fishermen, who were washing their nets (Luke 5:1–2).

It had been a long night. I don't know how many times we had thrown that net into the blackness and heard it slap against the sea. I don't know how many times we had held the twine rope as the net sank into the water. All night we had waited for that bump, that tug, that jerk that would clue us to haul in the catch . . . but it had never come. By daybreak, my arms ached. My eyes burned. My neck was sore. All I wanted was to go home and let my wife rub the knots out of my back.

But just as I was about to leave the beach, I noticed a crowd coming toward me. They were following a lanky fellow who walked with a broad swing and wide gait. He saw me and called my name. "Morning, Jesus!" I called back. Though he was a hundred yards away, I could see his white smile. "Quite a crowd, eh?" he yelled, motioning at the mass behind him. I nodded and sat down to watch.

He stopped near the edge of the water and began to speak. Though I couldn't hear much, I could see a lot. I could see more and more people coming. With all the pressing and shoving, it's a wonder Jesus didn't get pushed down into the water. He was already knee-deep when he looked at me. I didn't have to think twice. He climbed into my boat, and John and I followed. We pushed out a bit. I leaned back against the bow, and Jesus began to teach.

He got into one of the boats, the one belonging to Simon, and asked him to put out a little from shore (v. 3).

It seemed that half of Israel was on the beach. Men had left their work, women their household chores. I even recognized some priests. How they all listened! They scarcely moved, yet their eyes danced as if they were in some way seeing what they could be.

Then he sat down and taught the people from the boat (v. 3).

When Jesus finished, he turned to me. I stood and had begun to pull anchor when he said, "Push out into the deep, Peter. Let's fish."

[Jesus] said to Simon, "Put out into deep water, and let down the nets for a catch" (v. 4).

I groaned. I looked at John. We were thinking the same thing. As long as he wanted to use the boat for a platform, that was fine. But to use it for a fishing boat— that was our territory. I started to tell this carpenter-teacher, "You stick to preaching, and I'll stick to fishing." But I was more polite: "We worked all night. We didn't catch a thing."

Simon answered, "Master, we've worked hard all night and haven't caught anything" (v. 5).

He just looked at me. I looked at John. John was waiting for my cue . . .

I wish I could say I did it because of love. I wish I could say I did it out of devotion. But I can't. All I can say is there is a time to question and a time to listen. So, as much with a grunt as with a prayer, we pushed out.

"But because you say so, I will let down the nets" (v. 6).

With every stroke of the oar, I muttered. With every pull of the paddle, I grumbled. "No way. No way. Impossible. I may not know much, but I know fishing. And all we're going to come back with are some wet nets."

1. Read Luke 5:1–5. The Galilean shoreline was a place where rough-hewn, blue-collar types worked and hung out. Why did Jesus go *there* to look for disciples?

   _____

   _____

   _____

   _____

   _____

   _____

2. Why did Jesus choose Peter? What could Christ possibly have seen in him—not just as a disciple but also as a close friend?

   _____

   _____

   _____

   _____

   _____

3. What hope does that give for us "regular people" today?

   _____

   _____

   _____

   _____

4. Jesus got Peter's attention through the activity Peter knew best: fishing. How did Jesus get your attention when he called you?

   _____

   _____

   _____

   _____

PANDEMONIUM

Peter continues his story: *The noise on the beach grew distant, and soon the only sound was the smack of the waves against the hull. Finally we cast anchor. I picked up the heavy netting, held it waist-high, and started to throw it. That's when I caught a glimpse of Jesus out of the corner of my eye. His expression stopped me in mid-motion.*

He was leaning out over the edge of the boat, looking out into the water where I was about to throw the net. And, get this, he was smiling. A boyish grin pushed his cheeks high and turned his round eyes into half-moons—the kind of smile you see when a child gives a gift to a friend and watches as it is unwrapped.

He noticed me looking at him, and he tried to hide the smile, but it persisted. It pushed at the corners of his mouth until a flash of teeth appeared. He had given me a gift and could scarcely contain himself as I opened it.

"Boy, is he in for a disappointment," I thought as I threw the net. It flew high, spreading itself against the blue sky and floating down until it flopped against the surface, then sank. I wrapped the rope once around my hand and sat back for the long wait.

But there was no wait. The slack rope yanked taut and tried to pull me overboard. I set my feet against the side of the boat and yelled for help. John and Jesus sprang to my side.

We got the net in just before it began to tear. I'd never seen such a catch. It was like plopping down a sack of rocks in the boat. We began to take in water. John screamed for the other boat to help us.

It was quite a scene: four fishermen in two boats, knee-deep in fish, and one carpenter seated on our bow, relishing the pandemonium.

That's when I realized who he was. And that's when I realized who I was: I was the one who told God what he couldn't do!

"Go away from me, Lord; I'm a sinful man." There wasn't anything else I could say.

I don't know what he saw in me, but he didn't leave. Maybe he thought if I would let him tell me how to fish, I would let him tell me how to live.

It was a scene I would see many times over the next couple of years—in cemeteries with the dead, on hillsides with the hungry, in storms with the frightened, on roadsides with the sick. The characters would change, but the theme wouldn't. When we would say, "No way," he would say, "My way." Then the ones who doubted would scramble to salvage the blessing. And the One who gave it would savor the surprise.

> *They caught such a large number of fish that their nets began to break. So they signaled their partners in the other boat to come and help them, and they came and filled both boats so full that they began to sink (Luke 5:5–6).*

> *When Simon Peter saw this, he fell at Jesus' knees and said, "Go away from me, Lord; I am a sinful man!" For he and all his companions were astonished at the catch of fish they had taken (vv. 8–9).*

> *Jesus said to Simon . . . "From now on you will fish for people" (v. 10).*

5. Read Luke 5:6–11. What did Jesus do when Peter showed even the smallest amount of faith? What does this say about our obedience to God?

_____

_____

_____

_____

_____

6. Have you, like Peter, ever inadvertently tried to limit God or tell him what he couldn't do, whether it involved a health issue, a job situation, a personal relationship, or something else? Explain.

_____

_____

_____

_____

_____

7. Why do we often fall into the trap of thinking we know the full scope of what God is capable of doing? Why do we have difficulty seeing beyond the moment?

_____

_____

_____

_____

_____

_____

_____

_____

8. Why did witnessing the miracle prompt Peter to say he was sinful? In what ways has God brought you to this same realization in your life?

_____

_____

_____

_____

_____

_____

_____

_____

This was the first of several life-changing encounters Peter had with Jesus on or near water. In the next study, we'll see how Jesus used the same setting—a boat on the Sea of Galilee—to take Peter far outside his comfort zone.

━❧ POINTS TO REMEMBER ❧━

❖ It's never a good idea to tell God what he can and can't do.
❖ When we say, "No way," God says, "My way."
❖ If we're paying attention, we will see the miracles God brings into our everyday lives.

━❧ PRAYER FOR THE DAY ❧━

Father, thank you for the miracles—large and small, seen and unseen—
that you perform every day. Thank you for giving us stories like Peter's
to bolster our faith and strengthen our resolve as believers. May we be ever ready
to "lower our nets" when you give the word so we may enjoy the bounty of
your blessings. In Jesus' name, amen.

Day Two: Caught in a Storm

TIME TO GET SOME HELP

Peter was nitroglycerin. If you bumped him the wrong way, he blew up. He made a living with his hands and got in trouble with his mouth. If he had had a tattoo, it would have been a big, black anchor on his forearm. If they had had bumper stickers, his would have read, "I don't get mad; I get even." Yet while he might not have known everything about self-control, he knew one thing about being a fisherman. He knew better than to get caught in a storm.

And this night, Peter knows he is in trouble.

The winds roar down onto the Sea of Galilee like a hawk on a rat. Lightning zigzags across the black sky. The clouds vibrate with thunder. The rain taps, then pops, then slaps against the deck of the boat until everyone aboard is soaked and shaking. Ten-foot waves pick them up and slam them down again with bone-jarring force.

His disciples went down to the lake, where they got into a boat and set off across the lake (John 6:16–17).

The boat was already a considerable distance from land, buffeted by the waves (Matthew 14:24).

These drenched men don't look like a team of apostles who are only a decade away from changing the world. They don't look like an army that will march to the ends of the earth and reroute history. They don't look like a band of pioneers who will soon turn the world upside down. No, they look more like a handful of shivering sailors who are wondering if the next wave they ride will be their last.

[Jesus] saw the disciples straining at the oars, because the wind was against them (Mark 6:48).

A strong wind was blowing and the waters grew rough (John 6:18).

And you can be sure of one thing. The one with the widest eyes is the one with the biggest biceps—Peter. He's seen these storms before. He's seen the wreckage and bloated bodies float to shore. He knows what the fury of wind and wave can do. And he knows that times like this are not times to make a name for yourself; they're times to get some help.

That is why, when he sees Jesus walking on the water toward the boat, he is the first to say, "Lord, if it's really you, tell me to come to you, walking on the water" (Matthew 14:28 NLT).

They saw Jesus approaching the boat, walking on the water (v. 19).

"Lord, if it's you," Peter replied, "tell me to come to you on the water" (Matthew 14:28).

Now, some say this statement is a simple request for verification. Peter, they suggest, wants to prove that the one they see is really Jesus and not just anyone who might be on a stroll across a storm-tossed sea in the middle of the night. (You can't be too careful, you know.)

So, Peter consults his notes, removes his glasses, clears his throat, and asks a question any good attorney would. "Ahem, Jesus, if you would kindly demonstrate your power and prove your divinity by calling me out on the water with you, I would be most appreciative."

I don't buy that. I don't think Peter is seeking clarification; I think he's trying to save his neck. He is aware of two facts: he's going down, and Jesus is staying up. And it doesn't take him too long to decide where he would rather be.

Hear my cry, O God; listen to my prayer (Psalm 61:1).

Perhaps a better interpretation of his request would be, "Jeeeeeeeesus! If that is you, then get me out of here!"

1. Read Matthew 14:22–28. What was the disciples' first reaction when they saw Jesus walking on the waves? How did Jesus respond to them?

_____

_____

_____

_____

2. Peter's request to walk on the water betrays his fear of the situation. In this, he is among a long line of characters in the Bible who needed reassurance at times that God was there and was going to help them. Read the following passages and write down how God responded to each person's call for help.

Gideon: Judges 6:33–40

_____

_____

_____

David: Psalm 57:1–3

_____

_____

_____

Elijah: 1 Kings 17:17–22

_____

_____

_____

Jehoshaphat: 2 Chronicles 18:28–32

_____

_____

_____

Hezekiah: 2 Chronicles 32:16–21

_____

_____

_____

3. Maybe you've never been caught in a squall on open water, but chances are you've faced a situation like Peter's. That is, you faced circumstances you thought you had under control, only to watch them spiral into something scary or dangerous. Think about that situation. At what point did you realize you were in trouble? What was your first reaction?

_____

_____

_____

4. Peter stepped out of a boat in the middle of a raging storm at sea. How much are you willing to risk where your faith is concerned?

_____

_____

_____

NO OTHER OPTION

What is Jesus' reply to Peter's request? "Yes, come" (Matthew 14:29 NCV).

Peter doesn't have to be told twice. It's not every day that you walk on water through waves that are taller than you are. But when faced with the alternative of sure death or possible life, Peter knows which one he wants.

"Come," [Jesus] said. Then Peter got down out of the boat, walked on the water and came toward Jesus (Matthew 14:29).

The first few steps go well. But a few strides out onto the water, and he forgets to look to the One who got him there in the first place, and down he plunges.

Peter knows he is in trouble, and he knows Jesus is the only one who can save him. To his credit, he doesn't allow his pride to get in the way of admitting he has made a mistake. And while his response may lack class—it probably wouldn't get him on the cover of *Gentlemen's Quarterly* or even *Sports Illustrated*—it gets him out of some deep water.

When [Peter] saw the wind, he was afraid and, beginning to sink, cried out, "Lord, save me!" (v. 30).

"Help me!"

And since Peter would rather swallow pride than water, a hand comes through the rain and pulls him up.

The message is clear.

As long as Jesus is one of many options, he is no option. As long as you can carry your burdens alone, you don't need a burden bearer. As long as your situation brings you no grief, you will receive no comfort. And as long as you can take him or leave him, you might as well leave him, because he won't be taken halfheartedly.

Immediately Jesus reached out his hand and caught him. "You of little faith," he said, "why did you doubt?" (v. 31).

But when you mourn, when you get to the point of sorrow for your sins, when you admit that you have no other option but to cast all your cares on him, and when there is truly no other name that you can call, then cast all your cares on him, for he is waiting in the midst of the storm.

Cast all your anxiety on him because he cares for you (1 Peter 5:7).

5. Read Matthew 14:29–36. Peter had certainly seen a lot out on the Sea of Galilee during his years as a fisherman, but safe to say he'd never seen anyone strolling along the top of the water. What made him think he could do something unprecedented like that?

_____

_____

_____

_____

_____

6. No one else made a move to climb over the side of the boat. What set Peter apart from the rest of the disciples?

_____

_____

_____

_____

7. When was a time you took a risk for Jesus? What were the results? Did you ever start to sink? If so, what did you do?

_____

_____

_____

_____

8. What does it mean that if Jesus is one of many options, he is no option?

_____

_____

_____

_____

The bond between Jesus and Peter was solidified during their stroll on the Sea of Galilee. Evidence of that bond can be seen in Jesus' invitation to Peter to witness the Transfiguration, one of the most profound events of Jesus' earthly ministry. As we'll see in the next study, Peter's reaction to that event—as well as to Jesus' subsequent arrest and trial—secures his place as one of the easiest-to-identify-with people in Scripture.

⤳ POINTS TO REMEMBER ⤳

❖ The storms of life can help us to realize we are going down while Jesus is staying up.
❖ As long as Jesus is one of many options, he is no option.
❖ God is always waiting for us in the midst of a storm.

❧ PRAYER FOR THE DAY ❧

Father, thank you for calling us out onto the water with you—
for pulling us from our comfort zones, stretching us beyond anything
we consider possible, and filling our lives with purpose and adventure.
Give us the courage to let go of the things that seem safe and follow you
into the teeth of the storm. In Jesus' name, amen.

Day Three: Betrayal and Redemption

THE PRAYER RETREAT

It's the first scene of the final act in the earthly life of Christ. Jesus has taken three followers on a prayer retreat. "He took along Peter and John and James, and went up on the mountain to pray. And while He was praying, the appearance of His face became different, and His clothing became white and gleaming" (Luke 9:28–29 NASB).

Oh, to have heard that prayer. What words so lifted Christ that his face was altered? Did he see his home? Hear his home?

Maybe Jesus needed comfort. Knowing that his road home will pass through Calvary, he puts in a call. God is quick to answer. "And behold, two men were talking with Him; and they were Moses and Elijah" (verse 30 NASB).

The two were perfect comfort givers. Moses understood tough journeys. Elijah could relate to an unusual exit. So Jesus and Moses and Elijah discuss "His departure which He was about to accomplish at Jerusalem" (verse 31 NASB).

Peter, James, and John, meanwhile, take a good nap. All at once they woke up and saw how glorious Jesus was. They also saw the two men who were with him.

Moses and Elijah were about to leave, when Peter said to Jesus, "'Master, it is good for us to be here! Let us make three shelters, one for you, one for Moses, and one for Elijah.' But Peter did not know what he was talking about" (verses 32–33 CEV).

What would we do without Peter? The guy has no idea what he is saying, but that doesn't keep him from speaking. He has no clue what he is doing but offers to do it anyway. This is his idea: three monuments for the three heroes. Great plan? Not in God's book. Even as Peter is speaking, God starts clearing his throat.

Peter's error is not that he spoke, but that he spoke heresy. Three monuments would equate Moses and Elijah with Jesus. No one shares the platform

Jesus took Peter, James and John with him and led them up a high mountain, where they were all alone. There he was transfigured before them (Mark 9:2).

And there appeared before them Elijah and Moses (v. 4).

They spoke about his departure (Luke 9:31).

Peter and his companions were very sleepy, but when they became fully awake, they saw his glory and the two men (v. 32).

Peter said to Jesus, "Rabbi, it is good for us to be here. Let us put up three shelters—one for you, one for Moses and one for Elijah" (Mark 9:5).

(He did not know what to say, they were so frightened) (v. 6).

*We were eyewitnesses of [Jesus']
majesty. He received honor and
glory from God the Father when the
voice came to him from the Majestic
Glory, saying, "This is my Son,
whom I love" (2 Peter 1:16–17).*

"Listen to him!" (Mark 9:7).

with Christ. God comes with the suddenness of a fast-moving weather front and leaves Peter gulping. "This is My Son," he says (verse 35 NASB). Not *a son* as if he were clumped in with the rest of us. Not *the best son* as if he were valedictorian of the human race. Jesus is, according to God, "My Son, My Chosen One," absolutely unique and unlike anyone else.

In the synoptic Gospels, God speaks only twice—at the baptism and then here at the Transfiguration. In both cases he begins with "this is My beloved Son." But at the river he concludes with affirmation: "in whom I am well pleased" (Matthew 3:17 NKJV). On the hill he concludes with clarification: "Listen to Him."

1. Read Luke 9:28–36. What do you suppose was Jesus' reason for taking Peter (as well as James and John) with him for his rendezvous with Moses and Elijah? What did he want these three disciples to take away from the experience?

   _____

   _____

   _____

   _____

   _____

2. "Peter said to [Jesus], 'Master, it is good for us to be here. Let us put up three shelters—one for you, one for Moses and one for Elijah.' (He did not know what he was saying.)" (verse 33 NIV). What does Peter's response to seeing Moses and Elijah—and Luke's comment—tell you about Peter's personality?

   _____

   _____

   _____

   _____

3. Read Exodus 20:3–6. Based on this passage, what was the problem with Peter's plan to build three monuments to Moses, Elijah, and Jesus?

   _____

   _____

   _____

4. As the events surrounding the Transfiguration reveal, the Gospel writers tend to portray Peter "warts and all" instead of just focusing on his most admirable characteristics and heroic deeds. Why do you think they took this approach? What parts of yourself do you see in Peter? Explain.

   _____

   _____

   _____

   _____

INVITATION TO BREAKFAST

See the fellow hiding in the shadows? That's Peter. Peter the apostle. Peter the impetuous. Peter the passionate. He once walked on water. Stepped right out of the boat onto the lake. Fearless before friends and foes alike. But tonight he is weeping in pain. "Lord, I am ready to go with you to prison and even to die with you!" he had pledged only hours earlier. "But Jesus said, 'Peter, before the rooster crows this day, you will say three times that you don't know me'" (Luke 22:33–34 NCV).

His memories race as he relives the events of the anguished night: the clanking of the Roman guard, the flash of a sword, a touch for Malchus, a rebuke for Peter, soldiers leading Jesus away. He had followed the noise until he saw the torch-lit jury in the courtyard of Caiaphas. There he had stopped near a fire to warm his hands. The night had been cold. The fire was hot. But Peter was neither. He was lukewarm.

"Peter followed at a distance" (Luke 22:54 NIV). He was loyal . . . from a distance. That night he went close enough to see, but not close enough to be seen. The problem was, Peter *was* seen. Other people near the fire recognized him. "You were with him," they had challenged. "You were with the Nazarene." Three times people said it, and each time Peter denied it. And each time Jesus had heard it.

Denying Christ on the night of his betrayal was bad enough, but did he have to boast that he wouldn't? And one denial was pitiful, but three? Three denials were horrific, but did he have to curse? "Peter began to place a curse on himself and swear, 'I don't know the man'" (Matthew 26:74 NCV). And now, awash in a whirlpool of sorrow, Peter is hiding. Peter is weeping. And soon Peter will be fishing.

We wonder why he goes fishing. We know why he goes to Galilee. He had been told that the risen Christ would meet the disciples there. The arranged meeting place is not the sea, however, but a mountain (see Matthew 28:16). If the followers were to meet Jesus on a mountain, what are they doing in a boat? Two years earlier, when Jesus called Peter to fish for men, he dropped his net and followed. We haven't seen him fish since. We never see him fish again. Why is he fishing now?

Especially now! Jesus has risen from the dead. Peter has seen the empty tomb. Who could fish at a time like this? Were they hungry? Perhaps that's the sum of it. Maybe the expedition was born out of growling stomachs.

Or then again, maybe it was born out of a broken heart.

You see, Peter could not deny his denial. The empty tomb did not erase the crowing rooster. Christ had returned, but Peter wondered, he must have wondered, *After what I did, would he return for someone like me?*

We've wondered the same. Is Peter the only person to do the very thing he swore he'd never do? Then the rooster crows, and conviction pierces, and Peter has a partner in the shadows. We weep as Peter wept, and we do what Peter did. We go fishing. We go back to our old lives. We return to our pre-Jesus practices. We do what comes naturally, rather than what comes spiritually. And we question whether Jesus has a place for folks like us.

Peter [said], "I will lay down my life for you." Then Jesus answered, "Will you really lay down your life for me? Very truly I tell you, before the rooster crows, you will disown me three times!" (John 13:37–38).

They took Jesus to the high priest. . . . Peter followed him at a distance (Mark 14:53–54).

Simon Peter . . . struck the high priest's servant (John 18:10).

Peter replied . . . "I don't know what you're talking about!" (Luke 22:60).

Then [Peter] began to call down curses (Matthew 26:74).

"I'm going out to fish," Simon Peter told them (John 21:3).

You were taught, with regard to your former way of life, to put off your old self (Ephesians 4:22).

203

Jesus said to them, "Come and have breakfast" (John 21:12).

Jesus came, took the bread and gave it to them, and did the same with the fish. This was now the third time Jesus appeared to his disciples after he was raised (vv. 13–14).

Jesus said . . . "Follow me!" (v. 19).

Jesus answers that question. He answers it for you and me and all who tend to "Peter out" on Christ. His answer came on the shore of the sea in a gift to Peter. You know what Jesus did? Split the waters? Turned the boat to gold and the nets to silver? No, Jesus did something much more meaningful. He invited Peter to breakfast.

Jesus prepared a meal. Of course, the breakfast was one special moment among several that morning. There was the great catch of fish and the recognition of Jesus. The plunge of Peter and the paddling of the disciples. And there was the moment they reached the shore and found Jesus next to a fire of coals. The fish were sizzling, and the bread was waiting, and the defeater of hell and the ruler of heaven invited his friends to sit down and have a bite to eat.

No one could have been more grateful than Peter. The one Satan had sifted like wheat was eating bread at the hand of God. Peter was welcomed to the meal of Christ.

5. Read Matthew 26:31–75. For all Peter knew, his epic collapse when Jesus needed him the most was the end of his career as a disciple. In what ways did Peter stumble in this passage? What emotions did he likely experience in the hours that followed his betrayal of Christ?

_____

_____

_____

_____

_____

6. Peter had been in Jesus' "inner circle" along with James and John and up to this point had been one of the most fearless of the disciples. What was it about seeing Jesus taken into custody that had caused him to abandon his closest friend?

_____

_____

_____

_____

_____

7. Read John 21:1–14. Guilt and regret had caused Peter to return to his former way of life as a fisherman. How do Jesus' actions show Peter that he accepts him and still has a place for him in God's plan?

_____

_____

_____

_____

_____

_____

_____

_____

8. Perhaps you are sitting in a metaphorical boat like Peter, regretting a life decision you made and figuring that Jesus wants nothing to do with you. What do you think Peter would say to you? What steps would he tell you to take to get back in the game and return to Jesus' side?

_____

_____

_____

_____

_____

_____

_____

_____

Perhaps you've stumbled in the past and wonder if Jesus can ever look at you the same again. Perhaps you doubt that he still has a plan for your life. If so, just look at the story of Peter. He abandoned Christ and failed miserably as a disciple, yet Jesus met him on the beach, served him breakfast, and restored him back into fellowship. What's more, as we'll see in the next study, Jesus' plans for Peter had only just begun. And when Peter was given a second chance to serve Jesus—to be the kind of disciple he swore he would be—he seized it with both hands.

"I will restore you to health and heal your wounds," declares the LORD, "because you are called an outcast" (Jeremiah 30:17).

❧ POINTS TO REMEMBER ❧

❖ We must never forget that no one shares the platform with Christ.
❖ Like Peter, we're all guilty of doing the things we swore we'd never do.
❖ God is gracious and merciful to restore us when we fall.

❧ PRAYER FOR THE DAY ❧

Father, grant us the wisdom to learn from Peter's example. Convict us when we betray you with our words or actions and help us understand the consequences of our betrayal. Forgive our failures. Restore us to your service. And give us the opportunity to share with others the grace you show to us. In Jesus' name, amen.

Day Four: The Floodgates Open

WAITING IN THE RIGHT PLACE

Jesus' word to the doubting disciples before his ascension into heaven had been "wait." Before you go out, stand still. Prior to stepping forth, sit down. "Stay here in the city until the Holy Spirit comes and fills you with power from heaven" (Luke 24:49 NLT). So they do.

Peter and the rest of the disciples go to the upstairs room of the house where they are staying and wait. They have reasons to leave. Someone has a business to run or field to farm. Besides, the same soldiers who killed Christ still walk Jerusalem's streets. The disciples have ample reason to leave . . . but they don't. They stay.

And they stay together. As many as 120 souls huddle in the same house. How many potential conflicts exist in this group? Talk about a powder keg. Nathanael might glare at Peter for denying Christ at the fire. Then again, at least Peter stood near the fire. He could resent the others for running. So could the women. Faithful females who stood near the cross share the room with cowardly men who fled the cross. Bitterness, arrogance, distrust, chauvinism—the room is a kindling box for all four. But no one strikes a match. They stay together and, most of all, they all pray together.

One day passes. Then two. Then a week. For all they know a hundred more will come and go. But they aren't leaving. They persist in the presence of Christ.

Then, ten days later . . . "On the day of Pentecost all the believers were meeting together in one place. Suddenly, there was a sound from heaven like the roaring of a mighty windstorm, and it filled the house where they were sitting. Then, what looked like flames or tongues of fire appeared and settled on each of them. And everyone present was filled with the Holy Spirit" (Acts 2:1–4 NLT).

Doubters became prophets. God opened the floodgates on the greatest movement in history. It began because the followers were willing to do one thing: wait in the right place for power.

1. Read Acts 1:12–15. On the night of Jesus' arrest, Peter and the rest of the disciples had fled. What do you think compelled them to stay and follow Jesus' instructions this time in spite of the risks they faced?

_____

_____

_____

_____

"Do not leave Jerusalem, but wait for the gift my Father promised" (Acts 1:4).

The apostles returned to Jerusalem. . . . They went upstairs to the room where they were staying (vv. 12–13).

Peter stood up among the believers (a group numbering about a hundred and twenty) (v. 15).

They all joined together constantly in prayer (v. 14).

When the day of Pentecost came, they were all together in one place (2:1).

2. What were the disciples and the others doing while they waited? Why is this significant?

_____

_____

_____

_____

3. We live in a harried and busy world, but in the Bible we find commands to simply stop and wait on the Lord. Read each of the following passages and write down what it says to you about the importance of waiting on God.

Psalm 27:13–14: "I remain confident of this: I will see the goodness of the LORD in the land of the living. Wait for the LORD; be strong and take heart and wait for the LORD" (NIV).

_____

_____

_____

Lamentations 3:25: "The LORD is good to those who wait for Him, to the person who seeks Him" (NASB).

_____

_____

_____

Micah 7:7: "I will look to the LORD for help. I will wait for God to save me; my God will hear me" (NCV).

_____

_____

_____

James 5:7–8: "Therefore be patient, brethren, until the coming of the Lord. See how the farmer waits for the precious fruit of the earth, waiting patiently for it until it receives the early and latter rain. You also be patient. Establish your hearts, for the coming of the Lord is at hand" (NKJV).

_____

_____

2 Peter 3:9: "The Lord is not slow in keeping his promise, as some understand slowness. Instead he is patient with you, not wanting anyone to perish, but everyone to come to repentance" (NIV).

_____

_____

_____

4. Waiting is not the same thing as putting your life on hold. In fact, waiting doesn't have to be a passive pastime at all. What can you do while you wait on the Lord? How does God reward those who wait on him?

_____

_____

_____

_____

_____

LINGERING IN GOD'S PRESENCE

In the early-morning hours of Pentecost, a new sound was heard in the temple courts: Galileans were speaking various languages, praising God in tongues other than their own. A crowd gathered. Opinions and conclusions were reached. Then one of those disciples stood up and spoke. Peter, the transformed fisherman who had betrayed his Lord, delivered the first sermon, explaining from the Scriptures who Jesus really was and why he died. The results were remarkable.

A transformed group stood beside a transformed Peter as he announced: "Let everyone in Israel know for certain that God has made this Jesus, whom you crucified, to be both Lord and Messiah" (Acts 2:36 NLT). No timidity in his words. No reluctance.

What unlocked the doors of the apostles' hearts? Simple. They saw Jesus. They encountered the Christ. Their sins collided with their Savior, and their Savior won!

We're so reluctant to do what the disciples did. Who has time to wait? We groan at such a thought. But waiting doesn't mean inactivity. Waiting means watching for him. If you are waiting on a bus, you are watching for the bus. If you are waiting on God, you are watching for God, searching for God, hoping in God. Great promises come to those who do.

To those who still struggle, God says, "Wait on me." And wait in the right place. Jesus doesn't tell us to stay in Jerusalem, but he does tell us to stay honest, stay faithful, stay true. "If you rebel against the Lord's commands and refuse to listen to him, then his hand will be as heavy upon you as it was upon your ancestors" (1 Samuel 12:15 NLT). Are you illegally padding your pocket? Are you giving your body to someone who doesn't share your name and wear your ring? Is your mouth a Mississippi River of gossip? If you intentionally hang out at the bus stop of disobedience, you need to know something—God's bus doesn't stop there. Go to the place of obedience. "The Holy Spirit . . . is God's gift to those who obey him" (Acts 5:32 TEV).

While you're waiting in the right place, get along with people. Would the Holy Spirit have anointed contentious disciples? According to Peter, disharmony hinders prayers. He tells husbands, "Live with your wives in an understanding way. . . . Do this so that nothing will stop your prayers" (1 Peter 3:7 NCV). Waiting on God means working through conflicts,

All of them were filled with the Holy Spirit and began to speak in other tongues (Acts 2:4).

When they heard this sound, a crowd came together in bewilderment (v. 6).

Then Peter stood up with the Eleven, raised his voice and addressed the crowd (v. 14).

With minds that are alert and fully sober, set your hope on the grace to be brought to you when Jesus Christ is revealed at his coming (1 Peter 1:13).

If anyone, then, knows the good they ought to do and doesn't do it, it is sin for them (James 4:17).

Husbands . . . treat [your wives] with respect (1 Peter 3:7).

forgiving offenses, resolving disputes. "Keep yourselves united in the Holy Spirit, and bind yourselves together with peace" (Ephesians 4:3 NLT).

For ten days the disciples prayed. Ten days of prayer plus a few minutes of preaching led to three thousand saved souls. Perhaps we invert the numbers. We're prone to pray for a few minutes and preach for ten days. Not the apostles. Like the boat waiting for Christ, they lingered in his presence. They never left the place of prayer.

5. Read Acts 2:5–21. What was the crowd's response to the work the Holy Spirit was doing among the disciples? What was Peter's response?

_____

_____

_____

_____

6. Imagine that some of these people in this crowd had also been outside the high priest's residence on the night of Jesus' arrest. They would have seen Peter, the coward who had denied Jesus three times, now speaking with spiritual authority. What do you think their reaction would have been?

_____

_____

_____

_____

7. How do you think Peter would have explained this change to them? What would you need to do in order to transform the way he did?

_____

_____

_____

_____

8. What does it mean to "wait in the right place"? Why does waiting on God involve working through conflicts, forgiving offenses, and resolving disputes with others?

_____

_____

_____

_____

Peter and the other believers lingered in Christ's presence. They stayed in the place of prayer, and as a result they were filled with power from the Holy Spirit that enabled them to boldly proclaim the message of Jesus. However, that kind of boldness in first-century Israel carried severe consequences. As we'll see in the next study, Peter's second chance at honoring his commitment to Christ involved great danger and risk. This time, though, Peter didn't flinch.

Keep the unity of the Spirit through the bond of peace (Ephesians 4:3).

Those who accepted [Peter's] message were baptized, and about three thousand were added to their number that day (Acts 2:41).

⟿ POINTS TO REMEMBER ᴥ

❖ Waiting on God doesn't mean inactivity but rather actively watching for him to move.
❖ While you're waiting with your fellow believers in the right place, it's important to also get along with them.
❖ Incredible things happen when we linger in God's presence and stay in the place of prayer.

⟿ PRAYER FOR THE DAY ᴥ

Father, thank you for your unlikely choices. Only you saw the potential in Peter. Only you looked past his flaws to find the diamond within. We humbly ask that you do the same with us. Shape us and equip us to be used in ways we cannot anticipate, all for your glory. In Jesus' name, amen.

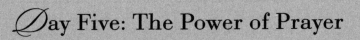

Day Five: The Power of Prayer

THE STRATEGY

[Herod] had James, the brother of John, put to death with the sword. When he saw that this met with approval among the Jews, he proceeded to seize Peter also (Acts 12:2–3).

[Peter was] guarded by four squads of four soldiers each. Herod intended to bring him out for public trial after the Passover (vv. 4–5).

In one of the last stories about Peter in the book of Acts, we find the disciple sitting (or rather, sleeping) in jail. King Herod, who suffered from a Hitler-level obsession with popularity, had just murdered the apostle James to curry favor with the populace. The execution bumped his approval rating, so he jailed Peter and resolved to behead him on the anniversary of Jesus' death. (Would you like a little salt with that wound?)

Herod placed the apostle under the watchful eye of sixteen Navy Seal sorts and told them, with no tongue in cheek, "He escapes, you die." (Quality control, Herod style.) So they bound Peter in chains and secured him three doors deep into the prison.

And what could the church do about it? The problem of an imprisoned Peter stood Goliath-tall over the humble community. They had no recourse: no clout, no political chips to cash. They had nothing but fear-drenched questions. "Who's next? First James, then Peter. Is Herod going to purge the church leadership?"

The church still faces her Goliaths. World hunger. Clergy scandal. Stingy Christians. Corrupt officials. Pea-brained and hard-hearted dictators. Peter in prison is just the first of a long list of challenges too big for the church. So our Jerusalem ancestors left us a strategy. When the problem is bigger than we are—we pray! "But while Peter was in prison, the church prayed very earnestly for him" (Acts 12:5 NLT).

They didn't picket the prison, petition the government, protest the arrest, or prepare for Peter's funeral. They prayed. They prayed as if prayer was their only hope, for indeed it was. They prayed earnestly for him.

"The night before Peter was to be placed on trial, he was asleep, fastened with two chains between two soldiers. Others stood guard at the prison gate. Suddenly, there was a bright light in the cell, and an angel of the Lord stood before Peter. The angel struck him on the side to awaken him and said, 'Quick! Get up!' And the chains fell off his wrists. Then the angel told him, 'Get dressed and put on your sandals.' And he did. 'Now put on your coat and follow me,' the angel ordered" (Acts 12:5–8 NLT).

Let's give this scene the chuckle it deserves. An angel descends from heaven onto earth. Only God knows how many demons he battled en route. He navigates the Jerusalem streets until he reaches Herod's prison. He passes through three sets of iron doors and a squad of soldiers until he stands in front of Peter. Brightness explodes like a July sun in Death Valley. But Peter sleeps through the wake-up call. The old fisherman dreams of Galilean sea bass.

The church was earnestly praying to God for him (Acts 12:5).

Suddenly an angel of the Lord appeared and a light shone in the cell. He struck Peter on the side and woke him up. "Quick, get up!" he said (v. 7).

1. Read Acts 12:1–8. What were the early believers' fears after hearing James had been executed and Peter imprisoned? How did they respond?

   _____

   _____

   _____

   _____

   _____

2. Chances are if you've followed Christ for any length of time, you've had to deal with some form of negative reaction from others because of your beliefs. What is the most severe consequence you've had to endure? How did it affect you?

   _____

   _____

   _____

   _____

   _____

3. How does Peter's story speak to you about the way God can work in your situation? What hope do you receive from it?

   _____

   _____

   _____

   _____

   _____

4. Think about a trial you are facing right now. What are some of the prayers you are sending up regarding the situation? Who else is praying for you? What response have you received?

_____

_____

GUARANTEED RESULTS

The apostle, who once wondered how Christ could sleep in a storm, now snoozes through his own.

"Peter," the angel says.

No response. "Peter!" Zzzzz. "Peter!!!"

The angel said to him, "Put on your clothes" (Acts 12:8).

Do angels elbow or wing people? Either way, shackles clang on the floor. The angel has to remind groggy Peter how to re-robe. First your sandals. Now your robe. Doors swing open in succession. And somewhere on the avenue to Mary's house, Peter realizes he isn't dreaming. The angel points him in the right direction and departs, muttering something about bringing a trumpet next time.

Then Peter came to himself and said, "Now I know without a doubt that the Lord has sent his angel and rescued me" (v. 11).

Rightly stunned, Peter walks to Mary's house. She, at that very hour, is hosting a prayer meeting on his behalf. His friends pack the place and fill the house with earnest intercession. Peter surely smiles as he hears their prayers. He knocks on the door. The servant answers and, instead of opening it, races back to the prayer circle and announces: "Peter is standing at the door!"

When this had dawned on him, he went to the house of Mary the mother of John (v. 12).

"You're out of your mind," they reply. But she insists. So they decide, "It must be his angel" (verses 14–15 NLT).

"You're out of your mind," they told her. When she kept insisting that it was so, they said, "It must be his angel" (v. 15).

I confess a sense of relief at that reading. Even the early followers struggled to believe God would hear them. Even when the answer knocked on the door, they hesitated. We still do. Most of us struggle with prayer. We forget to pray, and when we remember, we hurry through prayers with hollow words.

But Peter kept on knocking, and when they opened the door and saw him, they were astonished (v. 16).

Our minds drift; our thoughts scatter like a covey of quail. Why is this? Prayer requires minimal effort. No location is prescribed. No particular clothing is required. No title or office is stipulated. Yet you'd think we were wrestling a greased pig.

So: Let's pray, first. Traveling to help the hungry? Be sure to bathe your mission in prayer. Working to disentangle the knots of injustice? Pray. Weary of a world of racism and division? So is God. And he would love to talk to you about it.

Rejoice always, pray continually (1 Thessalonians 5:16–17).

Let's pray, most. Did God call us to preach without ceasing? Or teach without ceasing? Or have committee meetings without ceasing? Or sing without ceasing? No, but he did call us to "pray without ceasing" (1 Thessalonians 5:17 NKJV).

"My house will be called a house of prayer" (Mark 11:17).

Did Jesus declare: My house shall be called a house of study? Fellowship? Music? A house of exposition? A house of activities? No, but he did say, "My house will be called a house of prayer" (Mark 11:17 NIV).

No other spiritual activity is guaranteed such results. "When two of you get together on anything at all on earth and make a prayer of it, my Father in heaven goes into action" (Matthew 18:19 MSG). He is moved by the humble, prayerful heart.

The same God who heard the prayers from Jerusalem and set Peter free hears our prayers and sets us free. He is still listening. Are we still praying?

There was no small commotion among the soldiers as to what had become of Peter (Acts 12:18).

5. Read Acts 12:9–19. Peter's appearance at Mary's door was a gift from God—proof positive the believers' prayers were being heard and answered. So why did they doubt Rhoda's report that Peter was *actually* at their door?

_____

_____

_____

6. God could have sent Peter anywhere after his release, but he chose the house of Mary, a prayer warrior who at that very moment was hosting a prayer vigil for the apostle's release. What steps can you take this week to mold yourself into a prayer warrior like the early believers?

_____

_____

_____

_____

7. What steps can you take to pray *first* when you encounter a difficult situation? What steps will you take to pray *more*?

_____

_____

_____

8. Listening is perhaps the most important part of prayer. What will you do to build "listening time" into your daily routine?

_____

_____

_____

You have to love the story of Peter. After betraying Christ, he felt lower than a snake's belly. After Jesus gave him a second chance, he was the high hog at the trough. Even the angels wanted this distraught net-caster to know it wasn't over. The message came loud and clear from the celestial Throne Room through the divine courier: "Be sure and tell Peter that he gets to bat again."

Those who know these types of things say that the Gospel of Mark is really the transcribed notes and dictated thoughts of Peter. If this is true, then it was Peter himself who included those two words we find in Mark 16:7: "But go, tell His disciples—*and Peter*—that He is going before you" (NKJV,

Jesus said to Simon Peter, "Simon son of John, do you love me more than these?" (John 21:15).

"Yes, Lord," [Peter] said, "you know that I love you" (v. 15).

Five times I received from the Jews the forty lashes minus one. Three times I was beaten with rods, once I was pelted with stones, three times I was shipwrecked, I spent a night and a day in the open sea, I have been constantly on the move (2 Corinthians 11:24–26).

emphasis mine). If these really are his words, I can't help but imagine that the old fisherman had to brush away a tear and swallow a lump when he got to this point in the story.

It's not every day that you get a second chance. Peter must have known that. The next time he saw Jesus, he got so excited that he barely got his britches on before he jumped into the cold water of the Sea of Galilee. It was also enough, so they say, to cause this backwoods Galilean to carry the gospel of the second chance all the way to Rome where they killed him. If you've ever wondered what would cause a man to be willing to be crucified upside down, maybe now you know.

It's not every day that you find someone who will give you a second chance—much less someone who will give you a second chance every day.

But in Jesus, Peter found both.

A lot of things would happen to the early believers over the next few decades. Many nights would be spent away from home. Hunger would gnaw at their bellies. Rain would soak their skin. Stones would bruise their bodies. Shipwrecks, lashings, martyrdom. But there was a scene in the repertoire of memories that caused them to never look back: the betrayed coming back to find his betrayers—not to scourge them, but to send them. Not to criticize them for forgetting, but to commission them to remember that he who was dead is alive and they who were guilty have been forgiven.

❧ POINTS TO REMEMBER ❧

❖ The early church left us a strategy: when the problem is bigger than we are, we pray!
❖ Even the early followers, who witnessed wondrous miracles in their midst, struggled at times to believe God would hear them.
❖ No other spiritual activity—whether it's fellowship, music, or even preaching—is guaranteed the same results as prayer.

❧ PRAYER FOR THE DAY ❧

Father, thank you for the promises you provide to us in prayer.
Thank you that we can talk to you anywhere and at any time.
Help us to come to you first, to come to you more, and to pray boldly, confident that you will hear us. In Jesus' name, amen.

❧ WEEKLY MEMORY VERSE ❧

I have swept away your offenses like a cloud, your sins like the morning mist.
Return to me, for I have redeemed you.
ISAIAH 44:22 (NIV)

$\mathscr{F}$or Further Reading

Selections throughout this lesson were taken from *No Wonder They Call Him the Savior* (Nashville: Thomas Nelson, 1986); *Applause of Heaven* (Nashville: Thomas Nelson, 1990); *In the Eye of the Storm* (Nashville: Thomas Nelson, 1991); *He Still Moves Stontes* (Nashville: Thomas Nelson, 1993); *Traveling Light* (Nashville: Thomas Nelson, 2001); *Next Door Savior* (Nashville: Thomas Nelson, 2003); *Six Hours One Friday* (Nashville: Thomas Nelson, 2004); *Come Thisty* (Nashville: Thomas Nelson, 2004); *Outlive Your Life* (Nashville: Thomas Nelson, 2010).

$\mathcal{P}$AUL

NEVER TOO FAR GONE FOR A TURNAROUND

"MY POWER SHOWS UP BEST IN WEAK PEOPLE" (2 Corinthians 12:9 TLB). God said those words. Paul wrote them down. God said he was looking for empty vessels more than strong muscles. Paul proved it.

Before he encountered Christ, Paul had been somewhat of a hero among the Pharisees. He kept the law and order—or, better said, revered the Law and gave the orders. Good Jewish moms held him up as an example of a good Jewish boy. He had a "Who's Who in Judaism" paperweight on his desk and was selected "Most Likely to Succeed" by his graduating class. He was quickly establishing himself as the heir apparent to his teacher, Gamaliel.

If there is such a thing as a religious fortune, then Paul had it. He was a spiritual billionaire, born with one foot in heaven. This wild-eyed zealot was hell-bent on keeping the kingdom pure—and that meant keeping the Christians out. He marched through the countryside like a general demanding that backslidden Jews salute the flag of the motherland or kiss their family and hopes goodbye.

All this came to a halt, however, on the shoulder of a highway. Equipped with subpoenas, handcuffs, and a posse, Paul was on his way to do a little personal evangelism in Damascus. That's when someone slammed on the stadium lights, and he heard the voice.

When he found out whose voice it was, his jaw hit the ground, and his body followed. He braced himself for the worst. He knew it was all over. He felt the noose around his neck. He smelled the flowers in the hearse. He prayed that death would be quick and painless.

But all he got was silence and the first of a lifetime of surprises.

He ended up bewildered and befuddled in a borrowed bedroom. God left him there a few days with scales on his eyes so thick that the only direction he could look was inside himself. And he didn't like what he saw.

He saw himself for what he really was—to use his own words, the worst of sinners (see 1 Timothy 1:15). A legalist. A killjoy. A bumptious braggart who

If someone else thinks they have reasons to put confidence in the flesh, I have more . . . a Hebrew of Hebrews; in regard to the law, a Pharisee; as for zeal, persecuting the church; as for righteousness based on the law, faultless (Philippians 3:4–6).

I studied under Gamaliel and was thoroughly trained in the law of our ancestors (Acts 22:3).

I am the least of the apostles . . . because I persecuted the church of God (1 Corinthians 15:9).

As [Paul] neared Damascus . . . suddenly a light from heaven flashed around him (Acts 9:3).

"I am Jesus, whom you are persecuting" (v. 5).

Saul got up from the ground. . . . They led him by the hand into Damascus (v. 8).

217

claimed to have mastered God's code. A dispenser of justice who weighed salvation on a pan-scale.

That's when Ananias found him.

1. A *legalist,* like Paul was before he met Christ, believes that following rules and regulations will lead to salvation and spiritual growth. What is fundamentally wrong with this way of thinking?

_____

_____

_____

_____

_____

_____

_____

2. When in the past have you adopted a legalistic attitude? How has God gotten your attention and shown you the power of his grace?

_____

_____

_____

_____

_____

_____

_____

_____

_____

As renovation projects go, Ananias's was daunting. Saul of Tarsus hadn't just burned bridges with the Christian establishment—he had blown them up, and typically in advance of ever having reached them. He was Public Enemy #1 as far as Jesus' followers were concerned—a man to be feared and certainly not to be embraced as a brother. However, as we'll see in the next study, embracing Saul is exactly what Ananias had been called to do. He was given the task of preparing one of the most notorious enemies of first-century Christendom for . . . Christian service.

─◦ PRAYER FOR THE WEEK ◦─

Father, we praise you for the power of your forgiveness and redemption, for your ability to reclaim lives no matter what we've done with them. Thank you for the example of Saul in your Word. May we gain, during the next five days, a deeper understanding of your work in people's lives. In Jesus' name, amen.

$\mathcal{D}$ay One: A Tough Assignment

CAN'T BE TRUE

Ananias hurried through the narrow Damascus streets. His dense and bristling beard did not hide his serious face. Friends called as he passed, but he didn't pause. He murmured as he went, "Saul? Saul? No way. Can't be true."

He wondered if he had misheard the instructions. Wondered if he should turn around and inform his wife. Wondered if he should stop and tell someone where he was headed in case he never returned. But he didn't. Friends would call him a fool. His wife would tell him not to go.

But he had to go. He scampered through the courtyard of chickens, towering camels, and little donkeys. He stepped past the shop of the tailor and didn't respond to the greeting of the tanner. He kept moving until he reached the street called Straight. The inn had low arches and large rooms with mattresses. Nice by Damascus standards, the place of choice for any person of significance or power, and Saul was certainly both.

Ananias and the other Christians had been preparing for him. Some of the disciples had left the city. Others had gone into hiding. Saul's reputation as a Christian-killer had preceded him. But the idea of Saul the Christ follower?

That was the message of the vision. Ananias replayed it one more time. "Arise and go to the street called Straight, and inquire at the house of Judas for one called Saul of Tarsus, for behold, he is praying. And in a vision he has seen a man named Ananias coming in and putting his hand on him, so that he might receive his sight" (Acts 9:11–12 NKJV).

Ananias nearly choked on his matzo. This wasn't possible! He reminded God of Saul's hard heart. "I have heard from many about this man, how much harm he has done to Your saints in Jerusalem" (verse 13 NKJV). Saul a Christian? Sure, as soon as a turtle learns to two-step.

But God wasn't teasing. "Go, for he is a chosen vessel of Mine to bear My name before Gentiles, kings, and the children of Israel" (verse 15 NKJV).

Ananias rehashed the words as he walked. The name Saul didn't couple well with chosen vessel. Saul the thickhead—yes. Saul the critic—okay. But Saul the chosen vessel? Ananias shook his head at the thought.

1. Read Acts 9:1–16. What specifically did God tell Ananias to do? What was Ananias's response? How did God tell Ananias that he had plans for Saul?

_____

_____

_____

In Damascus there was a disciple named Ananias. The Lord called to him in a vision, "Ananias!" (Acts 9:10).

The Lord told [Ananias], "Go to the house of Judas on Straight Street and ask for a man from Tarsus named Saul, for he is praying" (Acts 9:11).

"Lord," Ananias answered, "I have heard many reports about this man and all the harm he has done to your holy people" (v. 13).

"Go! This man is my chosen instrument" (v. 15).

2. Ananias's mission was much like the one God gave to the prophet Jonah. Read Jonah 1:1–5. What did God tell Jonah to do? What was Jonah's initial reaction?

_____

_____

_____

_____

3. Turn to Jonah 4:1–3. What was Jonah's problem with his assignment? Why did he try to get out of following God's command by fleeing to Tarshish?

_____

_____

_____

_____

4. What can we learn from the stories of Ananias and Jonah about the importance of obeying God—regardless of whether we want to or not?

_____

_____

_____

_____

SOMETHING'S HAPPENED

Ananias went to the house and entered it (Acts 9:17).

By now Ananias was halfway down Straight Street and seriously considering turning around and going home. He would have, except the two guards spotted him.

"What brings you here?" they shouted from the second story. They stood at attention. Their faces were wintry with unrest.

Ananias knew who they were—soldiers from the temple. Traveling companions of Saul. "I've been sent to help the rabbi."

They lowered their spears. "We hope you can. Something has happened to him. He doesn't eat or drink. Scarcely speaks."

Ananias couldn't turn back now. He ascended the stone stairs. The guards stepped aside, and Ananias stepped into the doorway. He gasped at what he saw. A gaunt man was sitting cross-legged on the floor, half shadowed by a shaft of sunlight. Hollow cheeked and dry lipped, he rocked back and forth, groaning a prayer.

"How long has he been like this?"

"Three days."

Saul's head sat large on his shoulders. He had a beaked nose and a bushy ridge for eyebrows. The food on the plate and the water in the cup sat untouched on the floor. His eyes stared out of their sockets in the direction of an open window. A crusty film covered them. Saul didn't even wave the flies away from his face.

Ananias hesitated. If this was a setup, then he was history. If not, the moment was.

No one could fault Ananias's reluctance. Saul saw Christians as couriers of a plague. He stood near the high priest at Stephen's trial. He watched over the coats of stone throwers at the execution. He nodded in approval at Stephen's final breath. And when the Sanhedrin needed a hit man to terrorize the church, Saul stepped forward. He became the Angel of Death. He descended on the Christians in a fury, "uttering threats with every breath" (Acts 9:1 NLT). He "persecuted the church of God beyond measure and tried to destroy it" (Galatians 1:13 NKJV).

Ananias knew what Saul had done to the church in Jerusalem. What he was about to learn, however, was what Jesus had done to Saul on the road to Damascus.

For you have heard of my previous way of life in Judaism, how intensely I persecuted the church of God and tried to destroy it (Galatians 1:13).

5. Read Acts 9:17–19. For what reason did Ananias say God had sent him?

_____

_____

_____

_____

6. In Matthew 5:46–47, Jesus said, "If you love only the people who love you, you will get no reward. Even the tax collectors do that. And if you are nice only to your friends, you are no better than other people. Even those who don't know God are nice to their friends" (NCV). Why do God's plans often bring us into contact with people we otherwise might consider enemies?

_____

_____

_____

_____

7. What are the biggest obstacles we face in showing love and mercy to our enemies? What happens when we start to show love and mercy to them?

_____

_____

_____

8. What do you think Saul learned about Christians—the people he had been persecuting—from the way Ananias treated him?

_____

_____

_____

_____

As unsettling as the situation must have been for Ananias, imagine what it must have been like for Saul. He was a Christian exterminator on his way to eradicate an outbreak of conversions in Damascus. As we'll see in the next study, that zealous opposition lasted until the moment Jesus made himself known to Saul personally.

✑ POINTS TO REMEMBER ✑

❖ God will sometimes call us to places we wouldn't expect to go and to people we wouldn't have expected to see.
❖ God's chosen vessels do not always make sense to us, but we have to remember that he looks at the heart.
❖ We may not always know the transformation that Jesus has started to make in another person's life.

✑ PRAYER FOR THE DAY ✑

*Father, help us hide your Word in our hearts so we may be
difference-making ambassadors for you. Remind us of the story of
Saul when we are tempted to judge or dismiss others based on their reputation.
Give us the vision to see their potential—to recognize what
you can do in their lives—and the wisdom and patience to interact
with them accordingly. In Jesus' name, amen.*

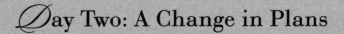

$\mathcal{D}$ay Two: A Change in Plans

AN ENCOUNTER WITH CHRIST

[Paul] went to the high priest and asked him for letters to the synagogues in Damascus, so that if he found any there who belonged to the Way, whether men or women, he might take them as prisoners to Jerusalem (Acts 9:1–2).

The trip had been Saul's idea. The city had seen large numbers of conversions. When word of the revival reached Saul, he made his request: "Send me." So the fiery young Hebrew left Jerusalem on his first missionary journey, hell-bent on stopping the church. The journey to Damascus was a long one, 150 miles. Saul likely rode horseback, careful to bypass the Gentile villages. This was a holy journey.

It was also a hot journey. The lowland between Mount Hermon and Damascus could melt silver. The sun struck like spears; the heat made waves out of the horizon. Somewhere on this thirsty trail, Jesus knocked

Saul to the ground and asked him, "Saul, Saul, why are you persecuting Me?" (Acts 9:4 NKJV).

Saul jammed his fists into his eye sockets as if they were filled with sand. He rolled onto his knees and lowered his head down to the earth. "'Who are You, Lord?' Then the Lord said, 'I am Jesus, whom you are persecuting'" (verse 5 NKJV). When Saul lifted his head to look, the living centers of his eyes had vanished. He was blind. He had the vacant stare of a Roman statue.

His guards rushed to help. They led him to the Damascus inn and walked with him up the stairwell. By the time Ananias arrived, blind Saul had begun to see Jesus in a different light. Christ had already done the work, and all that remained was for Ananias to show Saul the next step. "Brother Saul, the Lord Jesus, who appeared to you on the road as you came, has sent me that you may receive your sight and be filled with the Holy Spirit" (verse 17 NKJV).

Tears rushed like a tide against the crusts on Saul's eyes. The scaly covering loosened and fell away. Paul blinked and saw the face of his new friend.

He fell to the ground and heard a voice say to him, "Saul, Saul, why do you persecute me?" (v. 4).

When he opened his eyes he could see nothing (v. 8).

Placing his hands on Saul, [Ananias] said, "Brother Saul, the Lord—Jesus . . . —has sent me so that you may see again and be filled with the Holy Spirit" (v. 17).

Immediately, something like scales fell from Saul's eyes (v. 18).

1. Read Acts 9:1–2. What was the reason Saul was making this trip to Damascus? Why was he so adamant about exterminating followers of "the Way"?

   _____

   _____

   _____

   _____

2. The early believers had to face persecution and trials from people like Saul who believed Christianity was a threat to their faith. What do the following passages reveal about what we will endure for Christ and the purpose for doing so?

   Luke 6:22–23: "What blessings await you when people hate you and exclude you and mock you and curse you as evil because you follow the Son of Man. When that happens, be happy! Yes, leap for joy! For a great reward awaits you in heaven" (NLT).

   _____

   _____

   _____

   John 15:18–19: "If the world hates you, keep in mind that it hated me first. If you belonged to the world, it would love you as its own. As it is, you do not belong to the world, but I have chosen you out of the world. That is why the world hates you" (NIV).

   _____

   _____

   _____

   _____

1 John 3:13–14: "Do not be astonished, brothers and sisters, that the world hates you. We know that we have passed from death to life because we love one another. Whoever does not love abides in death" (NRSV).

_____

_____

_____

2 Timothy 3:12–14: "Indeed, all who desire to live a godly life in Christ Jesus will be persecuted, while evil people and impostors will go on from bad to worse, deceiving and being deceived. But as for you, continue in what you have learned and have firmly believed, knowing from whom you learned it" (ESV).

_____

_____

_____

1 Peter 3:17–18: "For it is better, if it is God's will, to suffer for doing good than for doing evil. For Christ also suffered once for sins, the righteous for the unrighteous, to bring you to God" (NIV).

_____

_____

_____

1 Peter 4:12–14: "Beloved, do not think it strange concerning the fiery trial which is to try you, as though some strange thing happened to you; but rejoice to the extent that you partake of Christ's sufferings, that when His glory is revealed, you may also be glad with exceeding joy. If you are reproached for the name of Christ, blessed _are you_, for the Spirit of glory and of God rests upon you" (NKJV).

_____

_____

_____

3. In Philippians 4:6 we read, "Do not be anxious about anything, but in every situation, by prayer and petition, with thanksgiving, present your requests to God" (NIV). What does this verse tell us is the best way to deal with trials?

_____

_____

_____

4. What can we learn from Saul's story to help us interact with people who oppose our faith?

_____

_____

_____

THE LIBERATOR IS BORN

Ananias's instructions to Saul are worth reading: "What are you waiting for? Get up, be baptized and wash your sins away, calling on his name" (Acts 22:16 NIV). He didn't have to ask twice. The legalist Saul was buried, and the liberator Paul was born. Within the hour he was stepping out of the waters of baptism. Within a few days he was preaching in a synagogue. The first of a thousand sermons.

Soon Paul is preaching from the hills of Athens, penning letters from the bowels of prisons, and ultimately siring a genealogy of theologians, including Aquinas, Luther, and Calvin. Stirring sermons, dedicated disciples, and six thousand miles of trails. If his sandals weren't slapping, his pen was writing. If he wasn't explaining the mystery of grace, he was articulating the theology that would determine the course of Western civilization.

All of his words could be reduced to one sentence. "We preach Christ crucified" (1 Corinthians 1:23 NIV). It wasn't that he lacked other sermon outlines; it was just that he couldn't exhaust the first one.

The absurdity of the whole thing kept him going. Jesus should have finished him on the road. He should have left him for the buzzards. He should have sent him to hell. But he didn't. He sent him to the lost.

Paul himself called it crazy. He described it with phrases like "stumbling block" and "foolishness," but chose in the end to call it "grace" (1 Corinthians 1:23; Ephesians 2:8 NIV). And he defended his unquenchable loyalty by saying, "The love of Christ leaves [me] no choice" (2 Corinthians 5:14 NEB).

Paul never took a course in missions. He never sat in on a committee meeting. He never read a book on church growth. He was just inspired by the Holy Spirit and punch-drunk on the love that makes the impossible possible: salvation.

The message is gripping: Show a man his failures without Jesus, and the result will be found in the roadside gutter. Give a man religion without reminding him of his filth, and the result will be arrogance in a three-piece suit. But get the two in the same heart—get sin to meet Savior and Savior to meet sin—and the result just might be another Pharisee-turned-preacher who sets the world on fire.

5. Saul the legalist had been buried, and Paul the liberator had been born. Read John 3:3–8. What did Jesus say about burying our past and being "born again"?

_____

_____

_____

_____

_____

_____

_____

Now what are you waiting for? Get up, be baptized and wash your sins away, calling on his name (Acts 22:16).

I returned to Jerusalem and was praying at the temple (v. 17).

The Lord said . . . "I will send you far away to the Gentiles" (v. 21).

We preach Christ crucified (1 Corinthians 1:23)

If we are "out of our mind," as some say, it is for God . . . for Christ's love compels us (2 Corinthians 5:14).

It is by grace you have been saved, through faith—and this is not from yourselves, it is the gift of God (Ephesians 2:8).

6. What does it mean to be "born of water and the Spirit" (verse 5 NIV)?

_____

_____

_____

_____

7. Turn to Psalm 103:11–12. What does it mean to you that God chooses not to remember what we were before we came to Christ?

_____

_____

_____

_____

8. Paul always remembered his life before Jesus: "I was circumcised when I was eight days old. I am a pure-blooded citizen of Israel and a member of the tribe of Benjamin—a real Hebrew if there ever was one! I was a member of the Pharisees, who demand the strictest obedience to the Jewish law" (Philippians 3:5 NLT). Why is it also important for *us* to remember what we were before Christ?

_____

_____

_____

_____

Paul's outlook changed 180 degrees when he encountered the risen Jesus. Yet his zeal and passion for the task at hand remained undiminished. As we'll see in the next study, the Lord helped Paul redirect the energy he had spent persecuting the church into helping to build and expand it.

ᴈ POINTS TO REMEMBER ᴂ

❖ Jesus should have left us all "to the buzzards," but instead he picked us up and called us his own.
❖ When the Holy Spirit is in charge, there is nothing we can't accomplish.
❖ Life-altering transformation happens when sin meets the Savior.

ᴈ PRAYER FOR THE DAY ᴂ

Father, thank you for removing our sins from yourself as far as the east is from the west. Thank you for giving us a clean slate—a moment we can look back on as the pivotal turning point in our lives. Work in our minds and hearts. Help us keep a balanced perspective of who we were—enough to maintain a spirit of humility, but not so much we struggle with guilt and shame over things we've been forgiven for. In Jesus' name, amen.

Day Three: The Impact of a Life

PAUL'S CALLING

Paul's calling took him first to the city of Antioch, where he ministered with Barnabas. From there the pair embarked on a missionary journey through Cyprus and what is today known as the country of Turkey. Returning to Antioch, Paul had a falling out with Barnabas that led to Silas and Timothy accompanying him on the next trip. This time, he and his companions would head into Greece.

In Philippi, a woman named Lydia becomes Paul's first convert in Europe. Paul and Silas are thrown in jail, but about midnight, as the two are singing worship songs to God, an earthquake breaks open the jail doors. "The jailer told someone to bring a light. Then he ran inside and, shaking with fear, fell down before Paul and Silas. He brought them outside and said, 'Men, what must I do to be saved?'" (Acts 16:29–30 NCV). The jailer becomes a believer, and Paul and Silas are set free.

From there it's on to Thessalonica, where he, Timothy, and Silas spend three fruitful weeks in the city. The result of their stay is a nucleus of believers. Luke provides a one-sentence profile of the church when he writes: "Some of them [the Jews] were convinced and joined Paul and Silas, along with many of the Greeks who worshiped God and many of the important women" (Acts 17:4 NCV).

An eclectic group attended the first church service: Some were Jews, some were Greeks, some were influential females, but all were convinced that Jesus was the Messiah. And in a short time, all paid a price for their belief. Literally. The young believers were dragged into the presence of the city leaders and forced to post bond for their own release. That night they helped Paul, Timothy, and Silas sneak out of the city.

Paul moved on, but part of his heart was still in Thessalonica. The little church was so young, so fragile, but oh-so-special. Just the thought of them made him proud. He longed to see them again. "We always thank God for all of you and mention you when we pray," he wrote (1 Thessalonians 1:2 NCV). He dreamed of the day he might see them again and, even more, dreamed of the day they would see Christ together.

> *[Barnabas and Saul] . . . went down to Seleucia and sailed from there to Cyprus (Acts 13:4).*

> *They had such a sharp disagreement that they parted company (15:39).*

> *The Lord opened [Lydia's] heart to respond to Paul's message (16:14).*

> *After Paul and Silas came out of the prison, they went to Lydia's house (v. 40).*

> *They came to Thessalonica (17:1).*

> *Some of the Jews were persuaded and joined Paul and Silas, as did a large number of God-fearing Greeks (v. 4).*

> *They dragged Jason and some other believers before the city officials. . . . The believers sent Paul and Silas away to Berea (vv. 6, 10).*

> *We wanted to come to you— certainly I, Paul, did, again and again (1 Thessalonians 2:18).*

1. What made Paul—formerly Saul, the enemy of the Christian faith—such an effective Christian evangelist?

_____

_____

_____

2. Read 1 Thessalonians 1:2–6. For what three things did Paul remember the believers in Thessalonica? What did Paul mean when he said that the gospel came to them "not simply with words but also with power" (verse 5 NIV)?

_____

_____

_____

_____

3. Jesus had told his disciples, "When the Helper comes, he will prove to the people of the world the truth about sin, about being right with God, and about judgment" (John 16:8 NCV). Why is it important to remember that the Holy Spirit is the One who makes people aware of their sin and their need for forgiveness?

_____

_____

_____

_____

4. Paul described his work in founding another church this way: "I planted the seed, and Apollos watered it. But God is the One who made it grow. So the one who plants is not important, and the one who waters is not important. Only God, who makes things grow, is important" (1 Corinthians 3:6–7 NCV). What is our role in reaching others with the good news of Jesus? What is the Holy Spirit's role?

_____

_____

_____

_____

WHEN CHRIST COMES

Indeed, you are our glory and joy (1 Thessalonians 2:20).

Note what Paul also says to the church in Thessalonica: "You are our hope, our joy, and the crown we will take pride in when our Lord Jesus Christ comes" (1 Thessalonians 2:19 NCV). The verse conjures up an image of an encounter between those freed and the One who led them to freedom. A moment in which those saved can meet the One who led them to salvation. This is not a haughty, look-what-I've-done pride, but rather an awestruck joy that declares, "I'm so proud of your faith."

We thank God . . . for all the joy we have in the presence of our God because of you (3:9).

In this case Paul will meet with the Thessalonians. He will search the sea of faces for his friends. They will find him, and he will find them. And, in the presence of Christ, they will enjoy an eternal reunion.

Imagine doing the same. Think about the day Christ comes. There you are in the great circle of the redeemed. Your body has been made new—no more pain or problems. Your mind has been made new—what you once understood in part, you now understand clearly. You feel no fear, no danger, no sorrow. Though you are one of a throng, it's as if you and Jesus are all alone.

And he asks you this question. I'm speculating now, but I wonder if Christ might say these words to you: "I'm so proud that you let me use you. Because of you, others are here today. Would you like to meet them?"

Chances are you'd be surprised at such a statement. It's one thing for the apostle Paul to hear such words. He was an *apostle*. We can imagine a foreign missionary or famous evangelist hearing these words—but us? Most of us wonder what influence we have. (Which is good, for if we knew, we might grow arrogant.) Most of us can relate to the words of Matthew 25, "Master, what are you talking about?" (verse 37 MSG).

At that point Jesus might—and this is just wild speculation—but Jesus might turn to the crowd and invite them. With his hand on your shoulder, he announces, "Do we have any here who were influenced by this child of mine?"

And one by one, they begin to step out and walk forward.

"Well done, good and faithful servant! You have been faithful with a few things; I will put you in charge of many things. Come and share your master's happiness!" (Matthew 25:23).

"You are the salt of the earth" (5:13).

5. Paul could look at the congregation in Thessalonica like a parent who is proud of his or her children's faith. Who serves as a Christian father or mother in your life? What do you envision them saying as they look at your life as a believer?

6. How many people in heaven would get credit for introducing you to Christ or helping you mature as a believer? What influence did each person have on you?

7. For which people might you be asked to step forward to receive recognition as a Christian influence?

8. Who are three people you would *like* to influence toward (or in) the Christian faith? What is a specific strategy you might use to make a difference?

The apostle Paul's concern for the members of his congregations didn't stop at their baptism. As we'll see in the next study, he exhorted first-century believers to live their lives in such a way they would bring honor and glory to the One who had saved them. In some cases, that meant confronting other believers who had gone astray or who had refused to give up their former sinful lifestyles.

❤ POINTS TO REMEMBER ❧

- ❖ There is a cost associated with following Jesus, but the eternal rewards far outweigh the earthly trials we will endure.
- ❖ When Christ returns, our minds and bodies will be made new—and there will be no more pain, fear, danger, sorrow, or problems.
- ❖ We may never know the people we have influenced for the gospel or the true impact our lives have had for God's kingdom.

❤ PRAYER FOR THE DAY ❧

Father, thank you for bringing the right people into our lives at just the right time to influence and guide us. Thank you for giving us, in turn, opportunities to make a difference in other people's lives. May we never take those opportunities for granted. Give us the wisdom, compassion, and courage to intervene in the lives of others, for your sake and your glory. In Jesus' name, amen.

$\mathcal{D}$ay Four: No Delight in Evil

STRONG WORDS

I am writing this not to shame you but to warn you as my dear children (1 Corinthians 4:14).

Not all of Paul's congregations gave him such comfort as the one in Thessalonica. The church in Corinth, for instance, handed the apostle all kinds of problems. One issue in particular, which Paul addressed in his first letter to the church, is shocking even today. Were this to air on a daytime talk show, I imagine the conversation would go something like this.

"So," says Christy Adams, the talk show host, "you discovered that your boyfriend had been sleeping with your mother?" The audience snickers. The teenage girl sitting on the stage ducks her head at the burst of attention.

Next to her sits her mother. She is a middle-aged woman in a too-tight black dress, her arm entwined with the skinny one of a boy in a sleeveless T-shirt. She waves to the crowd. He grins.

Christy wastes no time. "Do the two of you *really* sleep together?"

The mother, still holding the hand of the boy, looks at him. "Yes," she says. She goes on to explain how she's been lonely since her divorce. Her daughter's boyfriend had been hanging out at her house all hours of the day and night. And, well, one afternoon he plopped beside her on the couch, and the two started talking, and one thing led to another, and the next thing she knew they were . . .

Her face flushes, and the boy shrugs as they let the audience complete the sentence. The girl sits expressionless and silent.

"Aren't you worried what this might teach your daughter?" Christy inquires.

"I'm only teaching her the ways of the world."

"What about you?" Christy asks the boy. "Aren't you being unfaithful to your girlfriend?"

The boy looks amazed. "I still love her," he announces. "I'm only helping her by loving her mother. We are one happy family. There's nothing wrong with that!"

The audience erupts with whistles and applause. Just as the hubbub begins to subside, Christy tells the lovers, "Not everyone would agree with you. I've invited a guest to react to your lifestyle. He's the world's most famous theologian. Making his first appearance on the *Christy Adams Show*, please welcome controversial theologian, scholar, and author, the apostle Paul!"

Polite applause welcomes a short, balding man with glasses and a tweed jacket. He loosens his tie a bit as he settles his small frame in the stage chair. Christy skips the welcome. "You have trouble with what these people are doing?"

Paul holds his hands in his lap, looks over at the trio, and then back at Christy. "It's not how I feel that matters. It's how God feels."

Christy pauses so the TV audience can hear the "ooohs" ripple through the studio. "Then tell us, please, Paul, how does God feel about this creative tryst?"

"It angers him."

"And why?"

"Evil angers God because evil destroys his children. What these people are doing is *evil*."

1. Some people might say the apostle Paul's words are intolerant. How do you think he would respond?

_____

_____

_____

_____

It is actually reported that there is sexual immorality among you, and of a kind that even pagans do not tolerate: A man is sleeping with his father's wife (1 Corinthians 5:1).

And you are proud! Shouldn't you rather have gone into mourning? (v. 2).

I have already passed judgment in the name of our Lord Jesus on the one who has been doing this (v. 3).

2. On what other subjects are people today urged to show tolerance? When those topics come up in conversation, how do you deal with them?

_____

_____

_____

_____

3. The prophet Isaiah wrote, "But your iniquities have separated you from your God; your sins have hidden his face from you, so that he will not hear" (Isaiah 59:2 NIV). What does sin do to our relationship with God?

_____

_____

_____

_____

4. Read Psalm 51:7–14. How does David describe the feeling of being forgiven from the evil in his life? What does that compel him to do?

_____

_____

_____

_____

ANGRY AT EVIL

Hand this man over to Satan for the destruction of the flesh, so that his spirit may be saved on the day of the Lord (1 Corinthians 5:5).

Paul's strong words trigger a few hoots, some scattered applause, and an outburst of raised hands. Before Christy can speak, Paul continues, "God has left these two as a result of their actions and let them go their sinful way. Their thinking is dark, their acts are evil, and God is disgusted."

A lanky fellow in the front shouts out his objection. "It's her body. She can do what she wants!"

"Oh, but that's where you are mistaken. Her body belongs to God and is to be used for him."

"What we're doing is harmless," objects the mother.

"Look at your daughter," Paul urges her, gesturing toward the girl whose eyes are full of tears. "Don't you see you have harmed her? You traded healthy love for lust. You traded the love of God for the love of the flesh. You traded truth for lie. And you traded the natural for the unnatural . . ."

Christy can restrain herself no longer. "Do you know how hokey you sound? All this talk about God and right and wrong and immorality? Don't you feel out of touch with reality?"

"Out of touch? No. Out of place, yes. But out of touch, hardly. God does not sit silently while his children indulge in perversion. He lets us go our sinful ways and reap the consequences. Every broken heart, every unwanted child, every war and tragedy can be traced back to our rebellion against God."

God will judge those outside. "Expel the wicked person from among you" (v. 12).

People spring to their feet, the mother puts her finger in Paul's face, and Christy turns to the camera, delighting in the pandemonium. "We've got to take a break," she shouts over the noise. "Don't go away; we've got some more questions for our friend the apostle."

How does the above dialogue strike you? Harsh? (Paul was too narrow.) Unreal? (The scene was too bizarre.) Outlandish? (No one would accept such convictions.)

Regardless of your response, it is important to note that though the script is fictional, Paul's words are not.

God is "against all the evil and wrong things people do" (Romans 1:18 NCV). The One who urges us to "hate what is evil" (Romans 12:9 NCV) hates what is evil.

Hate what is evil; cling to what is good (Romans 12:9).

In three chilling verses Paul states: "God left them and let them go . . ." (Romans 1:24 NCV). "God left them and let them do . . ." (Romans 1:26 NCV). "God left them and allowed them to have their own worthless thinking . . ." (Romans 1:28 NCV).

God is angry at evil.

God gave them over in the sinful desires of their hearts (1:24).

For many, this is a revelation. Some assume God is a harried high school principal, too busy monitoring the planets to notice us. He's not.

Others assume he is a doting parent, blind to the evil of his children. Wrong.

Still others insist he loves us so much he cannot be angry at our evil. They don't understand that love is *always* angry at evil. As Paul put it: "Love takes no pleasure in evil but rejoices over the truth. Love patiently accepts all things. It always trusts, always hopes, and always endures" (1 Corinthians 13:6–7 NCV).

Love does not delight in evil but rejoices with the truth. It always protects, always trusts, always hopes, always perseveres (1 Corinthians 13:6–7).

5. Read 1 Corinthians 5:1–5. The believers in this church—like the audience of the fictitious *Christy Adams Show*—were actually *proud* of this evil taking place in their midst. How does Paul react to this attitude?

_____

_____

_____

_____

_____

6. Paul is clear the believers need to separate themselves from this type of evil. What does he tell them to do with the man? Why do you think he instructs them to take this course of action?

_____

_____

_____

_____

_____

_____

7. Paul urged believers to "live a life worthy of the calling" they had received from God (Ephesians 4:1 NIV). What are our responsibilities toward those who aren't living such a life? How do we speak the truth in love to those people?

_____

_____

_____

_____

_____

_____

8. How can you show that love is *never* tolerant of evil? How can you show that it always trusts, always hopes, and always endures?

_____

_____

_____

_____

_____

_____

_____

Paul's exhortations for Christians to confront sin and live godly lives are just a small part of his legacy. As we'll see in the next study, this former enemy of the church became a hero of the faith by listening to God's call and following his promptings—even when they resulted in imprisonment and martyrdom.

❧ POINTS TO REMEMBER ❧

❖ Evil angers God because evil destroys his children.
❖ God does not sit silently while his children engage in sin.
❖ We will always reap grief and pain when we sow evil.

❧ PRAYER FOR THE DAY ❧

Father, thank you for setting up a system of checks and balances within the body of Christ to make sure we live lives worthy of our calling. Give us the wisdom and courage to speak the truth in love to our loved ones, friends, and acquaintances who need to hear it. And give us the wisdom and humility to listen when others speak the truth to us. In Jesus' name, amen.

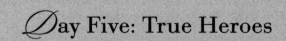

Day Five: True Heroes

IN THE PRISON

True heroes are hard to identify. They don't look like heroes. Take Paul, for example.

We find him finishing out his ministry in a Roman jail. His days are marked. The man who shaped history would die in the jail of a despot. No headlines would announce his execution. No observer would record the events. When the axe struck Paul's neck, society's eyes wouldn't blink. To them Paul was a peculiar purveyor of an odd faith.

Paul, a prisoner of Christ Jesus (Philemon 1:1).

Peer into the prison and see him for yourself: bent and frail, shackled to the arm of a Roman guard. Behold the apostle of God. Who knows when his back last felt a bed or his mouth knew a good meal? Three decades of travel and trouble, and what's he got to show for it?

It has become clear throughout the whole palace guard and to everyone else that I am in chains for Christ (Philippians 1:13).

There's squabbling in Philippi and competition in Corinth. The legalists are swarming in Galatia. Crete is plagued by money grabbers. Ephesus is stalked by womanizers. Even some of Paul's own friends have turned against him.

Dead broke. No family. No property. Nearsighted and worn out.

Everyone in the province of Asia has deserted me (2 Timothy 1:15).

Oh, he had his moments. Spoke to an emperor once but couldn't convert him. Gave a lecture at an Areopagus men's club but wasn't asked to speak there again. Spent a few days with Peter and the boys in Jerusalem, but they couldn't seem to get along, so Paul hit the road.

And never got off. Ephesus, Thessalonica, Athens, Syracuse, Malta. The only list longer than his itinerary was his misfortune. Got stoned in one city and stranded in another. Nearly drowned as many times as he nearly starved. If he spent more than one week in the same place, it was probably a prison.

I have labored and toiled and have often gone without sleep; I have known hunger and thirst and have often gone without food; I have been cold and naked (2 Corinthians 11:27).

He never received a salary. Had to pay his own travel expenses. Kept a part-time job on the side to make ends meet.

Doesn't look like a hero.

Doesn't sound like one either. He introduced himself as the worst sinner in history. He was a Christian killer before he was a Christian leader. At times his heart was so heavy, his pen drug itself across the page. "What a miserable man I am! Who will save me from this body that brings me death?" (Romans 7:24 NCV).

Christ Jesus came into the world to save sinners—of whom I am the worst (1 Timothy 1:15).

Only heaven knows how long he stared at the question before he found the courage to defy logic and write, "I thank God for saving me through Jesus Christ our Lord!" (verse 25 NCV). One minute he's in charge; the next he's in doubt. One day he's preaching; the next he's in prison. And that's where I'd like you to look at him. Look at him in the prison.

1. Read 2 Corinthians 11:16–31. How does Paul sum up his ministry in this passage? How is he able to "boast" in these sufferings?

   _____

   _____

   _____

   _____

2. Paul wrote, "Though I am free and belong to no one, I have made myself a slave to everyone to win as many as possible" (1 Corinthians 9:19 NIV). How was Paul's attitude instrumental in his success as a disciple?

   _____

   _____

   _____

   _____

3. What characteristics of the apostle Paul would you like to emulate in your life? Which traits would you rather avoid? Explain.

   _____

   _____

   _____

   _____

   _____

4. What do you think Paul would have identified as his biggest success? What would he have identified as his biggest regret? Explain.

   _____

   _____

   _____

   _____

AN UNLIKELY LEGACY

Pretend you don't know Paul. You're a guard or a cook or a friend of the hatchet man, and you've come to get one last look at the guy while they sharpen the blade.

What you see shuffling around in his cell isn't too much. But what I lean over and tell you is: "That man will shape the course of history."

You chuckle, but I continue.

"Nero's fame will fade in this man's light." You turn and stare. I continue.

"His churches will die. But his thoughts? Within two hundred years his thoughts will influence the teaching of every school on this continent."

You shake your head.

"See those letters? Those letters scribbled on parchment? They'll be read in thousands of languages and will impact every major creed and constitution of the future. Every major figure will read them. Every single one."

That would be your breaking point. "No way. He's an old man with an odd faith. He'll be killed and forgotten before his head hits the floor."

Who could disagree? What rational thinker would counter? Paul's name would blow like the dust his bones would become.

No level-headed observer would think otherwise. Courageous but small. Radical yet unnoticed. No one—I repeat, *no one*—bade farewell to this man thinking his name would be remembered more than a generation.

His peers simply had no way of knowing—and neither do we. For that reason, a hero could be next door and you wouldn't know it.

The fellow who changes the oil in your car could be one. A hero in coveralls? Maybe. Maybe as he works he prays, asking God to do with the heart of the driver what he does with the engine.

The day-care worker where you drop off the kids? Perhaps. Perhaps her morning prayers include the name of each child and the dream that one of them will change the world. Who's to say God isn't listening?

The parole officer downtown? Could be a hero. She could be the one who challenges the ex-con to challenge the teens to challenge the gangs. I know, I know. These folks don't fit our image of a hero. They look too, too . . . well, normal. Give us four stars, titles, and headlines. But something tells me that for every hero in the spotlight, there are dozens in the shadows. They don't get press. They don't draw crowds. They don't even write books!

But behind every avalanche is a snowflake. Behind a rock slide is a pebble. An atomic explosion begins with one atom. And a revival can begin with one sermon.

Heroes like Paul rarely know when they are being heroic. Rarely are historic moments acknowledged when they happen. (A visit to the manger should remind you of that one.) We seldom see history in the making, and we seldom recognize heroes. Which is just as well, for if we knew either, we might mess up both.

But we'd do well to keep our eyes open. Tomorrow's hero might be mowing your lawn. And the hero who inspires him might be nearer than you think.

He or she might be in your mirror.

People look at the outward appearance, but the LORD looks at the heart (1 Samuel 16:7).

[Paul] proclaimed the kingdom of God and taught about the Lord Jesus Christ—with all boldness and without hindrance! (Acts 28:31).

5. No one in Paul's day could have guessed the tremendous impact he would have on Christianity and the world. Think about the men of the Bible you have studied in these lessons. In what ways were they also unlikely heroes?

Noah (see Genesis 6:9–22; 9:20–23)

_____

_____

_____

_____

_____

Job (see Job 2:11–13; 42:1–6)

_____

_____

_____

Jacob (see Genesis 25:29–34; 27:15–29; 30:31–43)

_____

_____

_____

Moses (see Exodus 2:11–15; 4:10–17)

_____

_____

_____

David (see 1 Samuel 16:1–13; 2 Samuel 11:1–27)

_____

_____

_____

Joseph (see Matthew 1:18–24; Luke 2:1–21)

_____

_____

_____

Matthew (see Matthew 9:9–13; Mark 2:13–17)

_____

_____

_____

Lazarus (see John 11:17–45)

_____

_____

_____

Peter (see Matthew 26:69–75; Mark 14:66–72; Luke 22:54–62)

_____

_____

_____

6. Who are some of the people you encounter every day who could secretly be a "Christian hero"? Why do you think this could be the case?

_____

_____

_____

7. If you began to think of those people as potential Christian heroes, how would it affect the way you interact with them?

_____

_____

_____

8. If you knew people were looking at *you* as a Christian hero, how would it affect your . . .

decision-making and priorities?

_____

_____

_____

relationships with others?

_____

_____

_____

lifestyle choices?

_____

_____

_____

prayer life and spiritual life?

_____

_____

_____

self-image?

_____

_____

_____

God used Paul to touch the world. But remember that first he used Ananias to touch Paul. Has he given you a similar assignment? Has he given you a Saul?

A mother once talked to me about her son who was serving time in a maximum-security unit for robbery. Everyone else, even his father, had given up on the young man. But his mom had a different outlook. She really thought her son's best years were ahead of him. "He's a good boy," she said firmly. "When he gets out of there, he's going to make something out of his life."

Another Saul, another Ananias.

I ran into a friend in a bookstore. He recently celebrated his fiftieth wedding anniversary. He teared up as he described the saint he married and the jerk his wife married. "I didn't believe in God. I didn't treat people with respect. Six weeks into the marriage, I came home one day to find her crying in the bathtub about the mistake she had made. But she never gave up on me."

Another Saul, another Ananias.

And you? Everyone else has written off your Saul. "He's too far gone." "She's too hard . . . too addicted . . . too old . . . too cold." No one gives your Saul a prayer. But you are beginning to realize that maybe God is at work behind the scenes. Maybe it's too soon to throw in the towel . . . you begin to believe.

"My Father is always at his work to this very day, and I too am working" (John 5:17).

Don't resist these thoughts.

Joseph didn't. His brothers sold him into Egyptian slavery. Yet he welcomed them into his palace.

David didn't. King Saul had a vendetta against David, but David had a soft spot for Saul. He called him "the LORD'S anointed" (1 Samuel 24:10 NKJV).

Hosea didn't. His wife, Gomer, was queen of the red-light district, but Hosea kept his front door open. And she came home.

Of course, no one believed in people more than Jesus did. He saw something in Peter worth developing, in the adulterous woman worth forgiving, and in John worth harnessing. He saw something in the thief on the cross, and what he saw was worth saving. And in the life of a wild-eyed, bloodthirsty extremist, he saw an apostle of grace. He believed in Saul. And he believed in Saul through Ananias.

"Go and make disciples of all nations" (Matthew 28:19).

Don't give up on your Saul. When others write him off, give him another chance. Stay strong. Call him brother. Call her sister. Tell your Saul about Jesus, and pray. And remember this: God never sends you where he hasn't already been. By the time you reach your Saul, who knows what you'll find.

❧ POINTS TO REMEMBER ☙

❖ Heroes like Paul rarely know when they are being heroic—they simply obey God's call and follow his will.
❖ Paul's peers had no way of knowing he was a hero, just like we have no way of knowing whom God will raise up around us.
❖ The heroes who inspire us may be nearer to us than we think.

❧ PRAYER FOR THE DAY ☙

God, thank you for never giving up on us. Help us to see others the way you see them and never write them off as being a lost cause. Help us to do your will in all things so we can truly make a difference in this world.
In Jesus' name, amen.

～❧ WEEKLY MEMORY VERSE ❧～

In him we have redemption through his blood, the forgiveness of sins,
in accordance with the riches of God's grace.
EPHESIANS 1:7 (NIV)

For Further Reading

Selections throughout this lesson were taken from *The Applause of Heaven* (Nashville: Thomas Nelson, 1990); *In the Grip of Grace* (Nashville: Thomas Nelson, 1996); *When Christ Comes* (Nashville: Thomas Nelson, 1998); *When God Whispers Your Name* (Nashville: Thomas Nelson, 1999); *Outlive Your Life* (Nashville: Thomas Nelson, 2010).

Ten Men of The Bible

....

LEADER'S GUIDE

....

Thank you for your willingness to lead a group through *Ten Men of the Bible*. The rewards of being a leader are different from those of participating, and we hope you find your own walk with Jesus deepened by this experience. During the ten lessons in this study, you'll be helping your group explore the lives of ten fascinating characters in the Bible through inspirational readings by Max Lucado, thought-provoking group discussion questions, and practical takeaway exercises. There are several elements in this leader's guide that will help you as you structure your study and reflection time, so follow along and take advantage of each one.

Before You Begin

Before your first meeting, have the group participants get a copy of *Ten Men of the Bible* so they can follow along in the study guide and have their answers written out ahead of time. Alternately, you can hand out the study guides at your first meeting and give the group members some time to look over the material and ask any preliminary questions. During your first meeting, be sure to send a sheet around the room and have the members write down their name, phone number, and email address so you can keep in touch with them during the week.

Generally, the ideal size for a group is between eight to ten people, which ensures everyone will have enough time to participate in discussions. If you have more people, you might want to break up the main group into smaller subgroups. Encourage those who show up at the first meeting to commit to attending the duration of the study, as this will help the group members get to know each other, create stability for the group, and help you know how to prepare each week.

Note that each of the lessons begins with an opening story from Max Lucado that focuses on that week's Bible character. The two questions that follow serve as an icebreaker to get the group members thinking about the person and the topic at hand. Some people may want to tell a long story in response to one of these questions, but the goal is to keep the answers brief. Ideally, you want everyone in the group to get a chance to answer at least one of these opening questions, so try to keep the responses to a minute or less. If you have talkative group members, say up front that everyone needs to limit his or her answer to one minute.

Give the group members a chance to answer, but tell them to feel free to pass if they wish. With the rest of the study, it's generally not a good idea to have everyone answer every question—a free-flowing discussion is more desirable. But with the opening icebreaker questions, you can go around the circle. Encourage shy people to share, but don't force them.

Before your first meeting, let the group members know the lessons are broken down into five days' worth of reading material. The goal of structuring the material in this format is to encourage group members to spend time each day in God's Word. During your group discussion time the participants will be drawing on the answers they wrote down during the week, so encourage them to always complete these ahead of time. Also invite them to bring any questions and insights they uncovered while reading to your next meeting, especially if they had a breakthrough moment or if they didn't understand something.

Weekly Preparation

As the leader, there are a few things to do to prepare for each meeting:

❖ *Read through the lesson.* This will help you to become familiar with the content and know how to structure the discussion times.

❖ *Decide which questions you want to discuss.* Each lesson contains forty Bible study questions (generally eight per day), so you will not be able to cover every question. Instead, select two to three questions in each day's reading that especially stood out to you.

❖ *Be familiar with the questions you want to discuss.* When the group meets you'll be watching the clock, so you want to make sure you are familiar with the Bible study questions you have selected. You can then spend time in the passage again when the group meets. In this way, you'll ensure you have the passage more deeply in your mind than your group members.

❖ *Pray for your group.* Pray for your group members throughout the week and ask God to lead them as they study his Word.

❖ *Bring extra supplies to your meeting.* The members should bring their own pens for writing notes, but it's a good idea to have extras available for those who forget. You may also want to bring paper and additional Bibles.

Note that in many cases there will no one "right" answer to the question. Answers will vary, especially when the group members are being asked to share their personal experiences.

Structuring the Discussion Time

You will need to determine with your group how long you want to meet each week so you can plan your time accordingly. Generally, most groups like to meet for either sixty minutes or ninety minutes, so you could use one of the schedules on the following page.

SECTION	60 MINUTES	90 MINUTES
WELCOME (members arrive and get settled)	**5** minutes	**10** minutes
ICEBREAKER (discuss the two opening questions for the lesson)	**10** minutes	**15** minutes
DISCUSSION (discuss the Bible study questions you selected ahead of time)	**35** minutes	**50** minutes
PRAYER/CLOSING (pray together as a group and dismiss)	**10** minutes	**15** minutes

As the group leader, it is up to you to keep track of the time and keep things moving along according to your schedule. You might want to set a timer for each segment so both you and the group members know when your time is up. (Note that there are some good phone apps for timers that play a gentle chime or other pleasant sound instead of a disruptive noise.) Don't feel pressured to cover every question you have selected if the group has a good discussion going. Again, it's not necessary to go around the circle and make everyone share.

Don't be concerned if the group members are quiet or slow to share. People are often quiet when they are pulling together their ideas, and this might be a new experience for them. Just ask a question and let it hang in the air until someone shares. You can then say, "Thank you. What about others? What came to you when you read through the passage?"

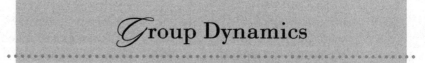

Group Dynamics

Leading a group through *Ten Men of the Bible* will prove to be highly rewarding both to you and your group members. However, that doesn't mean that you will not encounter any challenges along the way! Discussions can get off track. Group members may not be sensitive to the needs and ideas of others. Some might worry they will be expected to talk about matters that make them feel awkward. Others may express comments that result in disagreements. To help ease this strain on you and the group, consider the following ground rules:

❖ When someone raises a question or comment that is off the main topic, suggest you deal with it another time, or, if you feel led to go in that direction, let the group know you will be spending some time discussing it.

❖ If someone asks a question you don't know how to answer, admit it and move on. At your discretion, feel free to invite group members to comment on questions that call for personal experience.

❖ If you find one or two people are dominating the discussion time, direct a few questions to others in the group. Outside the main group time, ask the more dominating members to help you draw out the quieter ones. Work to make them a part of the solution instead of the problem.

❖ When a disagreement occurs, encourage the group members to process the matter in love. Encourage those on opposite sides to restate what they heard the other side say about the matter, and then invite each side to evaluate if that perception is accurate. Lead the group in examining other Scriptures related to the topic and look for common ground.

When any of these issues arise, encourage your group members to follow the words from the Bible: "Love one another" (John 13:34 NIV), "If it is possible, as far as it depends on you, live at peace with everyone" (Romans 12:18 NIV), and "Be quick to listen, slow to speak and slow to become angry" (James 1:19 NIV).

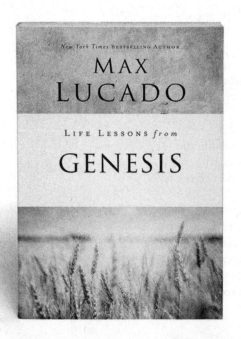

ALSO AVAILABLE FROM

MAX LUCADO

THE LIFE LESSONS
BIBLE STUDY SERIES

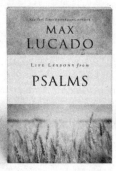

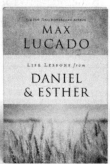

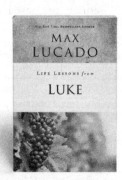

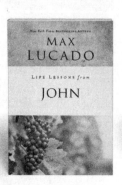

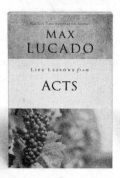

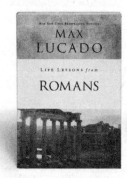

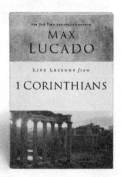

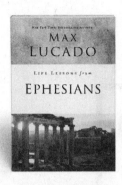
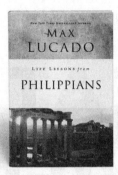
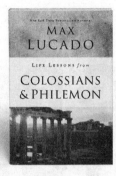
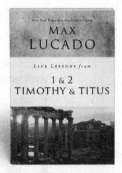

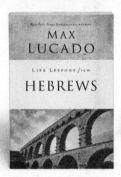
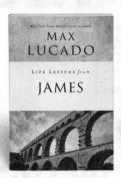
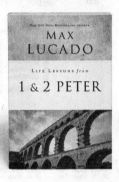
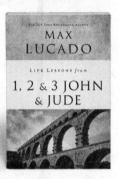

BIBLE STUDIES INCLUDE

Genesis
Psalms
Ezra & Nehemiah
Daniel & Esther
Matthew
Mark
Luke
John
Acts
Romans
1 Corinthians
2 Corinthians
Galatians
Ephesians
Philippians

Colossians & Philemon
1 & 2 Thessalonians
1 & 2 Timothy & Titus
Hebrews
James
1 & 2 Peter
1, 2, 3 John & Jude
Revelation

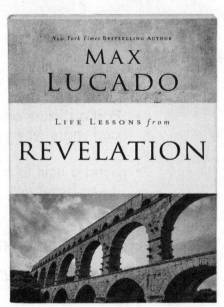

SCAN ME

HARPERCHRISTIANRESOURCES.COM

From the Publisher

GREAT STUDIES

ARE EVEN BETTER WHEN THEY'RE SHARED!

Help others find this study

- Post a review at your favorite online bookseller

- Post a picture on a social media account and share why you enjoyed it

- Send a note to a friend who would also love it—or better yet, go through it with them!

Thanks for helping others grow their faith!